Praise for

THE APPARITIONISTS

A *Publishers Weekly* Top Ten Book of the Year
An NPR Best Book of the Year
A *New York Times Book Review* Editors' Choice

"In *The Apparitionists*, Peter Manseau takes us on an expedition through the beginnings of photography and its deceptions ... Manseau has created an exceptional story of how photography intersects with the hope that some heretofore unexplored scientific process will reveal something about the nature of man and our limitations."
— **Errol Morris,** *New York Times Book Review*

"Manseau develops these threads so that *The Apparitionists* itself is like a photograph—each successive chapter adding depth and shade and specks of mystery, until the final result magically appears, provoking as many questions as it provides answers." — **Karen Abbott,** *Wall Street Journal*

"An incredibly rich, surprisingly relevant story."
— **Ron Charles,** *Washington Post*

"Manseau finds a clever balance of historical remove and the immediacy of suspense, and manages to maintain a—perhaps necessary—agnosticism when it counts. Because as diverting (and telling) a history as it is, in the end, *The Apparitionists* is a biography about why we believe." —NPR

"A sensitive, insightful history." — *The New Yorker*

"Wide-ranging and thought-provoking ...In our age of digital manipulation, it is more important than ever to scrutinize every photograph, whether or not they contain ghosts." — *San Francisco Chronicle*

"In this meticulously researched study of America's dalliance with spiritualism in the nineteenth century ... Manseau provides comprehensive context for his chronicle of Mumler, placing him at the intersection of the Spiritualist movement and the rise of the photographic art, and in the context of the Civil War, which acquainted Americans with death on an unprecedented scale."
— *Publishers Weekly,* starred review

"*The Apparitionists* is breezy, clever, and exuberant." —*Harper's Magazine*

"More than just a fraud, William Mumler was a pioneer in the new art of photography—a striking technology that not only offered new levels of immediacy but also immediately offered itself up to manipulation, provoking questions of authenticity even as its uncanny effects offered a tantalizing vision of the unknown. He was a huckster, but like all successful hucksters, he was a perfect reflection of his time. Peter Manseau's *The Apparitionists* recreates Mumler's life with a scholar's poise and a storyteller's grace, offering an enduring portrait of the nineteenth century through one of its most unlikely figures." —**Colin Dickey**, author of
Ghostland: An American History in Haunted Places

"Written like a novel but researched with academic rigor, this account of a photographer whose work seemed to incorporate images from the spirit realm stops short of either endorsing the veracity of the photographer's claim or debunking his work as a scam . . . A well-paced nonfiction work that reads more like a historical novel than an academic study." —*Kirkus Reviews*

"Manseau has become the foremost chronicler of the deep American desire to believe in the weird, the strange, and the oddly wonderful. His latest, *The Apparitionists,* is lighthearted and yet—in all senses—grave, a profound consideration of death and doubt illuminated by a nineteenth-century gallery of genius and ingenious deception. The dead speak in this brilliantly entertaining tale." —**Jeff Sharlet**, *New York Times* best-selling author of
The Family: The Secret Fundamentalism at the Heart of American Power

"Peter Manseau's smart new book . . . crystallizes a moment when photography was so unsettling it reshaped ideas about mortality." —*The Week*

"Peter Manseau's *The Apparitionists* tells us much more about the climate of gullibility and grief in the United States leading up to the Civil War and in its aftermath than it does about the charlatans who fed on human emotions. It's a masterful work of human deception." —*Counterpunch*

"Fascinating for reasons historic and contemporary . . . Manseau's book sticks closely to the facts of Mumler's case. But in our own era of war, 'fake news,' and spiritual unrest, the story feels more than merely suggestive." —**Jeff Chang**, *The Millions*

THE
APPARITIONISTS

A TALE OF PHANTOMS, FRAUD, PHOTOGRAPHY, AND THE MAN WHO CAPTURED LINCOLN'S GHOST

PETER MANSEAU

MARINER BOOKS

An Imprint of HarperCollins *Publishers*

Boston   New York

First Mariner Books edition 2018
Copyright © 2017 by Peter Manseau

marinerbooks.com

Library of Congress Cataloging-in-Publication Data
Names: Manseau, Peter, author.
Title: The apparitionists : a tale of phantoms, fraud, photography, and
the man who captured Lincoln's ghost / Peter Manseau.
Description: Boston : Houghton Mifflin Harcourt, 2017. |
Includes bibliographical references and index.
Identifiers: LCCN 2017018074 (print) | LCCN 2017021898 (ebook) |
ISBN 9780544745988 (ebook) | ISBN 9780544745971 (hardcover)
ISBN 9781328557063 (pbk.)
Subjects: LCSH: Mumler, William H. | Photographers—United States—
Biography. | Psychics—United States—Biography. |
Spirit photography—United States—History—19th century.
Classification: LCC BF1027.M86 (ebook) | LCC BF1027.M86 M36 2017 (print) |
DDC 133.9/2 [B]—dc23
LC record available at https://lccn.loc.gov/2017018074

Book design by Jackie Shepherd

Printed in the United States of America
3 2021
4500841044

For Gwen

CONTENTS

Contents

LIST OF ILLUSTRATIONS

List of Illustrations

AUTHOR'S NOTE

IN THESE DAYS when an unprecedented number of amateur image makers carry cameras everywhere they go, taking more than a billion photographs every day, it is my hope that this story of photography's infancy will provide a fresh view of a time shaped by war, belief, new technology, and a longing for connection across ever greater distances—a time not unlike our own.

The entwined narratives told here—concerning photography's coming of age and the ghostly visions peddled by a photographer of dubious repute—together form an account of how captured images, and the possibility of manipulating them, overtook all other means of recording memories, documenting history, and understanding the past.

While those portrayed throughout walked a line only then being drawn between fact and fantasy in the development of their art, this is a work of nonfiction. Wherever dialogue or quoted passages appear, they are taken from the historical record: letters, memoirs, public lectures, or transcriptions of court proceedings made by the indefatigable journalists of the nineteenth century.

I make no claims for the reality of the apparitions that hover over many of these pages, but let the women and men who believed in such hauntings speak for themselves.

Nothing can be so deceiving as a photograph.
— **FRANZ KAFKA**

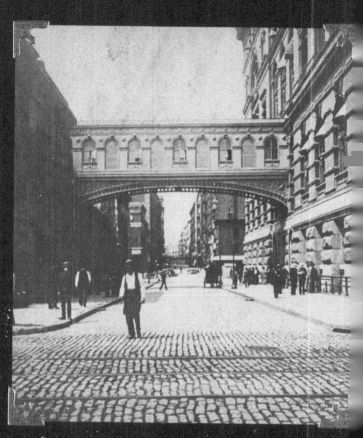

Late-nineteenth-century view of the "Bridge of Sighs"
at the Tombs prison.

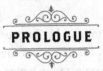

HAPPY IS THE MAN
WHO IS NOT THE CHOSEN ONE

New York City, April 12, 1869

THE ACCUSED MAN sat in a dark corner of the city known as the Tombs. Since its construction in the late 1830s, no one could remember a time when lower Manhattan's combined police court and detention center had not been so called. That the origin of the name was a mystery only made it seem all the more fitting. Some claimed the imposing granite complex had earned the macabre title due to its resemblance to an ancient Near Eastern mausoleum, complete with Egyptian columns suggesting forgotten pharaohs might be buried under the surrounding Five Points slum. A writer of the day proposed that the nickname had caught on because anyone who entered the "gray, begrimned" citadel instantly recognized it as "the tomb of purity, order, peace, and law," despite its official purpose as defender of such virtues. Others supposed it was called the Tombs simply because so many of those brought behind its walls were never seen again.

In any case, to the man listening to details of the charges made against him on an otherwise pleasant spring morning, the building's official name, the Halls of Justice, likely seemed no closer to the truth.

Though accused of attempting to swindle the public with photographs he claimed showed the souls of the dead keeping company with the living, William H. Mumler remained impassive, either oblivious to his surroundings or a true believer in the righteousness of his cause. As the words "fraud," "felony," "larceny," and, most unexpected in a place like this, "supernatural" echoed through the courtroom, Mumler sat with a stolid calm. Only the collar and tie straining around his thick neck suggested the bind in which the big man now found himself.

Each year, thousands climbed stone steps worn smooth by the footfalls of crime and punishment to reach the Tombs's entrance on Centre Street. On any given day, some four hundred men could be found crammed into a jail designed for half that number. There they lingered and suffered for weeks on end, before eventually making their way from holding cells to the spot where Mumler now sat, and then to the island lunatic asylum floating like a body in the East River, or to Sing Sing, the state penitentiary up the Hudson, or to the gallows assembled when needed in the cobblestone prison yard just beyond the courtroom's walls.

That this was a place of dire consequences was apparent all around him. Screams from the main holding pen, where ten dozen huddled as if in steerage, could be heard even through granite. Making his way to the arraignment that morning, Mumler would have seen wooden planks for the hangman's scaffold stacked and ready beneath an elevated gangway that the condemned ascended during their final walk on earth. In homage to the similar passage found in Venice, some doomed but worldly souls had taken to calling it *Ponte dei Sospiri*. The Bridge of Sighs.

"The Tombs has a history, and a very sad one," a reporter noted earlier that year. "Men have spent terrible days and nights there, with death, for which they were wholly unprepared, staring them in the face from the gallows' beam. What ghostly visions of murdered victims have trooped through those cells!"

Mumler saw no such visions during his stay in the Tombs. He did, however, bring ghosts of his own. If not for the specters that had followed him from New England to New York these past few years, and if not for the universal hunger for proof of their existence, he would be a free man.

———

THE COURTROOM THAT MORNING was crowded with other kinds of otherworldly figures as well, though these were indisputably made of flesh and bone. Pale, gaunt men with wild eyes and wilder beards shifted in their seats. Older women, dressed primly in the style of churches they no longer attended, wore looks of faraway concern. Though accustomed to exploring the darker corners of the spirit realm, they found something about these proceedings more disconcerting than the grave.

The defendant's assembled supporters claimed to feel the presence of the departed not only in a place as close to the veil between this world and the next as the Tombs was thought to be, but throughout the Empire City and the haunted nation around it. They filled the courtroom on a Monday morning in springtime not just because Mumler was in danger, but because they feared their beliefs might be.

Corpulent and full-whiskered, with a head of unkempt hair and a suit coat snugged tight to button over his barrel chest, Mumler was not as insubstantial as some of his gathered supporters. "He belongs to the heavy order of the Spiritualists, of which there are two kinds—the heavy and the fragile," a correspondent from Philadelphia wrote.

The meaty opposite of incorporeal, Mumler was an imposing man, sometimes called "athletic" or "robust" in the euphemisms of the day. Yet still there was a delicacy to him. Trained as an engraver, he had remade himself first as a chemist, then as an artist. He would be an inventor, too, before his time in the physical world was done. Each of these professions required fine work done by punctilious hands, and he had some success in all of them.

Though possibly safeguarded by his heft, he would likely not do well among the criminals the press labeled "hardened and degraded creatures" who were confined to the Tombs each night. Nor could he simply hope to blend in and go unnoticed. A telltale smell of lavender followed him into every room. Black stains lingered on his fingers — evidence that at least some of the charges made against him were true.

――――

THIS MUCH HE WOULD admit: William Mumler, late of Boston, recently of 630 Broadway, was guilty of making pictures.

Without question, he had used his camera and an array of potent chemicals to create images for those in need. Also true, in this work he had doubtless served some higher metaphysical purpose. He had frozen moments in time. He had used sunlight and silver to etch captured instants on rectangles of glass, which through some further alchemy of memory and imagination then became windows on love and loss for all who beheld them.

If there was a lawlessness to any of this, it was one to which the hundreds of photographers then working in New York City might also have pleaded guilty. His block of Broadway alone was among the most photographed acres on the planet, crowded as it was with tourists who never tired of seeing their own eyes stare up at them from newly varnished photographs, and the practitioners of this relatively new art eager to sell to them.

As for the accusation that he had convinced the gullible that he was able to make images not only of those who visited his studio, but of men, women, and children who had passed on to the next world — well, might it not be said that every photograph of a living person will eventually become a picture of the dead?

To bridge the chasm created by death had been arguably the single greatest change the art and technology of photography had brought to human experience. Just a generation before, a departed loved one's features began to decay in the mind's eye of the survivors with the final closing of the coffin lid. For the dead to remain in this world, even if only as a shadow, was to inch closer to immortality. The art had been born of this hope, and inevitably all the great photographers of the day had sought to depict death in ways that reframed the terror of oblivion for the limited comprehension of the living.

Hadn't the most celebrated image maker of the age, Mathew Brady, been lauded for displaying the casualties of war on Broadway, mere blocks from where Mumler had committed his supposed crimes? Hadn't Brady's Scottish protégé, Alexander Gardner, trailed doomed armies like a carrion eater across the battle-scarred South? And hadn't Brady's jealous rival, Jeremiah Gurney, hoped to one-up the master by training his camera on the corpse of Mr. Lincoln himself? Even Samuel Morse, father of both the telegraph and photography in America, acknowledged that his two distance-erasing inventions were born of the same hard fact: that death was the greatest separation of all.

It was not going too far to ask if photography itself might be complicit in this morbid fixation. From its earliest days scarcely thirty years before, it had been called the "black art"—a phrase referring primarily to the silver nitrate stains on a photographer's hands, but also suggestive of a possible connection to the much older "dark arts" of magic and sorcery.

To make images of any kind was to traffic in the uncanny; to make images of such perfection that they approached the divine was to invite the widespread belief that a camera somehow captured a sliver of its subject's soul. Every photographer was called upon to become a necromancer now and then.

To Mumler, the great injustice was that he alone had been arrested for making images that held a mirror up to the living and asked them to consider what lay beyond. If the root of his transgression was to be found in the notion that human ingenuity might be harnessed to once again see those who had passed on, why was it not all photography now on trial?

"The history of all pioneers of new truths is relatively the same," Mumler would later say, "and happy is the man who is not the chosen one to meet the prejudices of a skeptical world in the development of some new discovery."

―――――

ACROSS THE CITY, it had been a week full of consternation over other supposedly new spiritual discoveries. A few days before, at Christ Church in midtown, an Episcopal liturgy had been interrupted when the organist abruptly stopped playing and ran from the choir loft, complaining that "every fibre of his body rebelled" against taking part in worship he had suddenly realized was a "burlesque." On the same day, at a meeting of Methodists, debate on the question of allowing women to preach nearly brought the congregation to blows. And in Brooklyn, a hundred Spiritualists like those gathered in the courtroom on Mumler's behalf had met to hear an inspirational lecture on how their beliefs would soon rise to become the country's dominant creed.

"Spiritualism is the future church," the speaker had told them. "Its roof will be the stars; its walls the universe; the earth its foundation. Its choir the wild waving sea. Its idea the union of progress, steam, intelligence, and the locomotive; its aim God, Justice, and Immortality."

These were not beliefs held only by an oddball few. In the aftermath of the Civil War, during which more than three-quarters of a million were killed, the nation exploded with interest in the possibility of making contact with the spirit world.

Though often remembered as a fringe pursuit run by séance-holding hucksters, Spiritualism was a major cultural force. For a time, it seemed it would become one of the most widely held religious perspectives in America. Unlike other fast-growing religions in late-nineteenth-century New York—Catholicism and Judaism—the majority of Spiritualists were neither immigrants nor outsiders, but men and women from moneyed and established East Coast families. Their pedigrees couldn't protect them from the war and its emotional costs, and so in the war's wake many American cities became home to a form of spiritual searching as peculiar as it was poignant.

Mumler rarely became so expansive in his proclamations of faith, but he too believed, like the Brooklyn Spiritualist preacher, that the unimaginable transformations of this steam-fired, locomotive age would provide mortals with the keys to the life to come. Photography, in his view, offered truths unknown to earlier divine revelations. The images he had created were proof that scripture was now being, as the name of his art proclaimed, written with light.

Unfortunately for Mumler, the prosecutor assigned to his case was having none of this. If he had the authority, he soon told the court, he would put the whole "future church" of Spiritualism on trial, along with the notion that the speeding locomotive of technology could provide any answers to questions of faith.

Once the formal complaints had been entered into the record, the judge looked down at the defendant in his rumpled suit, his unruly beard. This Mumler was perhaps as unlikely a prophet of a new religion as had ever troubled the powers that be. But then, maybe being unlikely, rumpled, and unruly was a requirement of the job.

"What is it you've got to say to these charges?" the judge asked.

Though he would often be called "Mumbler" when his story began to find its way into the city's daily papers, and from there into news published around the world, Mumler spoke clearly enough now to be heard by members of the press spread among the ghostly crowd in the gallery.

In the weeks to come, these same seats would fill with

witnesses for the prosecution and defense: eminent photographers and others who knew far more about the "black art" than
his accusers ever could; the mayor's henchmen from Tammany
Hall, whose own large-scale corruption made them quick to
crack down on penny-ante crooks; the showman P. T. Barnum,
who hated all swindles except those he created and controlled;
and most important, Mumler's own satisfied customers, happy to
have been given the opportunity to purchase final reminders of
dear ones now gone.

"I have nothing to say," Mumler said.

"Do you pretend," the judge pressed, "that you take spirit photographs by supernatural means?"

"Have no answer to make to this question either," Mumler
replied. "I demand an examination."

No doubt the judge thought that even if the defendant might
be able to fool the world with his camera tricks, he would not be
taken in. Yet despite his desire to dispense quickly with criminals
of all kinds, he was intrigued by the figure before him, and likely
supposed others would be as well.

"The intensity of the interest manifested by the public in this
case," a reporter from the *New York Daily Tribune* soon wrote,
"has perhaps never been surpassed in reference to any criminal
investigation in this city." *Harper's Weekly* agreed: "The case of
the people against William H. Mumler is ... remarkable and
without precedent in the annals of criminal jurisprudence ... and
strange as it may seem, there are thousands of people who believe
that its development will justify the claims made by the spiritual
photographer."

"The accused does not know and has never pretended to
know by what power or process, other than that of producing
an ordinary photograph, these spirit photographs are produced,"
Mumler's attorney declared. "There are a great many intelligent
men and women who after careful investigation, are firm believ-

ers that the pictures are truly likenesses of the spirits of the departed, and every day the number of sitters, investigators, and
believers is increasing. He and such believers are of the opinion
that the taking of these pictures is a new feature in photography, yet in its infancy surely, but gradually and slowly progressing
to greater perfection in the future, requiring for such perfection
time and a scientific knowledge of the power that is operating."

It was a time when rapidly increasing scientific knowledge
was regarded not as the enemy of supernatural obsessions, but an
encouragement to them. Electricity had given credence to no-
tions of invisible energies operating beyond human comprehension. The telegraph had made communication possible over stag-
gering distances, which raised hopes of receiving messages from
the great beyond. Now came Mumler and his camera offering
sight beyond sight.

With other cases to get to on this busy Monday morning, the
judge instructed officers of the court to hold the spirit photographer in the Tombs until such time as a formal trial might begin.
As Mumler was led away to the jailhouse, the gathered Spiritualists dispersed into the streets. Passing by the Egyptian columns
and down the granite stairs, the troubled souls floated through
Manhattan like mist, as if a vast catacomb beneath the city had
creaked open at last.

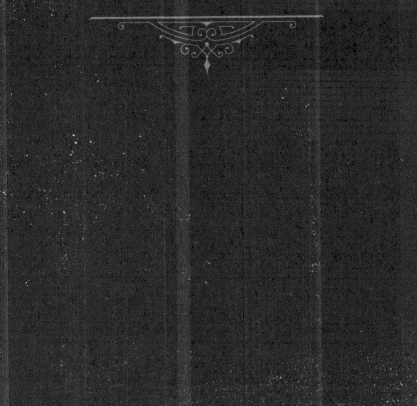

PART I
THE BLACK ART

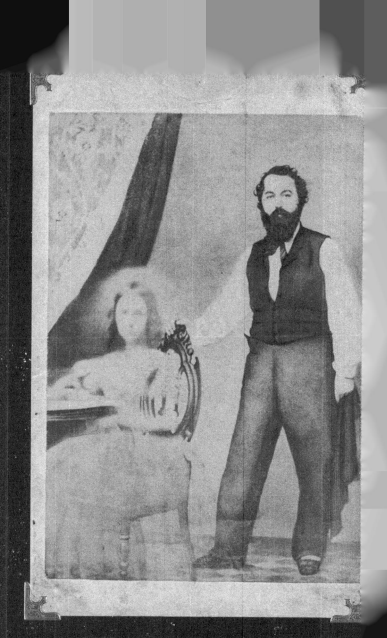

William Mumler's first photograph, 1862.

CHAPTER 1

PROCURE THE REMEDY
AT ONCE AND BE WELL

BEFORE THE SUMMER of 1862, William H. Mumler had never seen a ghost, but he had been bewitched by a woman.

It was under her spell that he first stood in front of a camera —his coat casually off, his thick arms holding the draping black lens cloth as a horseman might a saddle—and took an accidental self-portrait that would change his life. The image showed not only Mumler himself—a big man with an untamable mane bristling past his ears, and bushy whiskers that often obscured his bow tie—but also a faint figure sitting beside him in a room where he had thought himself quite alone.

At the time, Mumler was only dabbling in photography. An engraver by trade, he had for many years been gainfully employed by Bigelow Brothers & Kennard, Boston's premier fabricator and importer of high-end metal goods. Learning the craft of picture-making at a nearby studio was a weekend pastime, a way to fill the empty hours of a bachelor's Sunday afternoons.

The mechanical tinkering and chemical experimentation that then were part of the photographic process were not wholly alien to him, however. His paid work consisted of using fine tools and solvents to repair and add detail to jewelry, clocks and watches, sterling flatware, and the silver altarpieces favored by churches for liturgical use. In a city that had produced Paul Revere and still rang out with the tones of church bells the Revolutionary silversmith and bell founder had made, to work with metal was to be part of a respected tradition.

Mumler was an engaging if enigmatic sort. "A rather portly man, with an agreeable presence," in the view of one acquaintance. He was known for showing "a manner of somewhat reserved good-fellowship" and "a glance out of seemingly good-natured black eyes that yet conveyed the impression that they took in more than they gave out." His dark hair, while getting scarce on top, grew lavishly on his cheeks and chin through the end of his life, and probably beyond.

Despite his lumpy appearance, he was a careful man, and had done his job well enough to become the principal engraver for a successful and growing company—one that would stay in business another full century, in fact. Located at 219 Washington Street, a short stroll from the Boston Common and the Massachusetts statehouse, the showroom was a regular stop for ladies of leisure out for an afternoon of shopping. "Those desirous of making purchases of jewelry, watches, or articles of *virtu* will find one of the richest and best selected stocks at the store of Messrs Bigelow Bros & Kennard," a tourist guide to Boston recommended. "Their store is well-stocked, and their goods are all warranted of the best quality."

In an era when a laborer such as a blacksmith or carpenter counted himself lucky to make ten dollars per week, Mumler's specialized skills earned him as much as eight dollars a day. He might have enjoyed a long career with the firm and perhaps even followed another former employee of humble beginnings, Martin Kennard, into partnership with the founders John and Alanson Bigelow, and from there onto a higher social plane. "Although a self-made man," it was later said of Kennard, "he acquired rare culture and gained an unusually discriminating taste in art."

Mumler was on course for a similar ascension. Yet he was increasingly unsettled by a vague feeling of discomfort that determined he would take another path. "I had the reputation as an honest and trustworthy person," he recalled wistfully some years later of the turn his fortunes would soon take. With the full confidence of employers who provided luxury items for the nation's wealthiest families—far from merely a local concern, Bigelow Brothers had regular clients as far away as New Mexico—he was proud to note that he was often "entrusted with their valuables to a large amount." But, he lamented, "this reputation, which I had been years in establishing, vanished like a soap bubble."

At first his troubled spirit had manifested itself physically. The nature of his engraving work—long hours stooped over his bench, inhaling tiny shards of silver and polishing fumes—had brought about chronic gastrointestinal distress. Doctors were no help; as often as not, their prescriptions exacerbated existing symptoms and created new problems of their own. Mumler was not only an engraver, however, but a lifelong intuitive inventor with a well-developed understanding of chemical properties. Though he would eventually hold a handful of patents, the ability to mix a variety of ingredients to beneficial effect was a skill he had first learned in the hardscrabble mill town of Lawrence, some twenty miles northwest of Boston, where his parents worked as confectioners for a time, and his mother became known for "being the first to introduce into that place a superior article of molasses candy."

No stranger to taking precise measurements and blending compounds, he drew on the kitchen lessons of the Mumler household and soon concocted a series of digestive remedies to test on himself. So pleased was he with the eventual results, he placed an advertisement in the local papers offering to share his discovery with the world. "I am an engraver," he wrote. "My sedentary habits brought on Indigestion and Dyspepsia, from which I suffered terribly for a number of years." He then included a dubious-sounding backstory to give his new remedy a tried-and-true history with a dash of invented Old World provenance. "I tried various doctors and advertised nostrums to no avail: they only seemed to aggravate the disease, and I began to despair of finding relief, when I came into possession of an old German Receipt from an eminent German physician. I made the medicine and found instant relief. I have never suffered since I took the first bottle. I take this method to put it before the public, not to make money, but to relieve those who are suffering from the same disease."

Of course, he was not so invested in the relief of suffering dyspeptics that he intended to give his bottles away for free. Guessing his own experience might not be enough to inspire sales, he enlisted testimonials from others who had tried his treatment. Whether real or imagined, they were all similarly satisfied: "For the cause of suffering humanity," one wrote, "I consider it my Christian duty to place before the public, UNSOLICITED by any one, the wonderful cure in my case of dyspepsia, by the use of Mr. Mumler's *German Remedy*. I have been troubled over six years with this terrible disease, procured one bottle only and am a WELL MAN today. To those who have suffered as I have I say PROCURE THE REMEDY AT ONCE and be well."

Mumler apparently enjoyed enough success with his German remedy that he soon was able to leave his job behind and strike out on his own. He opened an engraving and copperplate printing business just up the road from the workshop where he had spent so many hours through the previous years. Washington Street then was still a dirt road, but it was well traveled and thick with commerce. To have his name on an awning alongside the likes of the Bigelow Brothers & Kennard and the hugely successful wallpaper merchant Samuel H. Gregory should have been a milestone assuring a bright future.

But the malaise that had troubled him lingered. As he grew older and the sweet smells of his parents' confectionary kitchen became an ever more distant memory, he was increasingly interested in what might be called a dyspepsia of the soul — a gnawing dissatisfaction with the possibility that, no matter whether he worked for himself or others, the labor of his days might add up to nothing. The war just begun in the southern states meant the end of certainty for nearly all men his age. Barely thirty, he was perhaps too young for a midlife crisis, but questions of mortality and meaning haunted him.

"After a man has passed into the middle age," he later wrote, "he looks forward, at the best, to but a few years of earthly existence, and naturally asks, 'Is this all of life?'"

The answer, Mumler soon found, was no. There was so much more to life — and death — than he had ever imagined.

To begin with, there was Hannah.

———

MRS. HANNAH GREEN STUART was the proprietress of a photographic studio and gallery in between Mumler's new and former places of business. When and how the two first met is not known, but given that such studios usually had large windows to let in natural light, it is possible he simply spotted her through the glass one day. The quality he soon described as her "magnetism" undoubtedly did the rest.

That she was now a few storefronts closer to his day-to-day activities than she had been was probably not a detail he had overlooked when scouting a location for his nascent printing and engraving enterprise. By all accounts, Mrs. Stuart was an intensely charismatic person. Her prominent brow and pronounced cheekbones had the look of a classical statue, while her dark hair parted down the middle and pulled to a loose bun in back was all New England. Boston at the time grandly regarded itself as the Hub of the Universe. To Mumler, Hannah was a Venus at the Hub's very center.

The proximity of Mrs. Stuart's studio, along with his skill as what was known then as a "practical chemist," soon led Mumler to take an interest in photography—or rather, to take an interest in Hannah's interest in the same.

There was plenty he might have found intriguing about this young married woman with an absent husband. They were roughly the same age, yet she seemed far more experienced spiritually, professionally, and otherwise. What became of Mr. Stuart remains unknown, though a name sometimes also associated with the Washington Street photographic studio, A. M. Stuart, may belong to one Adelbert M. Stuart, who enlisted as a private in Massachusetts's 53rd Regiment in 1862 and was killed in Louisiana the following year.

Given the discomforts with which he had recently contended, and the remedies he pursued as a result, Mumler was likely drawn first of all to the fact that Hannah, too, was an entrepreneur in the business of helping people. As a younger woman she had supported herself through the braiding of hair—not as a stylist or barber, but rather as a kind of midwife for the grieving, applying her skills to the sensitive work of weaving the hair of the dead. It was common practice of the time to save hair clippings from loved ones lost and craft them into elaborate keepsakes. In the years Hannah learned the art, one of the dozens of advertisements offering this service read: "Hair braided to order in the form of Guards, Necklaces, Bracelets, Vest Chains, Finger Rings, Crosses, etc, etc, with faithful attention to the identity of the person furnished."

A remnant of the pre-photographic era, this Old World craft had recently begun to incorporate the latest innovation, using small photographs in a cameo or locket attached to the braided hair. As an extension of the same consolation she had long provided to the bereaved, she started taking these photographs herself. While Mumler greeted his thirtieth year with dyspeptic dread, Hannah in the same stage of life acquired photographic equipment and opened her own studio.

The services she provided were not limited to enshrining the relics of the dead or capturing their likenesses, however. She also claimed to speak to the deceased as clearly as one might call to a lover in a nearby room.

Hannah, Mumler soon learned, was a medium. Not only did she claim to communicate with those who passed to the great beyond, she at times acted as a vessel for the voices of the departed. When her clients came to her with a lock of hair or a swatch of fabric and asked her to make something with which the loved one it came from might be remembered, Hannah offered far more—a direct connection, a hint of enduring love.

Naturally, for such barrier-breaching, any medium would ask a small fee. For a slightly larger payment, she might also diagnose the illnesses of the living through the use of psychic second sight. As a "natural clairvoyant for diagnosing and treating disease," Mumler noted, she "has been subject to this influence since her earliest recollection." Her mother, too, had shown signs of clairvoyance, but though the condition was apparently hereditary, for her diagnostic acuity Hannah relied on another source. When asked where her expert clinical opinions had come from, she often replied, "Dr. Benjamin Rush," the long-dead physician and Revolutionary patriot who she claimed had provided her with all the medical knowledge required.

For all Hannah's spiritual gifts, Mumler was most moved by "her wonderful magnetic powers." Summoning up the aptest compliment in an age newly enamored with electricity, and the possibility that energy of all kinds might be stored and used for ever greater spiritual purposes, Mumler considered Hannah "a perfect battery."

"What is electricity?" he once asked. "We know it is a force; it passes silent and invisibly over the wire and performs its work;

therefore we know it exists. But can this same electricity be made visible? Yes, by employing a medium, in the form of a vacuum tube, when by connecting with a battery, a stream of invisible electricity is made visible to the human eye, in its natural condition."

Standing at her place behind the counter of her photographic studio, a vision behind glass whenever he walked by on the packed dirt of Washington Street, Hannah was to Mumler the hidden forces of the universe suddenly made manifest. A cure at last to the existential maladies with which he had so long been afflicted.

"I have seen men faint," he recalled with perhaps a hint of jealousy, "under the peculiar reaction caused in their systems by imparting this wonderful, life-giving principle of *animal magnetism.*" For a man of scientific inclination, the popular notion that the mind could influence matter through the workings of electro-biology was perhaps the best explanation for what he had begun to feel. Speaking with greater intimacy, and possibly from personal experience, he described what it meant to be touched by someone of such obvious power. "On her placing her hands upon the head of a patient," he said, "the subtle current is felt distinctly coursing through every tissue of the body."

Mumler was not a Spiritualist when he met this wonderfully magnetic medium, nor did he think it possible to communicate with the dead even when he took his first spirit photograph. Mrs. Stuart, however, was nothing if not persuasive. Being in her presence made it difficult *not* to believe. She had introduced him to this strange new process of writing with darkness and light, but he still had much to learn about the art that was soon to take over his life. It had been haunted long before Mumler came along.

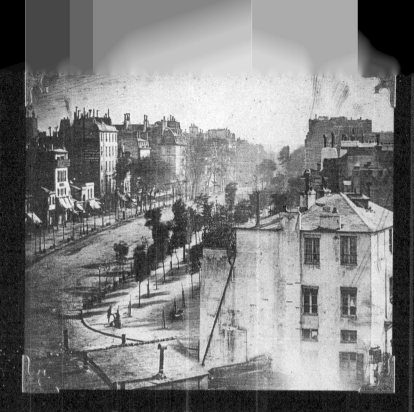

"Boulevard du Temple," the first known
photograph to include people.
Louis-Jacques-Mandé Daguerre, 1838.

CHAPTER 2

LOVE AND PAINTING ARE QUARRELSOME COMPANIONS

WHEN Louis-Jacques-Mandé Daguerre introduced his process for fixing images on silver-plated sheets of copper in 1839, he did not believe it would ever be used for portraits. The problem was in the eyes.

In the work of portraiture, the object looked upon by the camera—the human face—inconveniently insists on looking back. Unlike the dark pupil of a glass lens, the eye needs to blink. Exposure times for Daguerre's images might be as long as twenty minutes. The hundreds of tiny movements a face would make during that time resulted in pictures that were blurred at best and sometimes fully unintelligible. As a medium for capturing living moments, photography's original sin was that signs of life broke the camera's spell.

Daguerre discovered this himself during his earliest photographic efforts to document human activity. At eight o'clock one bright morning in 1838, he pointed his camera to the busy Boulevard du Temple in Paris. From his studio window he saw the crowded street, full as always with people and wagons going about the business of a new day. Yet despite what the artist's eye could behold, when he examined the image he had made after an exposure of about twelve minutes, he noticed that only two figures were apparent: the dark outline of a bootblack stooped before a customer standing tall over him on a walkway that appeared otherwise empty. As Parisians rushed around them, these two were as still as the buildings and trees, and so they alone remained fixed for the future to see.

The man who often claimed responsibility for bringing photography to the United States, Samuel Finley Breese Morse, met Daguerre in Paris shortly after each man had invented something that would change the world. The daguerreotype and the telegraph do not seem to have much in common, but in Morse's understanding they were technologies nearly identical in their ultimate effect. Each had succeeded in erasing distance; through their application there was no chasm too vast that could not now be closed.

Enshrined in American history as an inventor, Morse identified himself first of all as an artist. He had been born in Charlestown, Massachusetts, across the Charles River from Boston, some forty-five years before he began tinkering with electricity and chemicals, and had supported himself as a painter from his college days. While studying philosophy at Yale, he painted miniatures on ivory for five dollars apiece and expanded his understanding of shadow, light, and perception through experiments with a camera obscura, a darkened chamber in which the image of an object is received through a pinhole and focused on a facing surface. Specializing in portraits, he continued to make his living teaching art even after he conceived of the communication system that would permanently shrink the earth.

The son of a Calvinist minister who also wrote the nation's first geography textbook, Morse had been concerned with the question of distance all his life. He wrote home constantly during the extensive travels of his youth, and was often vexed by the time it took to convey thoughts and feelings. "I can imagine mama wishing that she could hear of my arrival, and thinking of thousands of accidents that may have befallen me," the young man called Finley by his family wrote from London when he was twenty years old. "I wish that in an instant I could communicate the information; but three thousand miles are not passed over in an instant and we must wait four long weeks before we can hear from each other."

There was at the time something of the artist's dreamy mysticism about such a wish, but he was not at all one for the supernatural. The Reverend Dr. Jedediah Morse had raised his three boys to be thoroughly orthodox in their Christian faith, observing the Sabbath and looking askance at all competing superstitions. In the same letter, Finley described events much like those that would convulse his own country decades later when Spiritualism was born, but he apparently had little patience for spirits at the time. "There has a ghost made its appearance a few streets only from me which has alarmed the whole city," he wrote. "It appears every night in the form of shriekings and groanings. There are crowds at the house every night, and, although they all hear the noises, none can discover from whence they come. The family have quitted the house. I suppose tis only a hoax by some rogue which will be brought out in time."

As he grew older, though, he learned something of the kind of loss that might make ghostly beliefs more difficult to resist.

He was a young father and husband when he fully embraced the notion that he would paint for his living. Like artists of any age, he felt keenly the financial uncertainty of his chosen profession even as he gained some early renown, and so he had counted himself extremely fortunate in 1825 when he received a commission to paint the French hero of the American Revolution, the Marquis de Lafayette, then in the United States to begin a tour commemorating the fiftieth anniversary of 1776.

Upon hearing that he had been selected from among several other prominent painters— including John Wesley Jarvis, John Vanderlyn, Charles Ingham, Samuel Waldo, and Rembrandt Peale—he wrote with great excitement to his wife that he expected to be paid "at least seven hundred dollars—probably a thousand." There would also be an engraving made from the finished portrait, and keepsake cards printed, sales of which would net him half the profits.

His one regret was that the work would take him from home for three weeks. The couple by then had settled in Connecticut, and Morse was to work with Lafayette in Washington. If it went as well as he thought it would, this portrait alone would allow the family to relocate to New York, where his artistic ambitions naturally led. "The only thing I fear," he said, "is that it is going to deprive me of my dear Lucretia."

Lucretia Morse was then a twenty-five-year-old dark-haired beauty, and the thirty-four-year-old Finley loved her with an intensity that he at times found frightening. Given the importance of light to an artist, it probably came as no surprise to those who knew him that he would fall for a girl said to "spread perpetual sunshine around every circle in which she moved."

"Love and painting are quarrelsome companions," Morse had claimed prior to meeting her. "The house of my heart is too small for both of them." But upon encountering Lucretia, the oldest daughter of a wealthy New Hampshire family, he apparently built an addition.

"The more I know of her the more amiable she appears," he told his parents early in their courtship. "She is very beautiful and yet no coquetry; she is modest, quite to diffidence, and yet frank and open-hearted." As he had previously fallen in and out of infatuations in a "harum-scarum" way, he feared his parents might object. This time, however, he assured them that he was approaching his newfound inclinations as a serious matter.

His parents were encouraging but understandably concerned with the speed with which this had all happened. The girl was young, after all, and they had known each other barely a month. "I wish to see the young lady who has captivated you so much," his mother said. "I hope she loves religion, and that, if you and she form a connection for life, some five or six years hence, you may go hand in hand to that better world where they neither marry nor are given in marriage."

They were married in September of 1818, having waited two years rather than the five or six Mrs. Morse had suggested. Lucretia was by then nineteen; she gave birth to a baby girl the following year, and a boy soon after. The years of their marriage were often financially strained, but Finley's artistic abilities flourished with her as his muse. That his passion for her did not wane can be seen in his brushstrokes. When he painted Lucretia and their two children in 1822, he captured a shine in her dark hair and rosy cheeks, and a glow seemed to emanate from her pale skin, blending with the sunlight that filtered through a cloud behind her.

Another son, Charles, arrived in January 1825, just days before Morse left to meet with Lafayette. It was to be the beginning of a prosperous new chapter in their lives.

Arriving in Washington on February 8, 1825, he planned on staying until the marquis departed on the twenty-third. That would leave just enough time, he hoped, to make a study of his subject's facial features, planning to use the resulting small sketches and rough paintings for a more formal full-length portrait when he returned to his New Haven studio.

As it happened, Morse had arrived in the capital at an exciting time. John Quincy Adams had just been elected the nation's sixth president. There had been no clear winner in the previous year's popular vote, nor in the Electoral College, and so after a tumultuous few months of politicking by the front-runners, the House of Representatives put a second Adams in the White House.

With an important portrait to paint and the political landscape shifting under his feet, Morse was kept busy. He met the current and future presidents, passed an evening with the writer James Fenimore Cooper, who then was well known for his recent novel *The Pioneers*, the first of his Leatherstocking Tales, and of course began his work with Lafayette, though not without some frustration. "He is so harassed by visitors and has so many letters to write," Morse noted, "that I find it exceedingly difficult to do the subject justice."

Yet for all this excitement, Lucretia was never far from his mind. He wrote to her as soon as he arrived, and continued to send notes, sometimes more than once a day, as on February 9:

> My Dearest Wife,
>
> The great contest is over, John Quincy Adams is the President of the United States, just elected on the first ballot this day. Expresses have gone off in every direction and I suppose you may have heard the intelligence before this reaches you, but as there is a moment before the mail closes, I thought I would let you know it as soon as the mail went. I was not present myself as I had an engagement with Gen. LaFayette; I have thus far succeeded to my mind; will write again soon. Love to all the children.
>
> In the greatest haste but with ardent affection as ever,
> your loving husband,
> Finley

The next day he was able to again secure some of Lafayette's time, and made careful observations of the face he would need to know intimately if he was to do his job well. "There never was a more perfect example of accordance between face and character," he said of the marquis. "He has all that noble firmness and consistency, for which he has been so distinguished, strongly indicated in his whole face." As the general's son was traveling with him, Morse soon made the acquaintance of Georges Washington de Lafayette, a man about ten years his senior. "This is Mr. Morse, the painter, the son of the geographer," the general told his son. "He has come to Washington to take the topography of my face." The obvious affection the elder Lafayette felt for him was yet another indication to Morse not only that he was "blest," but that the struggling part of his life was coming to an end.

Then a letter arrived from his father, four days after it had been sent.

February 8th, 1825

My affectionately beloved Son,

Mysterious are the ways of Providence. My heart is in pain and deeply sorrowful while I announce to you the sudden and unexpected death of your dear and deservedly loved wife. Her disease proved to be an affection of the heart—incurable, had it been known.

She was up about five o'clock yesterday p.m. to have her bed made as usual; was unusually cheerful and social; spoke of the pleasure of being with her dear husband in New York ere long; stepped into bed herself, fell back with a momentary struggle on her pillow, her eyes were immediately fixed, the paleness of death over-spread her countance, and in five minutes more, without the slightest motion, her mortal life terminated.

It happened that just at this moment I was entering her chamber door with Charles in my arms, to pay her my usual visit and to pray with her. The nurse met me affrighted, calling for help.

Your mother, the family, our neighbors, full of the tenderest sympathy and kindness, and the doctors thronged the house in a few minutes. Everything was done that could be done to save her life, but her appointed time had come, and no earthly power or skill could stay the hand of death.

It was the Lord who gave her to you, the chiefest of all your earthly blessings, and it is He that has taken her away, and may you be enabled, my son, from the heart to say: "Blessed be the name of the Lord."

Morse left Washington immediately. The study of Lafayette he had undertaken went unfinished, its brushstrokes ending abruptly with a corner of the canvas left unpainted.

He, too, was undone. Just days before, he had written to Lucretia in excitement about all they had to look forward to. He had detailed the bons mots he had exchanged with politicians and celebrities, described the meals he had eaten. He now realized that when he had last written to her, she was already dead.

What had it meant that he had thought he was communicating with her? Had she not been fully alive in his mind as he scratched his "ardent affection" across the page? "The confusion and derangement consequent on such an afflicting bereavement as I have suffered," he wrote, "have rendered it necessary for me to devote the first moments of composure to looking about me, and to collecting and arranging the fragments of the ruin which has spread such desolation over all my earthly prospects."

His "derangement" was no exaggeration. It was surely a kind of insanity to talk with such passion to someone who did not exist, to believe without question in her enduring presence. There could be no denying that she lingered in his thoughts as real as she had ever been. "Oh! What a blow!" he wrote. "I dare not yet give myself up to the full survey of its desolating effects. Every day brings to my mind a thousand new and fond connections with dear Lucretia, all now ruptured. I feel a dreadful void, a heart-sickness, which time does not seem to heal but rather to aggravate."

Two things haunted him. First, the days it took for him to hear the news—days when his wife lay dying, when his father carried their infant son to her bedside only to watch her fade away, when her body was lowered into the grave. Being there might not have prevented any of it. If the doctors were correct, her death was foretold by a defect in her heart that had been waiting to make itself known since it was formed in the womb. But hearing of it instantly would have made a great difference, at least to his own grief.

There was also the finality with which her face had simply vanished from his life.

"I am ready almost to give up," he wrote his parents two months later. "The thought of seeing my dear Lucretia and returning home to her served always to give me fresh courage and spirits whenever I felt worn down by the labors of the day. Now I hardly know what to substitute in her place."

Whether by choice or desperation, the answer for Morse proved to be work. He no longer sought greatness as a painter. Instead, he became a man driven by the conviction that the distances that had suddenly defined his life could be undone. With his wife's death he determined that no man should remain as unknowing for so long as he had been of his lover's fate, and should never more fear forgetting a single detail of her beauty.

The Spiritualist sisters Kate and Margaret Fox.
Thomas M. Easterly, 1852.

CHAPTER 3

TIES WHICH DEATH ITSELF
COULD NOT LOOSE

WHETHER ONE REGARDS it as a fad, a cult, a scam, or a sincere transformation of American belief, there is little disagreement over how Spiritualism began. Some fourteen years before William Mumler first touched a camera in 1862, when both he and Hannah Green Stuart were adolescents growing up on the outskirts of Boston, two other teenagers living some two hundred miles west of the Massachusetts border began to tell stories about things that went bump in the night.

As the movement's creation myth was eventually told, it started in the spring of 1848, when a family in the village of Hydesville, New York, not far from Rochester, noticed faint but persistent tapping sounds emanating from their floorboards and walls. The youngest children in the house, sisters Kate and Margaret Fox, age thirteen and fifteen respectively, insisted that their home was being visited by spirits. No one else took much notice until the girls convinced their older sister, thirty-four-year-old Leah, of the presence of a dead man who would not be ignored. The three Fox sisters then persuaded their parents to listen more closely.

"It sounded like someone knocking in the east bedroom, on the floor," their mother said. "We could hardly tell where to locate the sounds, as sometimes it sounded as if the furniture was moved, but on examination we found everything in order." She encouraged the girls to ignore the sounds of a settling house, and they all tried to sleep, but the noise persisted. "Although not very loud, it produced a jar of the bedsteads and chairs that could be felt when we were in bed. It was a tremulous motion, more than a sudden jar. We could feel the jar when standing on the floor."

On the following night, the disturbance intensified. "The noises were heard in all parts of the house," Mrs. Fox continued. "My husband stationed himself outside of the door while I stood inside, and the knocks came on the door between us. We heard footsteps in the pantry, and walking down-stairs; we could not rest, and I then concluded that the house must be haunted by some unhappy, restless spirit."

Mr. Fox agreed. "I do not know of any way to account for these noises as being caused by any natural means," he said. "We have searched every nook and corner in and about the house, at different times, to ascertain if possible whether anything or any body was secreted there that could make the noise, and have not been able to find anything which would or could explain the mystery. It has caused a great deal of trouble and anxiety."

For their part, the Fox girls seemed to regard the noises as an invitation. They called out questions to the "unhappy, restless spirit" and received further knocks and raps in return. Through this call and response they were soon able to ascertain that their home was haunted by a man—"aged 31 years . . . with a wife and five children, three sons and two daughters"—who had been murdered in the house a year before. He was, the spirit told them, buried in the cellar, ten feet below the packed earth.

When the neighbors heard about the strange happenings at the Fox farm, they came first by the dozen, then by the hundreds. The sisters demonstrated how the tapping and knocking seemed to follow them even when they moved great distances from the house, and a new religious movement was born.

It was no longer just one murdered man tapping in one up-state farmhouse. Apparently crowds of the dead vied for the attention of the living, longing to be heard. "There must have been a score of spirits who rapped one after the other, some on the table, some on the door, ceiling, windows, floor, etc," Leah Fox wrote. "Some were loud, some low, some rapid and some slower, and no two of them seemed quite the same. Many persons who are familiar with these signals frequently identify them by the sounds."

The three Fox sisters became the first hugely successful American mediums, and inspired others—many of them of similar age and rural background—to make known their own supernatural abilities. Spiritualism, they said, was a gift given to all. As such, it was quickly received and accepted by millions who had apparently been longing to talk with the dead all along. The movement's tenets were flexible enough—or unbearably vague, as critics said—to accommodate a range of practices and personality types. If it had a creed, it was, as one nineteenth-century description stated, "that disembodied human spirits sometimes manifest themselves, or make known their presence and power, to persons in the earthly body, and hold realized communication with them."

Wherever it went and however it was practiced, Spiritualism was embraced not only as a matter of faith but a matter of science, as in the first large public lecture explaining the new movement to the masses, delivered in New York City in November of 1850. The recent events near Rochester, the Reverend S. B. Brittan suggested to a packed crowd at the Stuyvesant Institute on Broadway, were an extension of the telegraph that had recently begun to connect the nation's cities. The messages received by the Fox family were sent by "telegraphy," he said, and the sisters themselves were the first "spiritual telegraph."

"As for the future of this great wonder, what the telegraph may become, or the means of intercommunion between the two worlds may develop, I confess I cannot even speculate upon,"

Brittan said. "The present is our own, and in that we have indeed good cause for congratulation; but beyond our own immediate day and hour who can venture to prophesy the probable future of what we call 'Modern Spiritualism'?" Despite this note of humility, he closed by expressing the task to which he thought all Spiritualists should be devoted: "A connecting bridge should be built between the mortal and immortal worlds," he said, "and a telegraph set in motion through which the ascended souls of earth should enlighten humanity on the actual conditions of the life hereafter."

For their part, the Fox sisters wanted to be clear about which means of communication—electromagnetic or spiritual—deserved to be spoken of first. "I soon received letters from various places," Leah Fox said of the spirit knowledge she had been given, "saying that it had been made known through clairvoyants, speaking mediums and seers, that the same signal had been given to all mediums. Thus we see that God's Telegraph antedated that of Samuel F. B. Morse."

"I well remember the time when the phenomena of spiritual manifestations were first introduced by the Misses Fox," Mumler later recalled, "and I did not, even at that early day, when Spiritualism was so little known and its promulgation so new and wonderful, do, as many others did and do now, scout its pretensions, for I saw the germ of a new era—one in which the human mind would become more free and expanded, and that it would do away with many false and cruel tenets in most of the popular creeds of the day. I was desirous, however, that others should study its reality and its claims to public confidence, as I had neither the time nor the inclination to search into such mysteries, for I had some fears that I might go too deep and that the subject might so involve my meditations as to unfit me for the actual duties of life, of which I had many responsible ones."

Decades later, the middle Fox daughter, Margaret, would acknowledge that it had all begun as a kind of game. As a lark to amuse themselves and give a fright to their family, the girls had learned ways to make tapping sounds without being seen. They had been surprised by the uproar it caused, but then reveled in the attention. In any case, it mattered little what had sparked such intense public interest in a few farm girls and their tall tales. Spiritualism was suddenly the fastest-moving fire of religious reinvention in American history. And like any wildfire, it did not burn in isolation.

In the 1830s—the decade in which William Mumler, Hannah Stuart, the two younger Fox sisters, and other mediums and metaphysical savants too numerous to name were born—the young United States was suffering a spiritual hangover. The period of radical religious fervor known as the Second Great Awakening had lasted forty years and was nearing its end. Though its earliest manifestations had been marked by explosive developments in Christian piety, its later stages moved expressions of faith even farther afield.

The Fox sisters were one embodiment of this trend. Another could be found in a self-taught "magnetic healer" by the name of Andrew Jackson Davis. Before the explosion of Spiritualism lit by the Rochester tappings, Davis had been a not particularly successful practitioner of mesmerism—the manipulation of animal magnetism made popular by the German physician Franz Mesmer in the previous century. In 1847, Davis had published a book that in retrospect seemed to herald the rappings upstate the following year—*The Principles of Nature, Her Divine Revelations, and a Voice to Mankind*—and then had successfully ridden the wave of interest in the Fox sisters to a reputation well beyond what anyone of his humble origins might expect. With the boom in spiritual interests in the 1850s, he became known as "the Seer of Poughkeepsie," the preeminent interpreter of the phenomena natural performers like the Foxes presented to the world. If they were the original evangelists of Spiritualism, Davis was its Saint Paul, providing an intellectual framework in which the pure appeal to emotion and sensation offered by séances might be understood.

As Davis and the Foxes began to travel on lecture tours spreading their new gospel, selling tickets all the while, the new faith extended from the hinterlands to urban centers, redrawing the map of the nation as a topography of ghosts.

And Boston was indisputably its capital. Of the more than one hundred Spiritualist periodicals that came into being in the decades following the Fox family's alleged haunting, the most widely read by far was the *Banner of Light*, whose offices through the 1860s were just two hundred feet north of Mumler's first employer on Washington Street. Soon boasting a circulation in the tens of thousands, the *Banner* promised to present Spiritualism "in all its varied phases, and furnish full and reliable statements of the all important events that may transpire in connection therewith."

From large public lectures to private séances held in "circles" hosted by mediums for hire, to loosely organized discussion groups that over time came to resemble the church services many of the spiritually curious had left behind in favor of more eclectic religious pursuits, the weekly *Banner of Light* and similar journals, like Andrew Jackson Davis's New York–based *Herald of Progress*, advertised thousands of such events held all over the country.

The *Banner*, moreover, was not just a newspaper; it was a religious institution in its own right. It was founded in 1857 by the printer Luther Colby and the journalist William Berry, who had met when both worked for the secular *Boston Daily Post*. In the 1850s, Berry had begun hosting séances in his Cambridge home, to which he soon invited a twenty-four-year-old medium, Fannie Conant.

Born Frances Ann Crowell, Fannie had been raised by a strict

Baptist mother known for troubling the members of her church with "wild delusions" about the presence of spirits in her home. When she was first introduced to the notion of talking to the dead, the medium in the making was just seven years old. Lying ill with a fever that had recently taken her baby sister, Fannie overheard her mother having a conversation in an empty room.

"Who are you talking with, mother?" she asked.

"Well, my dear," her mother replied, "I was talking to the angels."

"The angels, mother! I thought they lived in heaven."

"Yes, but they sometimes come to talk with us in this world."

Knowing what was said of her mother in their church, Fannie worried her mother had gone mad.

"Who are the angels, mother?" she asked.

"The angels, my daughter, are those who once lived on this earth, but who are now called dead. Your little sister is an angel."

"So you were talking to them?"

"Yes."

"What did they say?"

"Your little sister tells me that you are to recover."

Two decades later, Fannie Conant began to host regular séances with William Berry at the *Banner of Light* offices. The angels now spoke not only to her, but through her. Three times a week, believers would pose questions to her and she would reply in the voices of the dead. As one of her disciples later claimed, "She has been the channel through which more than ten thousand different spirits have sent messages to their kindred and friends on earth."

On Sundays, she fell into a trance state and delivered lengthy discourses on the subject of Spiritualism, though again, her words were presented as those of an outside intelligence merely making use of her ability to speak. Even her autobiography, she insisted, was not of her own creation, but of a spirit inhabiting her body.

"It is a simple, straight-forward narrative," one of her collaborators noted, "even though a dead man here describes the life lines of a living woman."

Mainstream papers covered colorful figures like Fannie Conant and Spiritualist developments around the country generally with alternating bemusement and alarm. Institutions both religious and scientific took formal positions on Spiritualist practices, issued in high dudgeon as in this dispatch from rural Ohio in 1853:

SPIRIT RAPPING AND NECROMANCY

One of the churches in the Presbytery of Chilocothe has suspended two of its members, who had been engaged in Spirit Rapping. The Presbytery adopted the following resolution in relation to the Rappings:

Resolved, That the practice of Spirit Rappings, (so called) as it prevails in many parts, is, in view of this Presbytery, a revival of the old abomination of necromancy, so decidedly condemned in the word of God.

As the movement spread and the spiritual marketplace became crowded with those offering connections to the dead, mediums specialized and diversified to set themselves apart. Some delivered messages by means of automatic writing, the practice of going into a trance while allowing a pen to move as if possessed with dramatic speed across a page. Others focused on channeling music, levitating tables, or reading messages in sealed envelopes. The Fox sisters' rapping and knocking were the seed from which a tree with a thousand branches and roots extended in every direction. By current scholarly accounting, as many as eight hundred cities became home to Spiritualist activities of one kind or another. None held nearly as many as the place William Mumler called home.

Among skeptical Yankees of a no-nonsense Puritan mindset, the very ubiquity of Spiritualists in Boston made it ripe for scorn and satire—that most Puritans had believed in witchcraft only furthered the desire of their descendants to distance themselves from what seemed its unwelcome reincarnation.

Well beyond New England, the fact that the Hub of the Universe was also the epicenter of an earthquake of floor rappings and wall knockings became widely noted. As far away as London, Charles Dickens's comic weekly *Household Words* ridiculed the city mercilessly for the growth in its metaphysical population. There were so many spirits and people eager to speak to them pouring into Boston that even the real estate market was seen to respond. "Spiritual phenomena of the medium kind are grown so common in that enlightened country," Dickens's correspondent wrote in 1858, "that furnished apartments are absolutely advertised upon the ground of their suitability for clairvoyant pursuits." He then reproduced one such ad as evidence:

ROOMS FOR MEDIUMS!

To let, at No. 6, Watner Square, two parlours,
furnished in handsome style.

Will be leased singly, or together. Also, an office
on the first-floor suitable for a Healing Medium.

Readers of *Household Words* also discovered that Boston was home to "medium apothecaries whose spiritual, clairvoyant, and mesmeric prescriptions are carefully prepared," as well as "highly gifted butchers, bakers, and candlestick makers of all kinds, anxious to secure the patronage of the spiritual public." If the reporter made no mention of photographers, it was only because Boston's spirits had not yet been taught to pose for the camera.

In the years leading up to the ghostly turn in Mumler's career, Boston's Spiritualist conflagration flared up and then seemed to smolder as memories of the excitement over the Fox family dimmed and as debunkers began to throw sand on the flames.

In a highly publicized visit in 1858, two of the Fox sisters and several local mediums were drawn into a public dispute over their abilities with a cohort of particularly dismissive members of the Harvard science faculty. It did not go well.

The organizer of the event, a well-known physician, H. F. Gardner, had taken up a challenge to produce signs of the supernatural for a prize of $500. Like many new religious movements, Spiritualists had by then developed an acute persecution complex. In their estimation, they were beset on all sides by naysayers who took great pleasure in denying the truths it was their duty to tell. Dr. Gardner's well-attended debate between the mediums and the professors was like Christians thrown to the lions. In the carefully controlled setting prepared by the nonbelievers, the raps and knocks that audiences had come to expect rang hollow. They were met not with reverent applause but doubtful silence.

For Spiritualism as a mass religious movement, the automatic writing seemed to be on the wall. But then came the Civil War, bringing with it death on a scale so vast that it gave the movement new life. What had begun in the innocence of a childish prank performed to relieve the monotony of life on an upstate farm had found in the battlefields of the South a seriousness of purpose beyond the scope or ambition of any early medium.

Like a water glass filled from a barrel, Spiritualism was a hokey parlor trick turned into the receptacle for the most intense collective grief the nation had ever known. Some reports suggest two million people became newly interested in Spiritualism in the wake of the Civil War. This figure may have been exaggerated, both by those who embraced the movement and by those who feared it, but nonetheless it speaks to a hunger that apparently was not being satisfied by traditional places of worship.

While church attendance dropped, private attempts to communicate with the dead soared. The war had left the country in "an impressionable state," the *Banner of Light* announced. "Death never was so generally thought of and talked about among the people." As the English-born Spiritualist Emma Hardinge Britten wrote of the movement whose grip she soon helped strengthen across the United States, "Never in any period of its brief history has it taken so deep and fervent a hold upon the hearts of a mourning people."

The time had come, many among Boston's mediums suggested, to offer the American people the solace of the belief that the sons, brothers, and husbands they'd lost were not gone forever. "Tendrils of love have bound them," Britten continued, "in ties which death itself could not loose."

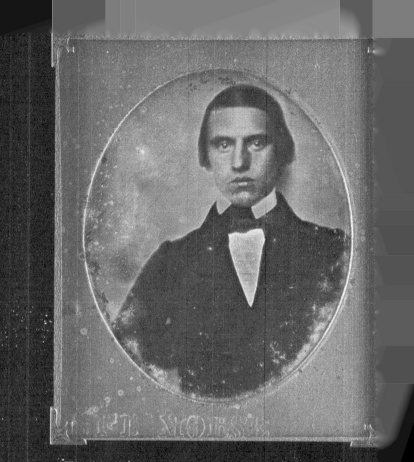

The first successful portrait photograph. Subject unknown.
Samuel Morse, 1840.

CHAPTER 4

A PALACE FOR THE SUN

AS A MAN who had endured such a great and sudden loss, Samuel Morse saw immediately the potential of the daguerreotype as a means of holding fast to cherished faces lost and moments that inevitably proved impermanent. As an artist, however, he could not help but look upon Daguerre's innovation first of all in terms of perspective: a question of distance and how it is perceived. "One of Mr. D.'s plates is an impression of a spider," he observed. "The spider was not bigger than the head of a large pin, but the image, magnified by the solar microscope to the size of the palm of the hand, having been impressed on the plate, and examined through a lens, was further magnified, and showed a minuteness of organization hitherto not seen to exist."

In Morse's view, this was similar to a comment he had once heard when testing his telegraph by tapping out words in the code that bears his name. "The next word you may write is IMMORTALITY," an admirer told him. "I see now that all physical obstacles, which may for a while hinder, will inevitably be overcome; the problem is solved."

Morse was under no illusion that an invention could bring about the end of death; some physical obstacles could never be overcome. But others could. Photography to Morse was essentially a tool for revealing levels of detail usually obscured by space and time. "In a view up the street," he explained, "a distant sign would be perceived, and the eye could just discern that there were lines of letters upon it, but so minute as not to be read with the naked eye. By the assistance of a powerful lens, which magnified 50 times, applied to the delineation, every letter was clearly and distinctly legible, and also were the minutest breaks and lines in the walls of the buildings, and the pavements of the street. The effect of the lens upon the picture was in a great degree like that of the telescope in nature."

In the grandest sense, the problem photography solved was bridging the distance between the known and the unknown.

The fact that Daguerre's invention allowed one to bridge this distance only when an object of interest was as still as the grave barely registered. Almost as an aside to a litany of rapturous praise for the daguerreotypes he had seen, Morse noted of Daguerre's famous Paris street scene, "Objects moving are not impressed. The boulevard, so constantly filled with a moving throng of pedestrians and carriages, was perfectly solitary, except an individual who was having his boots brushed. His feet were of course compelled to be stationary for some time, one being on the box of the boot black, and the other on the ground. Consequently his boots and legs are well defined, but he is without body or head, because these were in motion."

That would be photography's tradeoff: the ability to immobilize a vital scene allows it to be preserved and enjoyed, seemingly forever. Yet in that very immobility its vitality is lost. If a photograph is at once the product of the "black art," as its first practitioners called it, and an image "written with light," as its name suggests, it is so because it is always equally evocative of both movement and paralysis, life and death.

While meeting in Paris with Daguerre, Morse pressed him on how photography might be applied to human faces. "I specially conversed with him in regard to the practicability of taking portraits of living persons," Morse said. "He expressed himself somewhat skeptical as to its practicability, only in consequence of the time necessary for the person to remain immovable. The time for taking an out-door view was from fifteen to twenty minutes, and this he considered too long a time for any one to remain sufficiently still for a successful result."

Back home, however, Morse disregarded the more experienced image maker's opinion. He had by then relocated to New York City, and there he began trial-and-error research of his own. The experiments were in some ways simply extensions of those he had performed as a young artist when he was a student at Yale. "I don't know if you recollect some experiments of mine in New Haven, many years ago," he wrote his brother, "experiments to ascertain if it were possible to fix the image of the camera obscura. I was able to produce different degrees of shade on paper, dipped into a solution of nitrate of silver, by means of different degrees of light; but, finding that light produced dark, and dark light, I presumed the production of a true image to be impracticable, and gave up the attempt."

After being introduced to Daguerre's superior equipment and techniques, Morse brought his teenage daughter, Susan, and several of her friends to a Manhattan rooftop bathed in light. He then asked the girls to stand very still. Susan had been a subject of his artistic endeavors before. As a young child, she had posed beside her mother and brother; as an adult she would appear in his most ambitious work, a massive painting Morse called *The Gallery of the Louvre*, in which his daughter sat in the foreground of a canvas depicting more than three dozen masterpieces from the Paris museum. Most strikingly, as an adolescent she was the subject of one of his best portraits. In a painting often called *The Muse*, she is the image of her mother, the same glow on her pale skin seeming to light the sky behind her.

If his rooftop experiments were another way of summoning the dead, they were less successful. As he described the resulting images, "They are full-length portraits of my daughter, single and also in group with some of her young friends. They were taken out-of-doors, on the roof of a building, in the full sunlight, and with the eyes closed. The time was from ten to twenty minutes." These daguerreotypes have been lost, as has his first successful image, the Church of the Messiah, near Waverly Place in Greenwich Village, which undoubtedly stood as still as the cross no matter how long the artist needed to capture its image.

His only surviving daguerreotype is a portrait of an anonymous young man, taken in 1840. It's not known how long the subject had to stare motionless and unblinking into the camera, but much can be read in his expression. The way his pupils catch the light suggests the eyes are on the verge of tears. While most early photographic portrait artists used a vise-like apparatus that kept the head immobilized to prevent blurring, the young man's stillness seems all his own.

Despite this young man's impressive talent for maintaining a frozen expression during the long exposure of Morse's copper plate, the stillness required of subjects remained a barrier to taking living portraits. Seeing an opportunity in an obstacle, some photographers found the unmoving dead to be a perfect subject. This phenomenon had reasons practical—corpses don't blink—as well as commercial. For nearly half a century, posthumous memorial photographs became popular keepsakes for grieving families. To have an image of a child who died in infancy perhaps later served as the only indication that a brief life had indeed occurred. Even if taken after the child's last breath, a photograph was proof that the sleepless nights and early mornings were not a fantasy; it was evidence of a real son or a real daughter, no less missed though he or she otherwise left no trace.

That capturing an image seemed to have something to do with death went largely unspoken, yet half-serious suggestions of necromancy were often applied to the first generation of photographers. Writing twelve years after Daguerre's announcement of his invention, an American newspaper columnist speculated that the "bewildered astonishment" of the first human to look upon his reflection "could scarcely have exceeded the incredulous surprise with which even the most enlightened and scientific individual would have hearkened a dozen years since to a suggestion of the possibility of fixing and rendering permanent the impression upon a mirror." This work of "apparent necromancy" was "effected through the penetration, patience, and perseverance of the thaumaturgus of the age, Daguerre."

To call the original photographer a "thaumaturgus," a miracle worker, while simultaneously pondering his possible "necromancy" was to suggest his work was not merely a technological marvel, but a death-defying mystery whose alignment with the dark arts or the light remained to be seen.

It was said that the immediate result of the desire to produce lifelike portraits was "abortive efforts" by "an awkward squad of bunglers, whose crude attempts . . . presented a confused chaotic or distorted resemblance of the human countenance divine," but Morse continued his quest. He tried endless variations of chemical treatments and grades of metal, hoping to make possible an exposure window of a duration long enough to allow natural light to fix an image to the plate, but not so long that the open eyes of his subject would dry out and trigger a fit of tics and fidgets, wasting both materials and sunlight.

Morse enlisted another budding daguerreotypist, New York University professor of chemistry John William Draper, and together they constructed an innovative studio that they called "A Palace for the Sun." Within its clear walls they inadvertently created a major commercial enterprise and an indelible part of American culture. "Soon after, we commenced together to take portraits," Morse said, "causing a glass building to be constructed for that purpose on the roof of the University. As our experiments had caused us considerable expense, we made a charge to those who sat for us to defray this expense."

With that, the portrait photography business was born.

"As the Daguerreotype was not patented, but was free to all who would master the art," Morse's nineteenth-century biographer explained of the explosive growth that followed, "a large number of young men, with the enterprise of American youth, flocked to Professor Morse to be instructed in the mysteries of the process, that they might traverse the country and reap the first fruits of its introduction." One such budding student of photography wrote to Morse in 1840: "I learn, with equal astonishment and gratification, that you have succeeded in taking likenesses in ten seconds with diffused light. Pray reveal to me the wondrous discovery!"

Soon enough, Morse's discoveries were learned by thousands of working image makers who opened portrait studios across the nation. The millions who posed stiffly in their sitting rooms, acting dead before the camera for the sake of creating a living memory, also learned the artist's secret: stillness is photography's treasure, but it is also its price.

A photograph, Oliver Wendell Holmes wrote in the 1850s, is a "mirror with a memory." Yet the irrevocable nature of the change it had wrought on memory and forgetting, experience of the past and expectations of the future, suggested that the notion of sight as limited and time-bound would soon be forgotten. While photography was "the most audacious, remote, improbable, incredible" of all the marvels of the century, Holmes feared that in the sudden way its indelible images were becoming ubiquitous, "it has become such an everyday matter with us, that we forget its miraculous nature, as we forget that of the sun itself.

"We are wondering over the photograph as a charming novelty," he added. "But before another generation has passed away, it will be recognized that a new epoch in the history of human progress dates from the time when He who 'never but in uncreated light / Dwelt from eternity' took a pencil of fire from the hand of the 'angel standing in the sun,' and placed it in the hands of a mortal."

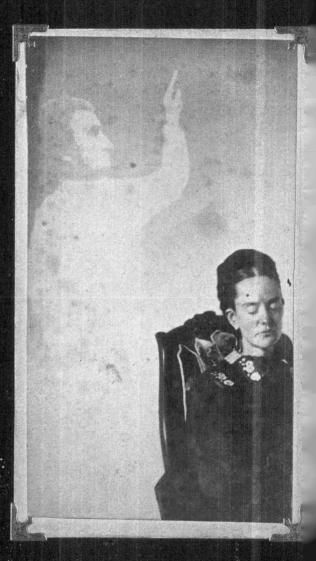

Unidentified woman (probably Hannah Mumler)
and an unidentified spirit image.
William Mumler, 1860s.

CHAPTER 5

I THOUGHT NOBODY
WOULD BE DAMAGED MUCH

THE CIVIL WAR had been raging for nineteen months, but William Mumler was not yet convinced that the swelling ranks of the dead walked among the living. Despite Hannah Stuart's unignorable magnetism and the tantalizing possibility of feeling electric currents coursing through his tissue at her touch, he held fast to the default skepticism of his scientific mind. "Not at that time being inclined much to the spiritual belief myself," he said, he thought nothing of having fun at the Spiritualists' expense. While no Dickensian wit, he considered himself as "being of a jovial disposition," and so was not above the kind of gentle ribbing *Household Words* had directed at the residents of his city. As far as most Spiritualists were concerned, he said, he was "always ready for a joke."

When it came to Hannah and her particular beliefs, however, there would be no jabs or jeers. For her, he wanted only to be helpful. If she asked him, as she did one Sunday in August, to organize developing chemicals in her darkroom and test the camera's focus, he could only say yes.

He had gone to the studio in the morning, Paul Revere's sixty-year-old church bell ringing out its call to prayer from the tower of the nearby South Church. As the Sabbath was still protected by law even in this increasingly eclectic and permissive age, all the other shops on Washington Street were closed. No one buying watches or monogrammed silver at Bigelow Brothers, no rolls of wallpaper to maneuver around as he passed by Samuel H. Gregory's shop.

After Mumler organized the chemicals, the morning light called out to him. He had lately been spending so much time in Mrs. Stuart's studio that he had learned the basics almost by osmosis. Somewhat coyly describing his ongoing infatuation and the artistic ambition it had inspired, Mumler acknowledged "being acquainted with, and somewhat interested in, parties engaged in the photographic business. By often witnessing the operation," he said, "I became familiar with the process of taking a picture."

He arranged a chair in the usual place where a sitter might pose, choosing a spot bathed in natural light, supplied to most studios by large windows cut in the ceiling for the purpose. Then he prepared the photographic plate, a process that itself had the air of conjuration about it. First he evenly coated the glass with collodion, a solution of ether and other chemicals mixed with cotton fibers barely visible to the eye. Next he bathed the plate in silver iodide before placing it in a container blocking all light until the instant of exposure. In front of the lens, a wooden slat waited to be removed to let in the sunlight that would fix the image on the glass. When all was prepared, he pulled the black cover from the camera and stepped quickly in front of it. He stood straight and still beside the chair, waiting a full minute before he moved an inch.

As he developed the negative in the darkroom, he thought he had made some mistake. Posed on the chair, which in the adjoining sitting room remained as empty as it had been all morning, sat a girl made of light.

One person who saw it at the time described Mumler's unexpected companion in detail. "The outline of the upper portion of the body is clearly defined, though dim and shadowy," Dr. H. F. Gardner, the same Spiritualist who brought the Fox sisters to Boston, wrote. "The chair is seen distinctly through the body and arms, also the table upon which one arm rests. Below, the waist (which apparently is clothed in a dress with low neck and short sleeves) fades away into a dim mist, which simply clouds the lower part of the picture." The photographer pictured, Dr. Gardner added generously, was an "active, rather athletic looking man," who gave every appearance of having just set the picture-making process in motion and then jumped into position before the lens. No fraud, his assessment suggested, would ever be so hastily concocted.

After he had seen it himself, Mumler found the image "unaccountable" and assumed he had improperly prepared the glass plate. It was possible, he noted, that "the negative was taken upon an old glass that had previously been used for the same purpose, but had been insufficiently cleaned." It was exactly the kind of careless error an amateur like himself would make.

When he told Hannah, however, he became less certain.

Not only was it a "portrait of a spirit," she said; it was the image of one "who had left her body behind yet had taken this method of communicating with those yet in bondage to the flesh."

"The picture was, to say the least, a novelty," Mumler admitted. He transferred the glass plate image to paper, to show to any friends who might stop in to see him at the engraving shop; presumably his old sense of humor about such things returned when he was not moved to suspend his disbelief in Hannah's presence.

Dr. Gardner happened to pay him a visit some days later. As Mumler would recall, he decided to show the prominent Spiritualist the image of the ghost child, "to have a little fun, as I thought, at his expense."

Mumler no doubt knew of the doctor's previous embarrassment involving dubious metaphysical manifestations, and so this recollection of his motives suggests either an uncharacteristic cruelty or, more likely, a lingering ambivalence about what exactly had happened when he had stood alone in the sunlight of 258 Washington Street. In any case, Dr. Gardner detected no malice in Mumler, and asked the budding photographer to write a brief account of the picture's creation on the back of the card-stock image.

"This photograph was taken of myself, by myself, on Sunday, when there was not a living soul in the room beside me," he wrote. Realizing that the spirit in the chair was not just anyone but a girl he once had known, he then acknowledged for the first time that he had begun to believe the camera had the ability to peer beyond the ultimate darkness. "The form on my right," he added, "I recognize as my cousin who passed away about twelve years since."

If one believes Mumler's account of these events, the matter might have ended there. It is of course entirely possible that all of this was a carefully orchestrated plan designed to launch a new business enterprise, either for the engraver who peddled digestive remedies on the side or for the medium who owned a photo studio and diagnosed illnesses with spectral assistance. Yet as the press all across the country would soon report the story, it all seems too haphazard to have been anyone's design.

Dr. Gardner took the picture away and Mumler went back to his engraving. A week later, Mumler received a copy of the *Herald of Progress* from New York. There he read not only a description of his short meeting with the doctor, but also the words he had jotted on the back of the photograph—published verbatim but without his consent.

The effect of finding his name prominently associated with so outrageous a claim brought all his doubts raging back. He knew practically nothing of photography, and even less of ghosts, yet here he was on record speaking with authority about both. "I felt, on reading this statement, considerably mortified in seeing my name in public print in support of what at that time I thought to be a kind of misrepresentation," he said. His only hope was that New York was far enough away that nothing more would come of it. With his own life largely confined to a short stretch of Washington Street, "I thought nobody would be damaged much," he said.

But then news of his peculiar photo appeared on the very block where he passed most of his days. The *Banner of Light* republished in full the story from the *Herald of Progress* and even supplied additional information. "It not only gave the description of the picture," Mumler realized with alarm, "but stated where in Boston it was taken."

There it was in the evening edition, in bold type, mailed to tens of thousands of homes: 258 Washington Street. Hannah's address.

He rushed to the studio to tell her what had happened. Fearing the worst, he intended to explain the "mischief" he had done, perhaps hoping it would not reflect badly on the business, and in turn not adversely influence its proprietor's patience with his presence. But it was too late. The gallery's reception room was packed with Spiritualists and the simply curious, all wanting to see the suddenly famous image and inquire about how it had been made.

He had not been a believer. Just a moment before, he had felt embarrassed to have his name associated with a story whose truth he questioned. But here were all these learned gentlemen insisting that he had done something extraordinary.

At her usual spot behind the counter, Mrs. Hannah Green Stuart was as magnetic as ever. She looked up as soon as he walked in. Despite his fears, she was pleased enough to see him that she called out over the din of the crowd.

"Here comes Mr. Mumler!" the future Mrs. Mumler said.

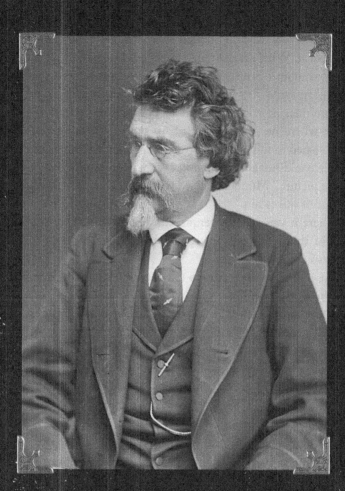
Mathew Brady, self-portrait, circa 1875.

CHAPTER 6

A LOUNGING, LISTLESS MADHOUSE

FOR THE FIRST generation of American photographers, Samuel Morse's studio was an open aperture letting in the light of a new way of seeing the world. By the early 1840s, the great inventor had relocated his experiments with chemicals and sunshine from the university rooftop where he had made closed-eyed portraits of his daughter Susan to a new space specially constructed for him by his younger brothers.

Richard and Sidney Morse had moved to Manhattan some years before, and together founded the *New York Observer*, which they published out of a six-story building they owned at 140 Nassau Street. The eldest child of Reverend Morse, Finley was still far less financially secure than the two youngest, but his siblings were intrigued by his forays into the scientific realm. On a newly added seventh floor, the Morse brothers built a glass-enclosed space for Finley's camera, then carved out a parlor on the third level where clients might inspect the images he had made while awaiting sittings of their own.

When Mathew B. Brady first met Morse in 1839 to learn from him the Daguerrean arts, his instructor was working tirelessly to support three children in an equal number of occupations. Though still new, Morse's rooms at the *Observer* were littered with archaeological layers of his many lives: paints, brushes, and canvases; spools of wire and wooden telegraph keys; chemical bottles of various volumes and playing card–sized plates of silvered copper, which then were procurable from any hardware store but rarely put to the purpose they found here.

Brady was just eighteen years old, an Irish immigrants' son from upstate New York. He had come to the city with dreams of becoming a painter and had shown a genuine youthful talent. During his adolescence he had come under the instruction of the artist William Page, an oil painter who had studied in Europe with the intention of becoming the American Titian. At the time Brady met him, Page had recently returned to art after briefly abandoning it to study for the Presbyterian ministry; his work maintained a theological tinge ever after, culminating in a controversy he caused with his painting *Head of Christ:* "It is the startling realism of the picture which most offends the multitude," a Boston arts journal said. Page's early influence likely got Brady interested in pursuing "startling realism" of a different kind —one he could learn only from Samuel Morse.

To a teenager from the hinterlands, Morse's studio would have seemed either a wizard's workshop or a laboratory for concocting new realities from scarce resources and endless research. In truth it was both. Morse by then was "tied hand and foot during the day endeavoring to realize something from the Daguerreotype portraits," while also painting the occasional canvas for money, and remaining hard at work preparing patents for his invention the telegraph and appealing to Congress to fund its implementation.

He would eventually get that funding in 1843, but not before the House of Representatives debated whether or not Morse's invention made use of forces more spiritual than electric. Delaying the vote on a bill authorizing $30,000 for "a series of experiments to be made in order to test the merits of Morse's electromagnetic telegraph," a congressman from Tennessee snidely proposed an amendment. "As the present Congress had done much to encourage science," Representative Cave Johnson said, he did not wish to see "the science of mesmerism neglected and overlooked." He therefore proposed that one half of the appropriation be given to the prominent mesmerist Theophilus Fisk so that he might carry out his experiments in electrobiology, elsewhere called "the latest and most profitable form of Scientific trickery."

A congressman from North Carolina meanwhile suggested he would accept this amendment if the gentleman from Tennessee was the experimental subject. The chair of the appropriations committee ended the discussion by saying that "it would require a scientific analysis to determine how far the magnetism of mesmerism was analogous to that to be employed in telegraphs."

Scientific shortcomings of Congress aside, that Morse was making progress simultaneously on the telegraph and the daguerreotype indicates something of the marvel of tenacity he had become in the fifteen years since Lucretia's death. Yet his achievements were rarely sufficient in his own estimation; they could never fill the void that had opened with her loss, even if he hoped one day to reach across it.

And all his effort came at a stiff price. Morse still maintained his university painting studio, but seldom visited it. A new resident of the same building in 1841—the year Brady arrived in the city—recalled once catching a glimpse inside its open door. "Every object in it bore indubitable signs of unthrift and neglect," he wrote. "The statuettes, busts, and models of various kinds were covered with dust and cobwebs; dusty canvases were faced to the wall, and stumps of brushes and scraps of paper littered the floor. The only signs of industry consisted of a few masterly crayon drawings, and little luscious studies of color pinned to the wall." A janitor at NYU explained, "You will have an artist for a neighbor, though he is not here much of late; he seems to be getting rather shiftless; he is wasting his time over some silly invention, a machine by which he expects to send messages from one place to another. He is a very good painter, and might do well if he would only stick to his business; but, Lord! The idea of telling by a little streak of lightning what a body is saying at the other end of it."

Though a budding painter himself, young Brady was not troubled that Morse had moved away from pure art. He was impressed by the potential of the operation he saw on Nassau Street and immediately signed on to become one of the master's students in the daguerreotype process. He likely paid for the privilege: another Morse pupil of the time noted that his teacher claimed with only slight exaggeration that if his students failed to pay on time, he might starve to death. To do his part in preventing this from happening, and to make his way in the city generally, Brady took a job as a clerk at Alexander Turney Stewart's Irish linens shop on Broadway, across from City Hall Park.

Neither his studies nor his employment lasted very long, and soon Brady struck out on his own. Good with his hands and mechanically inclined, he advertised two kinds of business at two different addresses by the time he reached his twenty-fifth year. He was at once a "jewelry, miniature, and surgical case manufacturer" at 187 Broadway and the sole proprietor of a Daguerrean gallery at 207 Broadway.

It was the latter that would make his name. Directly across from P. T. Barnum's American Museum, which by 1846 claimed nearly a half million visitors a year, Brady's studio was poised to capitalize on the seemingly endless foot traffic and establish itself as a new star of the arts in the fast-growing city. But first he needed to hone his craft as a portrait artist. That opportunity presented itself in a most unlikely place, and thanks to a woman who would become one of the leading lights of Spiritualism.

LIKE A MESSAGE IN a bottle bobbing in the East River, Blackwell's Island was crammed with the desperation of the lost.

Less than two miles long and a thousand feet wide, its 135 acres was home to New York City's penitentiary, almshouse, and lunatic asylum. The dangerous, the hated, the penniless, the forgotten —hundreds lived in dank cells of solitary confinement, hundreds more in vast halls as filthy and crowded as the steerage holds that had only recently brought most of them to America. Of the 1,239 prisoners in the penitentiary in 1846, the foreign born numbered 843; many of them had never set foot in Manhattan.

When Charles Dickens visited in the early 1840s, he was aghast. The island, he said, had "a lounging, listless, madhouse air, which was very painful." He watched a convict thrust his hands through a metal grate, grasping for air as if he could stuff it into his lungs. Another "flung down in a heap upon the ground, with his head against the bars, like a wild beast." With some of his bleakest works about the struggles of the London underclass still to come, he apparently found no shortage of inspiration in New York. "The moping idiot, cowering down with long dishevelled hair; the gibbering maniac, with his hideous laugh and pointed finger; the vacant eye, the fierce wild face, the gloomy picking of the hands and lips, and munching of the nails: there they were all, without disguise, in naked ugliness and horror," he wrote. "The terrible crowd with which these halls and galleries were filled, so shocked me, that I abridged my stay within the shortest limits, and declined to see that portion of the building in which the refractory and violent were under closer restraint."

Blackwell's Island itself had a rocky foundation from which the penitentiary's developers had dug deep quarries. After the prison had been constructed of this fine building stone, prisoners were put to work cutting more of it for use in the lunatic asylum and the almshouse, to which soon were added a hospital and workhouse. The workhouse made the island a moneymaker; its profits were published in the newspaper as evidence of civic money well spent.

To city planners, keeping the criminal, the mad, the sick, and the poor confined together on an island made perfect sense. The various institutions serving these diverse populations were "sufficiently contiguous to each other for all purposes of convenience," a report noted, and "sufficiently remote from the city to be protected from contagion."

For readers still struggling to form a mental picture, Dickens included a poetic aside: "Make the rain pour down, outside, in torrents. Put the everlasting stove in the midst; hot, and suffocating, and vaporous, as a witch's cauldron. Add a collection of gentle odours such as would arise from a thousand mildewed umbrellas, wet through, and a thousand buck-baskets, full of half-washed linen—and there is the prison, as it was that day."

That the author happened to see Blackwell's Island during a storm may have been a happy accident in terms of making its Dickensian nature immediately apparent. Outside the stone buildings, after all, the island might have seemed lovely to him on a sunny day. "The scenery upon it is unsurpassed for beauty by any in the vicinity of our city," an official report noted. But its true darkness had nothing to do with the landscape or the weather.

Four years after Dickens made his abridged tour of the penitentiary, young Mathew Brady was called to the same facility on an assignment that promised to produce images that would allow his work to be seen by the public for the first time.

Chastened by accounts like those Dickens published in his 1842 *American Notes,* the State of New York hired a reform-minded progressive to oversee one of its penal institutions. Eliza Wood Farnham, who like Brady and the oldest of the Spiritualist Fox sisters had been born in upstate New York in the first quarter of the century, arrived at America's first long-term lockup for women in the wake of a riot. "Violent battles are frequent," a contemporary report said; "knives have been known to be drawn." Opened in 1839 as the women's wing of Sing Sing, the Mount Pleasant Female Prison stood on a hilltop overlooking the Hudson, "a handsome building . . . with a Doric portico of imposing proportions."

Like the beauty of Blackwell's Island, however, its impressive architecture masked chronic abuse. For breaking the prison's rule of silence, women were put in straitjackets, doused with water until they nearly drowned, and gagged. Sing Sing's administrators regarded the latter punishment as a crucial difference between discipline in the men's and women's wings. "The gag has sometimes been applied," one prison official said, "but it has been only among the females that it has been rendered absolutely necessary!"

Eliza Farnham hoped to change all this. She came to the position through the influence of the liberal lawyer and future judge John W. Edmonds, who was then a state inspector of prisons. Edmonds had made it a point to limit such medieval practices as the use of the cat-o'-nine-tails for whipping prisoners, and Farnham followed along on the reforming path he had blazed. First she abolished the rule of silence and with it the hard punishments formerly used to enforce it. Next she allowed inmates to grow flowers, listen to music, and receive visitors — all of which were essential, she said, to maintaining order without the lash. Finally she opened a prison library and encouraged the reading of novels. A writer herself, she believed literature fostered moral development.

Her reading list for prisoners was not limited to fiction. She also encouraged books on phrenology, the hugely popular pseudoscience that claimed the shape of one's head was the key to understanding character and potential. She had been introduced to the practice by New York City's leading phrenological family, the brothers Orson and Lorenzo Fowler (authors of *The Illustrated Self-Instructor in Phrenology and Physiology*, which included directions on how to assess oneself), and Lorenzo's wife, Lydia Folger Fowler (author of *Familiar Lessons on Phrenology: Designed for the Use of Children and Youth*).

At the time she was appointed matron of Mount Pleasant, Farnham was particularly taken with an English pamphlet that applied head-measuring to her current work, Marmaduke B. Sampson's *Treatise on Criminal Jurisprudence Considered in Relation to Cerebral Organization*. Leveraging the status of her new position, she made up her mind to see Sampson's work published in the United States. She intended not only to republish it but to fully revise it for an American audience. She would write an introduction and appendices, doubling the length of the original text, and include copious footnotes quoting supporting materials. Perhaps most important in terms of marketing the book, she would commission illustrations designed to attract a wider audience than the usual "treatise" might. Living so close to the world's new daguerreotype capital, she recognized the power held by images—portraits particularly—when it came to winning public attention and introducing novel ideas in a sympathetic way. She only had to find the right photographer to go with her to Blackwell's Island to capture the likenesses of the city's castaways.

Farnham's publisher, D. Appleton & Company, was then right across the street from Brady's newly opened gallery. The founder's son, William Henry Appleton, was at the time overseeing the publications side of the family business, and walked by a sign reading BRADY'S DAGUERREAN SALOON whenever he entered his office at 200 Broadway.

The young artist likely got the job not because he was the best, but because he was nearby, and willing.

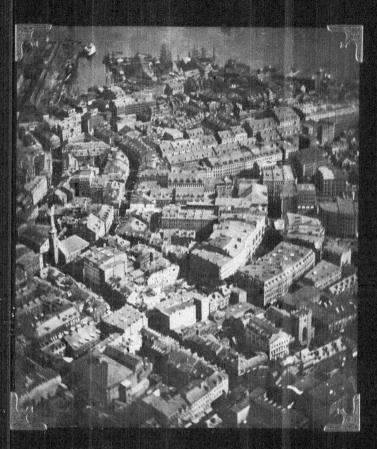

Balloon view of Boston, the first aerial
photograph of an American city.
James Wallace Black, 1860.

CHAPTER 7

MY GOD!
IS IT POSSIBLE?

EARLY ONE MORNING in October 1860, while the rest of Boston lingered under blankets to put off exposure to winter temperatures come early, a respectable middle-aged photographer named James Wallace Black prepared to ascend to the heavens.

It would be a bright and sunny day, but when Black arrived on Boston Common the grass was still stiff with frost. Together with his assistants, he carefully rolled out a massive pouch of stitched silk, then connected its open end to a portable hydrogen pump resembling an oversized casket on wheels. A fairly new contraption designed specifically for this purpose, the copper-lined wooden tank was filled with a solution of water and iron filings; adding sulfuric acid produced gas lighter than air that wanted nothing more than to escape the chamber in which it was born.

With the acid introduced to the tank, the photographer watched as the shroud of smooth fabric stirred to life. It seemed to breathe, growing gradually with each inhalation of gaseous hydrogen, and slowly mounded like a pimple on the face of the earth. Then all at once it stirred and rose from the frosted grass.

No expert balloonist, J. W. Black had spent half his years behind the camera, and all of them with his feet firmly on the ground. For guidance in this new interest, he turned to Samuel Archer King, New England's preeminent aerialist. King had traveled from Providence, Rhode Island, to help Black see Boston from above. The balloon, which King called "Queen of the Air," climbed more than twelve hundred feet over the common that day. The aerialist and the photographer floated beneath it in an attached basket for much of the afternoon, tethered by a rope to their launch site so they would not blow out to sea.

Black's images—the first aerial photographs taken anywhere in the United States—were a revelation. Within one frame, church steeples and storefronts, rooftops and alleyways, sailing ships and merchants' carts, all were collected like odds and ends in a junk drawer. As the balloon rose higher into the thinning air and Black made more exposures, the city came to resemble the interlocking gears and springs of a pocket watch with its back popped off. From the jumbled landscape emerged a world moved by designs too grand to be seen.

Not everyone found the images so astonishing. "The cow pasture character of our streets is finely presented," a journalist wryly noted upon seeing the pictures later that month. Bostonians, being Bostonians, rarely allowed themselves to seem too keenly impressed. The change in perspective Black's camera had provided, however, was not lost even on those sophisticates whose first impulse was bemusement.

Residents of the Hub of the Universe imagined their city filled with the greatest minds in the nation. The birthplace of John Adams, Ralph Waldo Emerson, Henry David Thoreau, Oliver Wendell Holmes, and other notables would, they imagined, always loom large in the life of the nation. And now, on a cold and quiet autumn Sunday, Black had gone up into the clouds and come back down with evidence of how small the city really was.

For a decade, new portrait studios had opened in Boston nearly as often as in New York, and indeed they soon seemed unremarkable in cities large and small. In these sorcerer's shops where mirrors learned to remember, Americans had been subtly taught to think of photography as a means of affirming their own individual importance. Through the duration of the long seconds of aperture, with the photographer staring intently as he slowly counted down, every sitter in every portrait studio became a still point in the turning world. Narcissus peering into the water until the currents pulled him down was not far from the experience of stopping in for a quick sitting only to drown in the parlor's lush curtains and the undivided attention of an artist who promised to turn every face into a masterpiece.

Yet to see images taken from high above was to realize photography might show far more than previously imagined. It did not merely erase distance, as Morse imagined it would; it proposed to control space and time. As the same wag who bemoaned the city's "cow pasture" streets noted, in Black's images "Boston looks very much like a toy town that a boy has built of painted blocks." What was the camera if not the all-seeing, eternally objective eye of God?

Of all the photographers working in the city, J. W. Black was in many ways the perfect person to pose this question. He had begun his career at the elbow of the brilliant Boston daguerreotypist J. H. Lerow, whose gallery thrived at 91 Washington Street beginning in the 1840s. None of his images survive, so his technical acumen cannot be known, but from the earliest toddling steps of the art he had understood what captured images might mean to those who stood within them. They were a means for ordinary people to make stories of their meandering days. And when your memories did not measure up to the requirements of narrative, photographs of other people could be purchased from a rack on two-by-three-inch cards, and their lives could become part of your own.

At around the time Black had learned the art from Lerow, the latter had placed in the newspapers a gripping yarn, likely written by himself, about a beautiful young woman who visited his studio one day. She was eager to have a picture taken for a locket she would give to her brother, who was headed out to sea the next day. Lerow sat her for a photograph, struck by features whose equal he had never seen. When sadly it came time for her to go — oh! — she discovered that she had lost her money. Lerow told her not to worry; she could have the photograph for free if she was willing to sit for another image, which he might keep for his shop's small gallery. A year later, when he'd forgotten it was there, a wealthy regular customer happened in. Seeing the photograph of the woman hanging on the wall, this "rich, well educated, not in any way dissipated" young man insisted he had to meet its subject. By great good fortune he was able to find her. Penniless but still lovely, on the verge of falling into ill repute at the hands of scoundrels, she married the gentleman "ere that month had passed."

This sentimental saga, called "Love at First Sight — or — The Daguerreotype," appeared in papers as far away as North Carolina. It filled five columns of a broadsheet and included a closing pitch, which of course was the hidden point of the whole tale. "We would be happy to remind them," the story said of the newlyweds, "Mr. L has a happy knack for taking family groups."

To visit 91 Washington Street was to entwine one's life with the rich and the beautiful, to participate in a fairy tale in which the rich received their due for virtue and the poor could find relief. As Black learned at Lerow's side, photography was an act of mythmaking.

Leaving his mentor's tutelage soon after, he worked as a plate buffer for various other daguerreotypists, including Luther Holman Hale, scion of a scythe-manufacturing fortune who operated a studio one biographer said was filled with a "palace-like magnificence," which included a pianoforte, various music boxes, and singing birds. Black then traveled as an itinerant photographer, where his open-air sitting sessions offered exposure to birds of other kinds. Through it all he was building toward taking pictures that suggested even the most intimate photographs could become windows on larger realities, ranging from celestial dramas — as when he turned his camera toward the night sky as a pioneer of astrophotography — to the national stage.

Black photographed John Brown in his own Washington Street studio in May of 1859, while the abolitionist was in Boston gathering resources for the raid on Harpers Ferry he planned for later that year. The preacher turned guerrilla fighter and anti-slavery crusader had previously visited Black three years before. At that time, he was smooth-cheeked and awkward-looking; his broad mouth pulled tight at the lips like a knife wound slashed laterally across the lower part of his face. He had recently suffered a mild stroke, and the image Black made then showed signs of Bell's palsy. It was later known as the "mad" photograph, proof that the zealot had lost his mind.

The John Brown who entered Black's studio in 1859 was by contrast as commanding a presence as a biblical patriarch. He had begun to grow a beard as a disguise in 1858, but the disguise had become the man himself. His beard flowed to the middle of his chest and called to mind, a soldier of his ragtag army later said, a "Puritan of the most exalted type." This is the John Brown who would be known by history. He wore the beard only during the last year of his life, including to his execution in December 1859, and yet, thanks to a single portrait, he will always be remembered with it. The story of his life became contained and defined by a single moment staring into a camera.

In his balloon and on the ground, Black showed how images could shape the past that came before them just as surely as what was yet to come.

WHEN JAMES WALLACE BLACK met William Mumler two autumns later, the former had been taking pictures for twenty years; the latter for about as many days.

H. F. Gardner, the local Spiritualist leader who had been so taken with Mumler's original ghostly photograph, sensed he had stumbled onto something important. But perhaps because he had suffered embarrassment years earlier when the Harvard professors publicly grilled Kate and Margaret Fox, he wanted to have his discovery independently verified.

As Mumler's first and most convincing advocate, Gardner insisted he had no doubts. His desire to believe was reinforced by what he witnessed when he had an image taken of himself. On the glass before him he saw clearly a picture of his deceased son, now years gone. There was no question in his mind about the abilities of the photographer, whom he took to be not an artist but a "peculiar medium." Despite his faith, however, he urged caution. "It behooves us as Spiritualists," Dr. Gardner told a gathering of his fellow believers in Boston, "to carefully investigate and candidly inquire what cause there is for faith in this thing and also what cause there is for doubt and opposition. I told Mr. Mumler that if he abused the gift of his remarkable power, it would be taken from him; to see well that he made a good, wise, and generous use of a valuable gift. Greater gifts than this will be soon given to the earth."

For a technical appraisal, he went to the best in the city, a man whose expertise and reputation among Boston photographers were unimpeachable. Conveniently, Black's studio was just blocks away from both Mumler's engraving shop and the Spiritualist newspaper the *Banner of Light,* which had recently spread news of the "spirit photographs" across the city. Gardner brought one such image—showing himself surrounded by four unidentified spectral forms—and asked Black if he would be able to create a similar one using either his usual photographic implements or any "mechanical contrivance." After scrutinizing the print, Black admitted that he could not.

But a man who would go up in a balloon for his art was not the sort who would leave further investigations to others. Black began his personal inquiry by sending his assistant, Horace Weston, down Washington Street to Mrs. Hannah Stuart's photo studio. There he was to request a sitting, giving no indication that his ulterior motive was to take notes and report back.

Mumler seated Horace for a portrait as he would any customer. Posing him by a large window, he took the young man's picture, developed it, and then supplied a photograph that seemed to show not only Horace's own likeness, but that of his deceased father.

Horace had been taught photography by the best in the city. If something was amiss in Mumler's process, surely he would have spotted it. And yet he had not. "All I can say to Mr. Black," he said to Mumler, admitting he had been sent there on a mission, "is that I have seen nothing different from taking an ordinary picture."

He left, but then returned a short time later, likely red in the face both from rushing up and down the street on this unusual errand and from embarrassment.

"When I went back, they all came around me to hear my report," he said of his coworkers at Black's studio. "And when I told them that I had got a second form on the negative, but had seen nothing different in the manipulation from taking an ordinary picture, they shouted with laughter." To his chagrin, they all thought he had been duped.

Horace asked if Mr. Black himself might pay a visit. "If you will allow him the same privilege of witnessing the operation that you did me," he said to Mumler, "and he gets a spirit form on the negative, he will give you fifty dollars."

"Tell Mr. Black to come," Mumler said.

A short time later, the great man arrived. For him the journey down Washington Street to Mumler's door would have been no less fantastical than lifting off into the air over the common. In the one known photograph of the esteemed photographer, Black presents himself as an informed and worldly man, impeccably dressed and reading a folded newspaper with spectacles on his nose. He sits with his legs crossed in a comfortable chair, as if fully at ease with the universe and his place within it. Now here was this rumpled amateur claiming he had captured more with a camera than Black had ever dreamed.

"Mr. Black, I have heard your generous offer," Mumler said by way of greeting. "All I can say is, be thorough in your investigations."

"You may rest assured of that."

Mumler had prepared the studio in advance. His camera stood at the ready. "That is the instrument I propose to take your picture with," he said. "You are at liberty to take it to pieces."

Black shrugged off the suggestion. He did not credit the man before him with enough knowledge to alter a camera's functioning sufficiently to produce the images Dr. Gardner and his assistant Horace had presented to him.

"That is all right," he said.

Next Mumler showed him the glass plate he intended to use.

"Mr. Black, I propose to take your picture on this glass; you are at liberty to clean it."

Black took the glass from Mumler and examined it for spots or other signs that it had been tampered with. Holding it close to his face, he exhaled sharply, his breath fogging the clear surface. He decided it was clean enough, but assured the supposed spirit photographer he would be watching all that followed very closely.

"I don't lose sight of this plate from this time," he said.

The two men then moved to the sky-lit sitting room. Black

sat facing a window for extra light while Mumler took his spot before him, poised beside the camera. He placed the plate in position, then raised the slide that would allow an image to be fixed on the glass.

"All ready," Mumler said.

With a quick tug, he removed the cloth cover from the lens. The two men waited in stillness and silence as light filled the camera and transformed all it could see into shadows more enduring than reality—a small miracle in itself no matter what other events might transpire that day.

"Mr. Mumler, I should be willing to bet one thing," Black said. "That you have got my picture."

"So would I," the spirit photographer replied.

"And I guess that is all."

"Very likely," Mumler agreed. "I do not get them every time."

Eager to give a skeptic as much control over the process as he wished, and perhaps in deference to his undoubtedly superior skills, Mumler led Black to the darkroom and suggested he might like to continue the developing process himself.

"I would rather you develop the negative, Mr. Mumler," Black insisted. "I am not acquainted with the working of your chemicals, and might spoil it." Just in case the younger man took this as a compliment, Black quickly added, "You are not smart enough to put anything on that negative without my detecting it."

"I am well aware of that," Mumler said.

Standing in the darkness of the tiny room, Mumler opened a bottle of developer. He then tipped the plate in his hand and poured the chemical solution over the glass. This would produce the negative, with the whitest spots appearing blackest, an inversion of all the ways the eye wants to see. To an experienced photographer, reading a negative is simply like switching to a language known since birth but used only on certain occasions.

Black watched as his own dark outline appeared on the glass, its form not unlike the photograph he'd had taken of himself seated with his newspaper. But then another shape began to emerge.

"My God!" Black said. "Is it possible?"

As Mumler would later remember, "Another form became apparent, growing plainer and plainer each moment, until a man appeared, leaning his arm upon Mr. Black's shoulder." The man later eulogized as "an authority in the science and chemistry of his profession" then watched "with wonder-stricken eyes" as the two forms took on a clarity unsettling in its intimacy.

Earlier, when he had heard his assistant Horace's account of seeing a dead parent revived on glass, he had likely been dismissive but not entirely unsympathetic. Black himself had been orphaned at the age of thirteen; his father's sudden death had set him on course to learn the art of the daguerreotype from Lerow, and then to become a self-made man who was brave enough to fly above the city with only silk and hydrogen as wings. He was a creature of experiment and certainty; the figure at his shoulder on Mumler's negative was the very shape of mystery.

Black did not remain long enough to ask questions, but he did ask if he could take the image with him. Mumler varnished it, as any portrait artist might, then handed the finished product to his fellow photographer.

"How much is to pay?" Black asked.

"Not a cent," Mumler said.

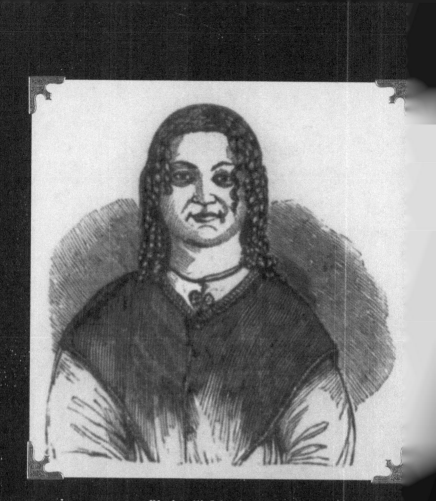

Blackwell's Island inmate.
Engraving from a daguerreotype by Mathew Brady, 1846.

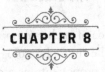

CHAPTER 8

SHE REALLY IS A
WONDERFUL WHISTLER

IT WAS THE kind of assignment one might take only for reasons of either desperation or true belief.

Mathew Brady's first significant job as a photographic artist would be to travel out over the dark waters of the East River to the prison, and there to spend enough time with criminals that he would be able to reproduce their images. Many of them dangerous, few of them pleasant, they had been convicted of crimes ranging from theft to arson to assault. As far as he knew, there were no murderers among them, at least no one who had been convicted of that crime. In the pre–mug shot era, the taking of such pictures was not standard procedure, and it would not be a rushed affair. Rather, Brady's work would be to create posed daguerreotype portraits requiring the same time, skill, and care as those offered to the New York gentry for several dollars apiece.

The ideological purpose of these portraits was immediately obvious. With his camera, Brady was to provide case studies bolstering the notion that "cerebral organization" was responsible for behavior, inclination, character, and even crime.

At the time Brady agreed to collaborate with prison matron Eliza Farnham, the pseudoscience of head measurement— "bumpology," as phrenology was sometimes derided in the press —was not yet primarily associated with racist prejudments about the physical characteristics of various ethnic and religious backgrounds. The seeds of such evil implications certainly were already there, but at the time phrenology was naively intended, by at least some of its proponents, as a compassionate development in the diagnosis and treatment of mental illness.

As it applied to crime and punishment, reformers like Farnham insisted that criminals should not be treated too harshly because they suffered from "moral insanity." Such unfortunates, it was believed, were no more responsible for their actions than one exposed to a disease was responsible for exhibiting its symptoms. In her view, the source of antisocial behavior was not a question of nature or nurture, but nature *and* nurture. Though social conditions played a role for Farnham, so much more depended on the physical position of the brain within the skull. "The form of head possessed by all dangerous and inveterate criminals is peculiar," says one source Farnham quotes. "There is an enormous mass of brain behind the ear, and a comparatively small portion in the frontal and coronal regions. Such a conformation always characterizes the worst class of malefactors and wherever it exists we find an excessive tendency to crime."

To make this case in print, Farnham's text would be supplemented not only with Brady's images but with rough sketches of various cranial shapes, all shorn of hair. For the drawings, the prison matron engaged a young artist named Edward Serrell. Like apparently all artists of the day, Serrell was also a budding inventor, and held the patent on a machine for making the lead pipes that Morse hoped to use for enclosing and protecting his telegraph wires. He, too, was a starving artist, however, and took whatever work fell his way.

On Farnham's instructions, Serrell journeyed to Sing Sing. Working in the office of a chaplain, who found the whole enterprise suspect and possibly un-Christian, Serrell measured the heads of convicts from both the women's and men's sections of the prison and then made line drawings detailing the various widths, points, and bumps that supposedly could provide a new window on the soul.

"No. 1 is the head of a very depraved person," Farnham wrote of Serrell's first subject. "The drawing indicates great firmness, with a very large development of the inferior propensities." Image and exposition were rarely enough for Farnham's purposes. She also included elaborate backstories attempting to demonstrate the real-world risks of those having such heads escaping proper treatment. "He has always been coarse and brutal in his conduct, an object of terror to children, and the dread of peaceable citizens," she said of No. 1. "His whole person is characterized by the rudeness and coarseness of his mind. He is 24 years old, and is under a sentence of ten years for arson in the third degree. The circumstances of his crime are strongly indicative of his character. He had made a bet of five dollars that at the next fire a certain engine company would be the first at the scene of action. The next night, he fired the building contiguous to their house in order to secure his bet."

Other unfortunates who submitted to Serrell's calipers and pen were no better off in Farnham's eyes. The owner of a perfectly unremarkable head with a smoothly arching crown was guilty of "some of the most daring burglaries ever committed in New York" due to overdevelopment of the "organ of destructiveness." Of a woman with a similarly ordinary-looking skull, it was decided, "She will doubtless spend her life in prison, for she is constitutionally a criminal." On the good-news end of the spectrum, the shape of one convict's cranium suggested to Farnham that there might be some small capacity within to know right from wrong, but "it is like the faintest gleam of starlight shining through the blackness of midnight."

Owing perhaps to the greater load required for his equipment, Brady was not asked to journey forty miles to Ossining to take his pictures, but just four miles from his studio. A ferry from

Manhattan crossed the East River to the city's nearest human dumping ground several times every day. Most passengers went in shackles; no ticket was required. Farnham's suggestion that Brady relocate his daguerreotype shop temporarily to Blackwell's Island could not have been taken lightly. From the moment its construction was completed in 1839, the island's penitentiary had occupied a mythic place in the city's vision of itself. The day-to-day terror of prisoners' lives went mostly unremarked upon and largely unnoticed except by reformers like Farnham, but the island featured regularly in the cautionary tales favored by the New York press.

Even a casual reader could recite a litany of colorful events that had occurred on that melancholy strip of land between Manhattan and Queens. For the most part these stories confirmed widespread stereotypes and suspicions of both the inmates and their minders. One day a cruel jailer buried a prisoner up to his waist for a minor infraction, leaving him in the ground for two days without food, as press reports noted, "except a little bread which was put into his mouth by a poor lunatic." In another strange incident involving untimely interment, an Irishman dug a hole in the prison yard and buried himself so he might be concealed while guards searched for him. When he later climbed free, he made his way to a pub in Five Points, where he buried himself in booze until he was apprehended.

The battle-hardened, too, found the prison nearly too much to bear. "An old Pole between 70 and 80 years of age was sent to Blackwell's Island," one newspaper reported. He had fought with Napoleon at Waterloo, returned to his homeland in time for the November Uprising against Russia, then embarked for America to fight as part of the Florida army in the Seminole War. "The survivor of many fields of blood and carnage," the man found his time in the penitentiary the worst ordeal of all.

Brady would not have visited the island on a lark. Yet having seen the poverty Morse endured, he was undoubtedly pleased to have the job.

Though less onerous than the journey to Sing Sing, the trip from his Broadway studio to the ferry waiting room at the foot of Seventieth Street still would have required some planning. And the river crossing, too, could be an experience. "The Blackwell's Island ferry has indeed a pitiable class of passengers," a newspaper lamented. "The up trip carries the convicts under sentence, while the returning boat brings those that are released." Weighed down with his camera, chemicals, and plates, Brady became the rare commuter seen equally on each leg of the crossing.

Once on the island, visitors were often conveyed from one site to another in smaller boats manned by prisoners, like gondoliers in traditional jailhouse garb. "Dressed in a striped uniform of black and buff," Dickens had noted, "they looked like faded tigers." If spotted rowing toward freedom, they could thus be shot from a distance with minimal risk to their passengers. Corpses of would-be escapees bobbed to the river's surface with alarming regularity.

While Brady encountered no such drama on his way to the penitentiary, inside its walls was another story. One after another, convicts entered his makeshift studio and sat before the camera. The daguerreotype process required that these sittings be undertaken in abundant natural light, which no doubt presented challenges within the prison's thick walls of quarried stone. While Farnham would later thank "the officers of the Penitentiary on Blackwell's Island for their politeness in furnishing me with facilities for taking the daguerreotypes," it's safe to say they did not build the temporary prison photographer his own "palace of the sun."

Joining Brady in these sittings were Eliza Farnham herself, whose subsequent character sketches of the convicts suggest lengthy conversations, and Farnham's phrenological mentor,

Lorenzo Fowler. The two men were likely already acquainted. Fowler had gone into business around the same time the aspiring photographer arrived in the city, opening his first "Phrenological Rooms" on the very block of Broadway that was soon to be home to Brady's studio, Appleton's publishing house, and Barnum's museum. In his shop, Fowler and his colleagues offered services ranging from "examining the heads and describing the character of their numerous visitors," to creating three-dimensional depictions of these visitors' skulls. "The new mode of taking busts in plaster," he insisted, "is perfectly safe to every age and sex" and "sure to give a perfect likeness." While not direct competitors, Brady and Fowler tilled adjoining fields.

Their work at Blackwell's seems to have progressed with Fowler hunting among the prisoners for heads representing a range of shapes and rap sheets providing a full menu of misconduct. Farnham then interviewed each convict to see if the contours of their heads comported closely enough with Fowler's expectations of their characters. Finally, Brady posed each case study appropriately to achieve the desired effect.

Nineteen portraits—engravings taken from Brady's plates —ended up in the finished book. Given the high failure rate for daguerreotype images that continued into the 1840s, many more prisoners likely sat for Brady than made the final cut. Among those who did, Farnham first told the story of a man selected by Fowler who had been born a slave but emancipated himself —the text does not note how—and then had lived "free" in the North for several years, most of them locked up on Blackwell's Island.

M.B., as he is called, is "a man of great determination and fixedness of mind and character; can scarcely be thrown off his guard, or induced to do any thing which his own mind does not deliberately consent to. He possesses great strength of purpose, strong powers of reason, and much capacity to plan, as well as

energy to execute." He was "esteemed by his officers an oblig-
ing, good man," and sat patiently for Brady, staring slightly away
from the camera as if reluctant to meet its gaze.

After Brady's picture was done, the collaborators inspected
it closely. Then the prison matron and the phrenologist read it
like tea leaves for hidden meanings their understanding of cerebral organization might make plain. "The head indicates very
strongly all these characteristics," Farnham wrote of M.B. "With
a very powerful temperament, are combined a large brain, well
developed in the intellectual region, particularly the superior fac-
ulties, large self-esteem, firmness, caution, and secretiveness. He
has the capacity to be made a very useful or a very desperate and
dangerous man."

Next came an inmate they called S.S. A vagrant and a former
prizefighter, he was an Irishman—like Brady's father. He was
first sent to state prison for assault with intent to kill. After serving five years, he moved in and out of smaller city and county
jails. "Before his mind became deranged," Farnham wrote, "he
exhibited great energy of passion and purpose, but they were
all of a low character, their sole bearing being to prove his own
superiority as an animal." Brady's daguerreotype, in her estimation, showed S.S. to have "a broad, low head, corresponding with
such a character . . . If the higher capacities and endowments of
humanity were ever found coupled with such a head as this, it
would be a phenomenon as inexplicable as that of seeing without
the eye, or hearing without the ear."

In the women's section of the island, they met C.P., "a half-
breed Indian and negro woman, under confinement for the fourth
time." An inveterate thief, she apparently was able to acquire a
carving knife during one of her incarcerations. She used it to attack a guard, who "was compelled to fell her with a loaded cane."

"In her head," Farnham wrote, "destructiveness is enormously
developed."

On and on. Brady aimed his camera repeatedly at people who had likely never seen such a contraption before. They had all been brought together in a crowded room of the stone prison so that Fowler could walk among them and pull aside specimens useful for demonstrating the phrenologist's art. For the most part, the selected inmates stared off to the daguerreotypist's side as M.B. had done. Among those who looked directly back were five children from the juvenile detention facility known as Long Island Farms (one noted for his "love of fun"), who appear utterly unimpressed, and a woman who decided to share a tune as she sat unexpectedly in the daylight.

"A Jewess of German birth," the woman called T.Z., Farnham explained, "sometimes appears to be insane, and is generally, I believe, esteemed to be so by her fellow prisoners." Yet she gave no outward signs of any affliction during her sitting. "She is exceedingly ingenious, displays great skill in many feminine arts, such as embroidery, drawing, etc."

"I much like music," T.Z. told them in heavily accented English. "I sing, play guitar, piano, and very much like to whistle."

Her picture, the phrenologists believed, indicated "a large development of the perceptive, the mechanical and musical powers." Perhaps covering their bases, they added that her head also suggested "excessive secretiveness and destructiveness."

When and how she decided to demonstrate her love of music can't be known, but something during her time before the camera led Farnham to comment on it. "And she really is a wonderful whistler," the prison matron said.

Following the illustrations of supposedly deranged, destructive, and deficient cerebral organization, the phrenologists inserted a few examples displaying "great mental power and refinement of feeling." The two male specimens "are taken from the busts of gentlemen distinguished for ability." The female representative, "known in her circle as a woman of superior mind, and a pattern of moral excellence and domestic affection," bears a striking resemblance to Lydia Folger Fowler, the phrenologist's wife.

When the work was done, Farnham thanked her mentor "for aiding me in the selection of cases," and Brady for his "indefatigable patience with a class of the most difficult of all sitters."

Rationale of Crime and Its Appropriate Treatment, Farnham's edition of Sampson's book, was met with mixed reviews when it was issued in 1846. The most scathing called it a product of "quackery" and "humbug." Were Brady better known at the time of its publication, he might have been charged with the same. Surely these were labels the owner of a fledgling business seeking clients would do everything possible to avoid, and Brady managed to do so, but his collaborator Lorenzo Fowler made no effort to distance himself from the project. His reputation only rose in the years after the book's release. He opened a bigger and more successful enterprise, which he advertised far and wide:

THE PHRENOLOGICAL CABINET
129 and 131 Nassau Street, New York

Contains Busts and Casts from the heads of the most distinguished men that ever lived; also Skulls, of humans and animals, from all quarters of the globe—including Egyptian Mummies, Pirates, Robbers, Murderers, and Thieves; also numerous Paintings and Drawings of Celebrated Individuals, living and dead; and it is always FREE to visitors, by whom it is continually thronged.

While Brady never expressed sympathy for Farnham's phrenology or the eclectic beliefs she would later embrace, putting his camera in their service for the duration of her project on Blackwell's Island could not have been wholly inconsequential to his development as an artist.

Phrenology was a humbug on the order of table-rapping Spiritualism, but its basic premise—that something of the interior life could be gleaned from exterior appearance — was almost universally accepted among that class of people who called themselves artists. This notion might be considered the single most important ingredient in the next stage of Brady's career, and indeed of the whole photographic industry, which was spreading as quickly as one of Morse's electromagnetic pulses across a country newly mapped with telegraph wires.

Just as Fowler filled his Nassau Street Phrenological Cabinet with "Busts and Casts from the heads of the most distinguished men that ever lived," Brady began to plan a project he called the *Gallery of Illustrious Americans,* which similarly would provide ideal types "representative" of "genius and patriotism" against which the public might measure themselves. And as Fowler included the counterexamples of "Pirates, Robbers, Murderers, and Thieves," Brady also began making images for his neighbor P. T. Barnum, whose human oddities were at once novelties to gawk at and unfortunate figures who might allow the average man and woman to feel superior. The shadows of phrenology in the rising celebrity cult were made plain when Barnum brought Lydia Fowler to speak on the subject at the most popular lecture ever offered by his American Museum.

Eliza Farnham did not fare as well. Led by the prison chaplain, who had been annoyed to discover a sketch artist had been measuring heads in his office, a movement against her phrenologically inspired reforms accused her of abusing the authority invested in her by the state. Her infractions were alleged to include "use of improper books," "unlawful use of prisoners' time and labor," and perhaps most damningly, "infidelity." Though at the time she would not have called herself anything other than a Christian, Farnham lost her job at Mount Pleasant in part because she was suspected of having religious beliefs that strayed far from the orthodox.

Eventually this charge would be proven correct. Within a few years, Farnham embraced the gospel of the Fox sisters, becoming an ardent believer in ghostly visitations and otherworldly communication. The man who had brought her to Sing Sing, John Edmonds, likewise became an evangelist for the new faith and, as he rose through the ranks of New York City jurists, was largely responsible for its increasing social acceptance.

Farnham meanwhile shook the dust of New York and Sing Sing from her feet. By the middle of the 1850s, she was both a successful author and a popular lecturer on the séance circuit. She traveled west with a number of single women in search of new lives, and husbands, on the frontier, and would be widely credited with introducing Spiritualism to California.

The three who collected the stories and images of convicts did not work together again. Brady was on the verge of becoming the most successful photographer in the city, presiding over a grand gallery and studio where he would later photograph Lorenzo Fowler in conditions infinitely better than those available at Blackwell's Island. He would not find himself in the same place as Eliza Farnham until 1863, when the fates and the war would conspire to bring the photographer and the prison matron together under worse conditions than either could have imagined.

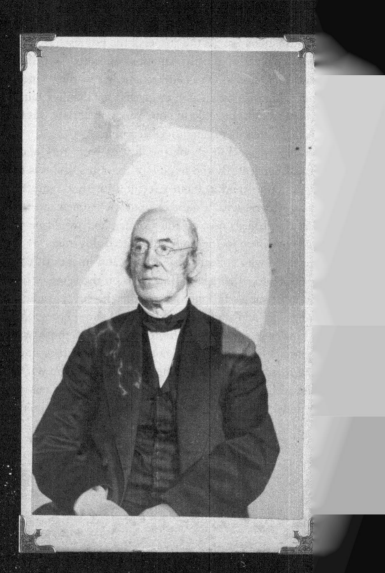

Abolitionist William Lloyd Garrison with a shackled spirit, William Mumler, 1862–1875.

CHAPTER 9

NO SHADOW OF TRICKERY

J. W. BLACK WAS not the only Boston photographer flummoxed by the images emanating from 258 Washington Street. One of Black's former employers, L. H. Hale, tried to re-create the process and produce spirit photographs of his own. But as the *Banner of Light* reported, Hale could imitate Mumler's ghosts only through the use of two negatives and by printing one image atop the other. "He says he cannot see how they can be produced on the card with only one negative," the Spiritualist paper noted with some delight, "which is the case with all Mumler's spirit pictures."

With the local photographic elite unnerved, more credulous souls flocked to Mumler's door, which, though it still was called Mrs. Stuart's studio, was now known to all as the workplace of Mr. and Mrs. Mumler.

When William and Hannah married, their partnership instantly became as much professional as domestic. Always a presence behind the counter at the gallery, she now stepped in front of it, participating in the theater surrounding Mumler's art.

If the spirit world refused to cooperate and the ethereal images could not be fixed upon the glass, the photographer or the sitters themselves would eventually ask Mrs. Mumler, "Do you see any spirits present?"

"Yes, I see a beautiful spirit," she would reply, and then describe in detail the ghostly form whose portrait would soon be written in light.

Her magnetism was as strong as ever. In fact, it was she alone for whom Mumler first claimed supernatural abilities. His role in the excitement that had become their livelihood and life's work, he insisted, was as mysterious to him as to anyone. To some doubters, his frequent befuddled failure to produce spirit images was a clear suggestion that this was a man without guile. "I have seen several pictures and there is a real look about them all. I examined the process of taking, and could find no shadow of trickery," a correspondent for the venerable abolitionist newspaper the *Liberator* noted. "The medium's air and manner, his non-success, his disappointment, all indicate reality."

Not that Mumler was wholly without explanations for the wonders over which he presided. To him, as miraculous as this new moment in the relationship between the realms of the living and the dead might be, its photographic manifestation was simply a matter of science. "One of the most frequently repeated arguments brought against the possibility of spirit-photography," he said, "is the assumption that what the eye cannot see cannot be photographed."

This, Mumler argued, was far from the case. Consider electricity, the unparalleled marvel of the age. When one passes an electric charge through a vacuum in a dark room, if the current is strong enough it will be seen by the naked eye. If the current is weak, it will seem to human observers to be nonexistent. If allowed a long enough exposure time, however, a camera will record its low-wattage life. "This is a remarkable fact," Mumler said; "indeed, it borders on the wonderful, that a phenomenon invisible to the human eye should have been, so to speak, seen by the photographic lens."

For further evidence, one had only to ask those who emerged blinking in the sunlight of Washington Street with a photograph by Mumler wrapped in brown paper. Impossible to make it home without opening the package on the sidewalk, so great was the hunger to see the unseen. Among his satisfied customers: Mr. Ewell of Boston had a beloved sister who died of consumption, but now again beside him together they stood. Mr. Miller of Malden mourned a son small enough to dandle on his knee, and here the boy was, still sitting right there. Mr. Stebbins lost a child. Dr. Main lost a wife. Mr. Hazard lost a wife. Each entered the Mumlers' studio with a private ache and left with a heart filled.

They counted among their early clients some of Boston's most influential families—men and women of means who came to the spirit photographer because of either a recent loss or a nagging emptiness they could not name.

In the latter category, the unassuming Alvin Adams stood out as a thoroughly practical man who suddenly felt himself haunted by the implications of his success.

Since 1839, while the nation's artists and dreamers had concocted fantastical ways of erasing distance with sunlight and copper wire, Adams had done much the same with nothing but a carpetbag. He had been thirty-five years old when he offered to fill as large a case as he could carry with parcels and transport them by steamship and train between New York and Boston. The business he started with that trip, Adams Express, soon became the largest shipping firm in the country.

In a dozen years, Adams's company grew from one man with a big bag to three hundred employees and offices as far away as San Francisco, Australia, and Japan. In 1854, the company moved gold, silver, cash, and other valuables totaling more than a million dollars a day. By the 1860s, it had so much currency in circulation it served as a de facto bank, financing much of the construction of California during the Gold Rush and handling payroll for both the Union and the Confederate armies when the Civil War broke out.

The war had of course hampered the shipping business, but not as badly as one might expect. When it became unlawful for Adams Express to ship goods to the Confederacy, the company split in two—one branch for the North, one branch for the South, both owned by Alvin Adams.

The war had other effects as well. Inevitably, Adams and his agents shipped weapons south. But as the fighting raged on, some unexpected shipments also began to come north. "Those ominous, long pine boxes, that betoken the dead remains of those who went to the war, now dead and long lost, crowd the office of Adams Express Company," one account said.

Death was, Adams no doubt realized, a growth industry. And when the dead couldn't come to Adams, Adams would go to the dead. He opened satellite offices near the places where the greatest number of casualties could be found. Controlling the majority of shipping throughout much of the country, his firm was the natural choice to facilitate the Union army's corpse recovery service. The surgeon in charge of Fort Monroe in Virginia asked those interested in locating the remains of loved ones to contact Adams Express directly. At a cost of $30 for digging, boxing, and shipping, he said, "they will exhume the body and send it wherever desired."

Detailed instructions were published regarding the certification Adams Express required to prove a body had been properly disinfected and packed. Other reports noted with macabre fascination that the metal coffins preferred by the shipping agents were often seen as more valuable than their contents. "The corpse was placed in the casket," an Adams employee explained of one such instance, "and as the weather was warm and the train did not leave until the next morning, the case was placed on the platform at the depot. What was our surprise the next morning to find the corpse lying on the platform and the casket gone!"

Whether shipping weapons to the front or carrying bodies

back home, Adams was paid nicely in either direction. To a man closed to all concerns except for the bottom line this might not have registered. But Adams was a committed Spiritualist and had been almost from the beginning.

Some still recalled with joy a séance held at his residence in Watertown, outside Boston, several years before. A one-thousand-pound piano with three men sitting on top was said to have risen off the ground with the aid of unseen spiritual agents. "The instrument was handled with such masterly freedom," one witness claimed, "that the invisible agents therewith beat the time to 'Hail Columbia.'" A skeptic among the believers that night insisted it must be a collective hallucination, but for that line of argument the Spiritualists had a ready answer. "When the piano is raised, slip your foot under it," they told the unbeliever, "and if your toes are not pinched, you may safely infer that the psychological hypothesis is the true one."

Such merriment, however, came long before the war. When Adams visited Mumler and asked for a sitting, he had more serious matters in mind.

Mrs. Mumler led him to a chair lit by the sun and notified her husband that conditions seemed right for an apparition to appear. A few minutes later, the shipping magnate was not surprised to discover a spirit emerge on the glass. Though he had posed by himself and had noted only the photographer and his wife in the room, beside him on the image he saw "a boy seated, and intently reading a book." A nephew who had died, he believed, was now appearing in a form "as perfect as if one in the flesh had sat before the camera." It was a vision of youth interrupted, as it had been for the occupants of all those metal boxes he moved across the country like coins on a table.

No less haunted was Eliza Babbitt, widow of the great inventor and entrepreneur Isaac Babbitt, who had died shortly before Mumler took his first picture. Like Mumler, Babbitt had been trained as a metalworker, primarily a goldsmith. He had branched out far more lucratively throughout his career, however. As a young man he had successfully forged the first American-made brass cannon, and later developed a flexible alloy known as Babbitt metal, which was considered so essential to the rise of industry in the northern states that Congress awarded him $20,000. He filed patents for a number of inventions, including an improved method of honing blades without a sharpener's wheel, and developed soap powders sold throughout the nation. "Babbitt's Cytherean Cream of Soap," one advertisement declared, "is intended to take the place of all other soaps." Because his recipe could cheaply produce mass quantities of disinfectant of the kind required by armies on the move, it would become useful in unforeseen ways. In 1860, he sold the formula for Boston Chemical Soap Powder for $6,000, a small fortune at the time.

As it had for Adams, the dissolution of the Union corresponded with the most successful time in Babbitt's career. His cannon-making years were well behind him, as was the need to personally oversee the sometimes dangerous processes of smelting metals and mixing chemicals, but they caught up with him as the war began. In the parlance of the day, Babbitt lost his mind. He was given over to the care of a mental institution, and he died there soon after. Though a lifetime spent inhaling toxic fumes may have contributed to his madness, his obituary noted, "the fact that Isaac Babbitt died in an insane asylum does not detract from the merits of his formulas."

Mumler made a picture for Eliza Babbitt showing her husband as she had known him: a proud self-made man before he had been undone by the lingering effects of the labors of his youth. His head had been shaved at the asylum, and sure enough, his spirit appeared bald in the image — a detail that was, Mumler claimed, "a remarkable test" of its veracity. The widow wrote a note of thanks to Mrs. Mumler, which quickly found its way into the Spiritualist press:

> This is to certify that I, Mrs. Isaac Babbitt, have a Spirit Photograph of my husband, taken at your rooms, by Mr. Mumler. It is recognized by all that have seen it, who knew him when he was upon earth, as a perfect likeness, and I am myself satisfied that his spirit was present, although invisible to mortals.
>
> Yours, with respect,
> Mrs. Isaac Babbitt

The Adams and Babbitt families were only the most noteworthy of the many who came to see Mumler during the first few weeks of his renown. The throng became so insistent that he was forced to limit himself to four sittings a day. After that, he said, the spirits were still willing, but his flesh was too weak to go on.

Parents saw visions of children gone for years. Widows who had seen husbands broken by dementia before death found them whole again. Widowers who missed wives as intensely as Samuel Morse missed his Lucretia looked upon their faces at last. And tears pooled on Washington Street like collodion on photo glass.

Mathew Brady advertisement,
New York Herald, August 21, 1856.

CHAPTER 10

A CRAVING FOR LIGHT

BY THE TIME Mathew Brady finished his work on Blackwell's Island, his First Premium Daguerrian Miniature Gallery was just one small booth in the most crowded marketplace in the city. Instant image makers were now ubiquitous. Reformed painters, former jewelry makers, lapsed corner-store chemists, mechanical tinkerers of every kind, they all wanted a piece of a faddish pastime that was becoming a booming industry. "There is hardly a block in New York that has not one or more of these concerns upon it," one tourist noted, "and some of them a dozen or more."

The stretch of Broadway chosen by Brady was firmly in the latter category. Since the introduction of daguerreotypes a few years before, photography studios had proliferated across lower Manhattan at such an alarming rate that one wag, writing for the penny newspaper *Brother Jonathan*, clucked that there were now just two types of New Yorkers: "the beggars and the takers of likeness by daguerreotype." It would soon be impossible, he continued, to find anyone who had not had "his likeness done by the sun."

Like Brady, the many self-taught cameramen now selling portraits on Broadway had chosen the spot because it was the most bustling thoroughfare in the city. The corner of Fulton Street especially attracted a steady stream of not only native New Yorkers but out-of-towners eager to take in such sights as P. T. Barnum's American Museum. Since its opening in 1841, the vast curiosity cabinet had been among the nation's most popular tourist destinations. Locating his studio directly across the intersection was the first and perhaps best marketing decision Brady would ever make.

Occupying nearly half a block at the corner of Broadway and Ann Street, the American Museum was a vast temple of diversion, and was to many visitors from the hinterlands the only reason the stench and danger of New York were worth the trip. Across the bustling intersection, the Ionic columns of St. Paul's Church gave the area the appearance of upright piety, but the stretch of roadway between the chapel and the museum was well known as "the standing-place for all kinds of cheats and robbers," as one contemporary chronicler recalled, "all on the watch for stray countrymen, strangers, and other green and unwary travelers."

Of such grifters, Phineas Taylor Barnum was indisputably king. His museum was either the greatest collection of novelties and amusements in the greatest city on earth, or it was, as highbrow scoffers complained of this constantly evolving populist cathedral, an "ill-looking, ungainly, rambling structure" containing a "paltry collection of preposterous things." Either way, Mathew Brady had scored a coup in opening his gallery so close to an address that was the cause of constant conversation.

Unfortunately, he was not alone. Of the two hundred photographic studios in the city, the lion's share were within the same square quarter mile. None were as close to the museum as Brady's, but all were an easy stroll for potential clients on the hunt for better images at a lower price. To begin with, there was the local salon of John Plumbe, who by the mid-1840s operated studios not only at 251 Broadway, but in Philadelphia, Baltimore, Albany, and Boston as well. A few doors down there was Edward Anthony, soon to become the largest supplier of photographic chemicals in the United States. Down at number 57, the agent of Monsieur Daguerre himself had set up shop, as if to remind Americans of the Frenchman's claim as the founder of the art.

Many of Brady's other nearby competitors proved to be talentless bumblers producing inferior products, and as a result did not stay in business long. Yet as further bad luck would have it, the very best in the city was less than a block away.

Jeremiah Gurney, ten years Brady's senior, had established himself as a high-end practitioner well before the younger man had taken his first mug shots on Blackwell's Island. Gurney had likewise been a student of Morse, and he considered himself heir to the professor's position at the top of the profession. He was master not only of technique, but in selling himself to a public that for the most part did not know what to expect from a visit to a photo studio. With ever more aspiring daguerreotypists setting up shop around him, Gurney reassured the cautious consumer by noting his experience whenever possible. "As in every art and science," he said in one advertisement, "years of study and practice are necessary to success . . . Especially is it indispensable in an art that has progressed so rapidly as the Daguerreotype."

In his own first advertisements, Brady was barely willing to engage in such salesmanship. He hoped his product would speak for itself, failing to grasp the necessity of first bringing potential clients to his door.

FIRST PREMIUM NEW YORK
DAGUERRIAN MINIATURE GALLERY
Corner of Broadway and Fulton Street, entrance third floor.

> Where may be had miniatures which, for beauty of color, tone and effect can at all times commend themselves; and if not superior, are equal to any that have been heretofore taken. Mr. B. does not claim superiority for himself, but leaves his pictures to the criticisms of a just and intelligent public, who, as well as strangers, are invited to call at the Gallery before going elsewhere, whether they intend sitting or not.

On a city block teeming with people, in large part due to the hyperbolic P. T. Barnum and those who had learned to emulate his swaggering style of self-promotion, *"Mr. B. does not claim superiority"* was not likely to draw a crowd.

Still in his mid-twenties, Brady had reason to be humble, and it was not just his age. As ever in the work of portraiture, the problem was the eyes. Usually this meant the eyes of the photographer's subject, which could not bear to remain open long enough to achieve a clear exposure. Yet for Brady, the most problematic eyes were his own.

Since adolescence he had experienced trouble with his vision. He had no difficulty arranging scenes for photographs in his studio or outside in the sunshine. Yet the precision of sight necessary to focus a lens or make adjustments to light and shadow was gradually leaving him. His round, steel-rimmed spectacles helped only so much; he remained limited by the malady that had so darkened his earliest days that he once remembered of his childhood, "I felt a craving for light."

In order to compete with the likes of Gurney, Brady had to think in bigger terms than the competition. He considered what the public wanted when it sought a photograph. In a way, it was something not unlike what he had provided to Eliza Farnham and her phrenologist colleagues: a rendering of inner lives written with exterior details. While a convict might be pictured in such a way that those who chose to do so could read any personal or psychological failing into the contours of his face, those with means and time enough to acquire their own portrait, or that of a person they admired, often had a similar desire: to see virtue reflected in the slope of a nose, the jut of a chin.

Every portrait studio worthy of the name featured not just a posing salon where clients might face the camera, but an elegant waiting room with dozens and sometimes hundreds of portraits on display. Brady began to remake his humble Daguerrian Miniature Gallery into the much-grander-sounding National Gallery of Daguerreotypes.

In his advertisements, the humility of a photographer going nearly blind fell away, replaced by a voice that proposed this was a site of significance to the entire country. He boasted that his walls now were home to "The President and Cabinet ... Members of the United States Senate and House of Representatives, Justices of the Supreme Court at Washington, and many other eminent persons." He continued, "The Proprietor, being much of his time in Washington, has the advantage of adding to these portraits many others that may interest the public."

Having cut his photographic teeth on criminals and lunatics, Brady took to politicians right away. In 1850, he published twenty-four images in a lithographic series that would allow his customers to display the heroes of the still young nation on their own walls: "This collection embraces portraits of the most distinguished men of this country," he claimed—and the claim had the curious effect of leading many who believed they should be counted among the "most distinguished" to seek out his services.

By the end of the decade, he had eclipsed even Gurney—almost literally so. He greatly expanded the studio to take up much of the block across from the American Museum, making "Brady of Broadway" a natural stop for thousands of tourists. With new sky-facing windows installed above the photographic rooms, he seemed also to harness all available light. "This establishment is one of the most extensive in the world," he wrote. "Its facilities for the production of portraits by the Daguerrean art unrivalled. It now occupies two large buildings, 205 and 207 Broadway. The operating department is arranged in the most scientific manner, and directed by persons of acknowledged skill in the profession. Strangers and citizens will be interested and pleased by devoting an hour to the inspection of Brady's National Gallery."

If the inventor of the telegraph planted the seed of the portrait photograph industry in America, Mathew Brady cultivated it, harvested it, and brought it to market. Exploiting the beginnings of celebrity culture and the possibilities it promised to those able to come close to the famous, Brady offered "strangers and citizens" the opportunity to sit before the very camera where the great men of the nation had sat, to be seen as they were seen. To sit before the camera, Brady realized, was to imagine oneself, if only for a few moments, the very center of the world's attention. The hub of the universe in the flesh.

It was also to dabble in the transformative magic of the art, which even then was beginning—a decade before Mumler would summon ghosts to his plates—to experiment with the innate sorcery of crafting images of light. It was not uncommon at the time to see advertisements for "composite photography," which involved looking at two photographs side by side in a viewer called a stereograph. With each eye focused on a different image, the mind would attempt to make sense of them by melding their forms into one. "I have taken a gentleman's picture on one plate and a lady's on the other, and by placing them in the stereoscope they were blended together, producing the most astonishing effect," one Philadelphia photographer wrote. "The resulting picture is not a true likeness of the one or the other, yet possesses the most prominent features of each, making a picture wonderfully like one of their children. All true lovers," he confidently predicted, "by having their daguerreotypes side by side in the stereoscope, will possess a perfect infantometer, and be enabled to anticipate the precise style of beauty which is to rise up and gladden their double blessedness."

The space between what was real and what was imagined was the art form's natural terrain, and Brady realized this better than anyone. Perhaps inevitably, he became the photographer of choice for P. T. Barnum, whose gravity and celebrity pulled the young photographer into still higher orbit. For the most part,

Brady's rise helped other nearby studios, permanently establishing Broadway as the single best place in the country to visit for those hoping to take part in the marvel of photography.

Gurney did not see it this way, however. Brady was not a threat to his livelihood, but he was to his reputation, previously unchallenged, as the nation's photographer.

After the election of Franklin Pierce to the White House in 1852, Brady landed the lucrative portrait of the new president. Brady had also made a daguerreotype of Pierce's vice president William R. King, but King would die less than a month after taking office. Annoyed that he had not had the opportunity to make an image of the new president himself, and perhaps taking some small comfort in the likelihood that Brady had printed hundreds of vice presidential portraits that would never sell, Gurney placed a clever advertisement in the papers that he imagined would remind readers who was the preeminent photographer in the country.

"Poetry is in decline but the muse still sings of Daguerreotypes," he wrote, then continued:

> *General Pierce is a popular person at present.*
> *United almost were the Yankees for Frank*
> *Rather new for this people—for him no less pleasant;*
> *Now, in favors and fame, who is second in rank?*
> *Every eye turns toward you, the greatest artist renowned*
> *Your daguerreotype runs everything off the ground.*

With no vice president, who was second to the commander in chief in terms of prestige? With no surplus of humility, Gurney's acrostic asserted that it was he himself. In an era in which classified ads filled dozens of columns in every paper with monotonous litanies of nearly indistinguishable advertisements for goods sold, services rendered, and situations sought, Gurney made playful use of their potential, showing the creative spark that had for so long secured his place at the top of his profession.

He had not recognized, however, that though Brady was a fine photographer, the younger man had become a truly tireless competitor, a man who would not be outdone. Gurney's use of poetry to spell his name had taken up six lines in the daily papers. By the time the next presidential contest began, Brady had begun placing ads that ran beyond a hundred lines of type, spelling out his name with hundreds of words in advertisements that came as close as one could get in nineteenth-century newsprint to putting his name in neon lights.

Brady was quick to align himself with the latest advances in photographic technology, leaving it to his potential clients to determine that his rivals were wedded to older ways of making images. If Gurney wanted to boast that his "daguerreotype runs everything off the ground," Brady was perfectly willing to let him. Only a decade after the miraculous discovery had become known in the United States, the daguerreotype was already becoming passé, replaced by ever more complex techniques.

Adding injury to the insult of being supplanted as the preeminent photographer for the great and distinguished, during the years of Brady's rise with these new methods, Gurney was laid low by an affliction associated with the now dated art. The same year he claimed that his skill with Daguerre's process made him "the greatest artist renowned," he came down with mercury poisoning, an occupational hazard of the days when developing plates involved the use of mercury fumes. In further contrast to Gurney, the image Brady portrayed—despite the limitations of his own eye affliction—was of vigor and the health of better days ahead.

By the presidential campaign of 1860, there was no question of whom the ambitious young lawyer from Illinois would choose to take his picture on the day of his first major address in New York, at the Cooper Union for the Advancement of Science and Art, commonly known as the Cooper Institute.

When Abraham Lincoln visited Brady of Broadway on February 27, 1860, the latter's reputation was well established, the former's only beginning its ascent. The photographer approached this portrait as he had so many others before: with an understanding of how a single instant captured on glass might come to represent a man's very soul.

With his gaunt face bobbling high above his shoulders and his hair somewhat wild from the winter winds that blew like a gale in the intersection of Broadway and Fulton, Lincoln did not look much like a statesman as he stood in Brady's posing room. The photographer drew up Lincoln's collar to shorten the appearance of his neck, and determined that he could put his artists to work taming Lincoln's hair after the image had been developed. They also might smooth the crags in his face — whatever might be done to make him appear more presidential. As a final touch, Brady placed Lincoln's hand on a book, as if he were already taking the oath of office.

When an image was needed to illustrate press accounts of Lincoln's successful address, an engraving made from Brady's photograph ran in newspapers across the country. It was the first most Americans had seen of the man. Later that year, after it became clear he would rise to the White House and all that lay beyond, Lincoln declared, "Brady and the Cooper Institute made me president."

This assessment no doubt had something to do with Brady's winning the chance to photograph the new first lady soon after. Mary Todd Lincoln visited Brady's studio in March of 1861. Famously concerned about her appearance in photographs, Mrs. Lincoln thought she looked too stern and matronly, and that her hands were too big. As he had with her husband, Brady posed his nervous subject, finding the best possible angle with which to display her profile. He then carefully arranged her hands to seem more dainty, diminished by a white kerchief he placed beneath her woven fingers. After developing the image, he instructed his artists to paint over the back of her dress, removing several inches from her waistline.

Half fantasy, half reality, it was one of her favorite photographs of herself.

PART II
PHILOSOPHICAL INSTRUMENTS

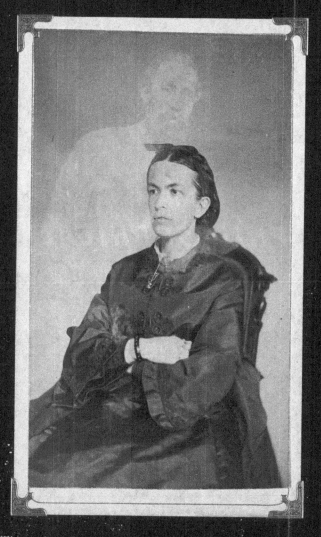

The medium Fannie Conant with a spirit image of her brother.
William Mumler, 1862–1875.

CHAPTER 11

THE MESSAGE DEPARTMENT

LESS THAN A MONTH after his initial discoveries, William Mumler was the talk of Boston, an object of fascination for the living as well as the dead. Among the spirits who gathered at the offices of the Spiritualist newspaper on Washington Street, only the war was a more heated topic of conversation.

On Mondays, Tuesdays, and Thursdays each week, a meeting room at the headquarters of the *Banner of Light* became crowded with the sitters of Fannie Conant's "circle," a gathering of Spiritualists who acted not only as an audience for the medium's channeling of spirits, but, it was said, as a "battery" providing the energy needed to maintain the connection between this world and the next.

In the beginning, the *Banner's* cofounder William Berry had proved a sufficient battery to release Mrs. Conant's gifts. They would sit together for hours, Fannie in a trance state, William enraptured by her spiritual powers. "Mr. Berry conceived the idea that the seances must be held strictly in private," her spirit-written autobiography later recalled, "only himself and Mrs. C being at the table." Acting as both battery and recorder, Berry raced to write down every word spoken.

On certain occasions, she became "so thoroughly depleted of vital force by reason of her ministrations" that the only way in which communications could be given through her was to allow her to fall into a deep slumber and then place a pen in her hand. The spirits would then write the messages they wished to convey, with Berry at Fannie's side, "moving the paper as fast as it became necessary."

Though this collaboration produced remarkable results in Berry's estimation, his partner Luther Colby soon suggested it was their responsibility to share Fannie's gifts with others who might benefit. Moreover, he argued, her powers as a medium had become so great that she needed a bigger battery.

Berry eventually agreed, but insisted he should remain intimately involved in the expanded circles. Fannie found his ongoing attentions a mixed blessing, however. She considered it his job to maintain a meditative calm in the increasingly crowded séance room, the better to keep open a channel of communication to the vasty deep. "At first the manifestations of spirit intelligence, and the management of the circles for the same, were not as quietly ordered, or systematically arranged as afterward," she later said. "It required practice for Mr. Berry and his unseen coadjutors to perceive the proper conditions to be observed on either end of the telegraphic wires. Mr. Berry, on his part, would often allow persons to enter the room, or retire, while the seance was going on, thus submitting the medium to the severest shocks, and almost unfitting her to continue."

Soon the room became so full it was difficult for eager Spiritualists to pass through without bumping into each other. If a stray hand should jostle Fannie's arm while she was summoning a spirit, "the nicely adjusted magnetic surroundings were so thoroughly disturbed that no further manifestations could be obtained." Sensing Fannie's displeasure, Berry made sure the doors closed at three o'clock sharp to avoid undue disturbances. On more than one occasion, he was forced to find a bigger room.

The biggest room of all proved to be the pages of the *Banner of Light*. While at most only a few dozen could attend even the largest séance circle, thousands would read the medium's messages in written form. Berry had dutifully copied hundreds by then, and began publishing them in a dedicated section of the paper known as the Message Department.

The otherworldly communications shared by Mrs. Conant were soon the *Banner of Light*'s most popular feature. She became the paper's star, and William Berry her most ferocious defender. "The great unpopularity of Spiritualism in its opening days," Fannie Conant's biography recalled, "caused much trouble to be made by the relatives of those communicating through Mrs. Conant, concerning the publication of their messages to the world. Those who felt specially aggrieved, frequently called in ruffled mood upon Mr. Berry, but gained no comfort from that gentleman, as he assured them, that whatever came as a message through the medium which was within the bounds of reason, he should most certainly publish."

BY THE TIME William Mumler appeared on the Boston Spiritualist scene, the *Banner of Light*'s circles had gone on in much the same fashion for five years. The only change was that Fannie Conant had begun to host them alone.

With the start of the Civil War, William Berry had enlisted as a sergeant in the 1st Company of the Massachusetts Sharpshooters. Part of a movement among Spiritualists to show their loyalty to the Union, many northerners who shared his beliefs had become concerned that Confederate mediums were supplying otherworldly information to Robert E. Lee and other rebel leaders. As the *Boston Daily Evening Transcript* reported, "The Spiritualists, or at least some of them, think that the rebels get their intelligence of the designs of the Union Generals through mediums, who are able to get into their thoughts and swindle them out of their plans."

At the age of thirty-six, Berry was a bit old to muster into service but driven to provide the Union with some Spiritualist muscle of its own. Though his civilian work had been largely limited to journalism, he headed for the front lines and quickly proved his worth at battles including Ball's Bluff, the Siege of Yorktown, and Savage's Station. He was promoted to first lieutenant within six months, while the *Banner* séance circle tried to ensure that the spirits of the dead would watch over him.

The war came up often in the circle. Men killed in battle frequently held court, and other spirits offered their ethereal opinions on the meaning of conflict and the good that might come of it.

"I've got somebody I want to speak to, living," Fannie Conant said in the voice of a young boy. His words came quietly, a result of the lung fever that, the medium explained, had caused his death. "My father was killed at the battle of South Mountain. I've been away most a year. I was eight years old, and my name was John Dixon. My father's name was Nathan. My mother's got Jenny with her, and she's most tired. She don't know how to live; she's so tired of working. And my father couldn't come to speak, and said I must. He's sober here; he isn't never drunk here. He'll talk to my mother, if she'll let him. I don't like to come here."

"You mustn't be afraid to come to this place," Mrs. Conant said in her own voice.

"I ain't afraid but I don't like to come."

"You ought to be willing to come for your mother's sake."

"She's crying all the time," the boy's voice said.

"You will do her much good by coming here today, I dare say."

Such communications usually included references to living readers of the *Banner,* who then would alert the family of the visiting spirits that contact had been made. On many occasions, Conant spoke not only with her own voice and that of the recently deceased, but in the name of a spirit who identified himself as Captain Gibbs, an old salt of a seafaring man who may or may not have died as a pirate. So taken was she with this persona that when traveling by water she would argue with steamship skippers about weather and the tides, insisting her nautical knowledge had come from the great beyond. Fallen soldiers preferred to talk to the spirit of Gibbs through the medium, apparently more at ease speaking with a man of military rank than to a woman.

One evening after she had fallen into a trance, she called out in the voice of one of the Union dead.

"Captain?"

"Sir," she replied in Gibbs's voice.

"I was here a little while ago. My name was Philip Guinon. Do you remember me?"

"I do."

"I was killed at Fair Oaks," she said. Also known as the Battle of Seven Pines, fought in Henrico County, Virginia, on June 1, 1862, it was a day with eleven thousand casualties, nearly equally split between North and South.

"I got the privilege of coming here a few minutes this afternoon to thank those kind friends who went to see my wife and children," the medium continued in the dead soldier's voice. "Bless 'em! If only they knew how—I said I'd keep calm so I will —but if they only knew how much good it did me, as well as my wife and children, they'd be glad they went. I thank 'em. It's all I can do, now, Captain, but I'll pay 'em by-and-by."

———

FOR BOSTON'S SPIRITUALISTS, the war's righteousness was a matter of faith supported not by scripture but by the voices of spirits who told them the struggle must continue. In the *Banner of Light* séance room, questions of why the war must be fought, or how long it would go on, were less important than what the conflict might signal in the unfolding relationship between the living and the dead. Though Fannie Conant spoke in the voices of those killed on both sides, there was little doubt which side she believed had the favor of the world to come.

In the case of William Mumler, however, readers of the paper's Message Department found that the woman speaking for the dead did not want to be pinned down on matters as quick to change as technology. Where spirit photographs were concerned, her ghostly friends insisted, it was too soon to tell.

"There is much that is genuine true, beyond the possibility of doubt, surrounding this recent unfoldment of spirit-power," the spirits said through the medium. "There is also much that is untrue, and which has its origin not in the world spiritual, but in the world material. The false or untrue was never born of Nature; on the contrary, it originates in what we call art." They continued, "It is not only your duty but your right, as rational and intelligent beings, to study this new spiritual unfoldment closely, and to draw the line of demarcation between the two."

"This is your work, and not ours," the spirits said. "Inasmuch as you have the faculty to divide the right from the wrong, the false from the genuine, it is your duty to exercise it, and to weigh the balances of your own judgement all that is presented you from the spirit-world, or from the world in which you now live."

When the séance ended, Fannie Conant fell silent, as if exhausted from the effort of viewing mortal quandaries from someplace far above.

———

WHILE MUMLER'S PHOTOGRAPHS were so preoccupying Boston, Fannie Conant had other reasons to feel spiritually exhausted. News from the front came that Lieutenant William Berry was dead. Killed along with seven thousand others at the

Battle of Antietam, he had apparently not been protected by spirits that day. But the overall loss of life proved to be a boon for Spiritualism itself. So many corpses lying in farmers' fields drew journalists like flies, soon followed by photographers, whose images would make death a fitting subject of polite conversation as never before.

As much as those in attendance at the *Banner of Light*'s circle may have been pleased by this in theory, the reality of the end of Berry's corporeal life came as a shock. As it was later reported by the Message Department, it took his spirit nearly a month to travel from Maryland to Massachusetts. "On the evening of October 11, the spirit of Wm. Berry," the column noted, "gained partial control of the medium, and attempted to make himself recognized."

On that night, Fannie moved her hand as if it held a pen, miming writing to give some impression of who the spirit now controlling her might be. When no one present could identify him, he left the circle. If any feared they had heard the last of him, they did not have long to wait.

"The next evening, October 12, he came again, going through the same motions, but I was still at a loss to identify," Berry's former partner Luther Colby wrote.

Again the spirit moving the woman at the front of the séance hall said very little, but managed to announce that Berry had recently been killed in battle.

"At this point," Colby continued, "I was strongly impressed with the presence of Brother Berry and when I pronounced the name, he shook my head violently, in token of glad recognition. Although the notice of his death had just appeared in the *Banner*, I was the only one in the room that had seen it."

Fannie Conant continued to move as if she were momentarily possessed by the spirit of her lost collaborator, the man who had recognized her gifts and helped her reach the wider world. She managed to speak only a few words.

"To the friends of the *Banner*," Colby wrote, "he wished me to say his past experiences had elevated him to the place of greater usefulness in the future, where he was content to dwell."

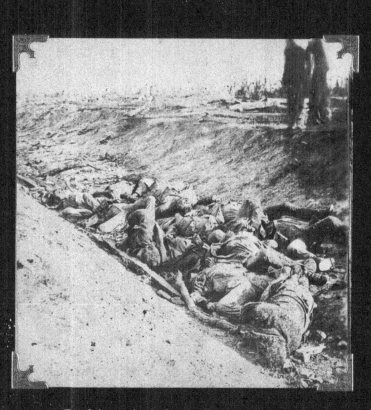

Confederate dead after the Battle of Antietam.
Alexander Gardner, 1862.

CHAPTER 12

A BIG HEAD FULL OF IDEAS

FROM HIS POSITION on the north bank of the sunken roadway, Alexander Gardner could see no fewer than sixteen bodies.
This one with legs bent at the knees like he was riding a bicycle;
that one with his hand resting gently on a comrade's thigh. They
clogged the bottom of this deep wagon gully cut between farmers' fields like logs floating down a river. Anonymous all, nearly
every man had his features hidden by earth, a flap of coarse wool,
or the shielding limbs of other bodies. Only one faced upward
and unobscured. He stared into sunshine that made this a good
day for photography, his dry mouth open like an aperture taking
in the vast September sky.

Gardner pointed his camera down into the ditch, positioning
it so the dead men appeared upside down on the ground-glass
focus screen. He adjusted his view until all four corners of the
image contained only unremarkable details, the better to frame
the remarkable horror at the center.

In the finished photograph, the lower right would show the
bloody dirt upon which the closest body seemed to be crawl-
ing. At the lower left, a ravaged hillside. The upper corners were
filled with empty air, beneath which a scorched cornfield would
give the photograph a swatch of necessary darkness, allowing
the lighter shades to stand out in stark contrast. Traversing the
picture's focal point, a stripe of commingled corpses and debris
would stretch to the left edge and beyond, as if to eternity.

The two men now watching Gardner work from across this dark chasm would inevitably appear blurred, but this would likely not read as a failure on the artist's part. In their abstraction they could be anyone, allowing the viewer to imagine standing and gawking just so. They would also provide two strong verticals to offset the photograph's multiple horizons, the layered lines of grass, corn, sky, and death. Important to balance the elements of such an unpleasant landscape—the eye wants symmetry, especially when faced with a mangled moment like this.

Satisfied with the tableau he had composed, Gardner moved to his wagon to prepare a plate. He had been trained as a portrait photographer, and perhaps would never shake the instinct to tell his subjects to remain still. Nonetheless, he knew he could take his time. He and his colleague James Gibson were the only photographers on the job, and the Union burial crews saw to their own first. To capture an image of these Confederate dead where they fell was in some ways easier than it was to pose a society matron in a Washington studio. Only the late-afternoon sun, slanting dramatically on the gray uniforms, reminded him he did not have all the time in the world.

In the darkness of his wagon, Gardner balanced a rectangle of glass on his fingertips, poured the collodion, and blew it dry. Ten by fourteen inches; it was a challenge for any novice to coat such a large plate just so—absolutely vital not to roll the pool of sticky liquid over itself—but Gardner was no novice. The precise tilt and rock of the wrist required was second nature to him, remembered by his muscles as reliably as any other man might move a pen to write his name.

Once the plate was prepared, he placed it inside a lightproof box and carried it carefully back to the camera. The focus window pulled forward to receive it and snapped back in place with a spring-loaded grip. Gardner then opened the aperture and began to count.

One. Two. Three. Four . . .

Had any of the dead men suddenly awoken, they might have thought Christmas had come early. Despite his dark hair, Gardner was the very image of a young Saint Nicholas. Not only did the Scotsman have a Viking's brawn, he also had a jovial air fully out of place with the surroundings. Once told he looked the part of a half-wild mountain man, he playfully obliged by dressing in fringed leather and a beaver fur hat for a self-portrait. In person, his brogue would have given the illusion away, but in the photograph he could have been born and raised on the frontier. Who was to say what illusions the photographs he now was making would maintain?

Five. Six. Seven. Eight . . .

Exposures in the field could take up to half a minute. With every second, the outlines of the bodies appeared more solidly on the glass. Soon they would be carted away, rolled into shallow graves. By the time grass grew above them, the best of Gardner's images might be reproduced as engravings in the press or sold for a dollar apiece. Some might call the war photographer's work ghoulish, but it was through his efforts alone that these few fallen did not merely disappear.

———

GARDNER HAD COME TO America looking for utopia; he found battlefields instead. Though he was physically imposing and clearly built for the latter—in his friend Walt Whitman's estimation, he was "large," "strong," and "mighty," and possessed a "splendid neck"—Gardner was temperamentally far more suited for the former, and had spent the better part of his life searching for it. Whitman further said that the photographer was "a man with a big head full of ideas." He had meant it as a compliment, perhaps not knowing that it was a characteristic that had proven dangerous.

By his fortieth year, Gardner had lost several members of his family to his ideas—specifically, to a plan launched with the best of intentions that had gone disastrously awry. This same plan would eventually lead him to the heart of a war for the future of a nation not his own.

Gardner was born in the town of Paisley in the Scottish Lowlands, to a family, one biographer would note, that had given many ministers to the local kirk. He entered not the ministry but the workforce, and he did so early, as nearly all children of his social station did at the time. In the particulars of his employment, however, he had been luckier than most. As a teenager in the 1830s, he had apprenticed as a silversmith—a good fit for a young man with artistic leanings and a precise, scientific mind. By then relocated to Glasgow, in his off hours he took classes in botany, chemistry, and astronomy, alive to the details and variations in the world around him.

In a city then entering the industrial age, he was also aware that the new world being created behind factory walls was not always so lovely. A social reformer of the day lamented, "I have seen human degradation in some of the worst places both in England and abroad, but I did not believe until the wynds of Glasgow, that so large an amount of filth, crime, misery, and disease existed on any one spot in any civilized country." The "wynds" were alleyways creating a maze-like warren surrounding the city's tenements. They were often too narrow for a cart to pass through, and so those living along them survived on what little could be carried in by hand.

"In the lower lodging houses," the reformer continued, "ten, twelve, sometimes twenty persons, of both sexes, and all ages, sleep promiscuously on the floor, in different degrees of nakedness. These places are generally, as regards dirt, damp, and decay, such as no person of common humanity . . . would stable his horse in . . . No efficient aid can be afforded them under existing institutions, and hundreds in a year become inured to crime, and pass through the rapid career of prostitution, drunkenness, and disease, to an early grave."

In the 1830s, successive outbreaks of typhus and cholera took thousands of lives a year, including Gardner's father. A teenager at the time, young Alexander looked for other paternal figures and soon found one in the Welsh reformer Robert Owen, who was then making waves across Britain with his advocacy for the downtrodden and his open endorsement of a revolution to overturn the existing social order.

Shortly before Gardner's birth, Owen had made the then radical suggestion that "no Male or Female shall be employed in any such Mill, Manufactory, or Building, until he or she shall have attained the age of Ten years." For those over ten but not yet adults, he proposed that they should not be permitted to work more than twelve and a half hours a day.

Reasonable though such recommendations now seem, Owen's ideas were at the time brushed aside. "The employments of these Children in Cotton Mills," one critic argued, "is not sedentary. It is neither laborious, nor such as tends to cramp their limbs, to distort their bodies, or to injure their health."

Like other radicals of the day, Owen soon lost hope in the possibility of changing society as a whole other than slowly, and by example. He established factory communities designed around the revolutionary concept of regarding the lives of workers and their families with something other than the bottom line in mind.

Gardner grew up hearing of the reforming communities Owen established, not only in Scotland, England, and Ireland, but in the United States, where Owen purchased thirty thousand acres on which to begin a fully self-sustaining utopian community. Ultimately it proved as successful as most other utopian experiments, and he lost nearly all his fortune as a result of its failure.

Following in the reformer's footsteps when he was not yet thirty years old, Gardner persuaded a cohort of acquaintances to pool their resources and make a new life in America, with the goal of establishing "by means of the united capital and industry of its partners, a comfortable home for themselves and families where they may follow a more simple, useful and rational mode of life than is found practicable in the complex and competitive state of society from which they are anxious to retire."

They settled on Iowa, and the first to go were Gardner's brother James, several in-laws, and a handful of family friends, who together made up an enterprise they called the Clydesdale Joint Stock Agricultural and Commercial Company. Alexander planned to join them a few years later. Until then he would serve as adviser and administrator of the expedition while raising funds and gathering other interested parties in Scotland. Though ostensibly the expedition's leader, he would never see most of them again.

GARDNER HAD ARRIVED AT Antietam earlier that day, September 19, 1862. Two mornings before, Union general Joseph Hooker gave orders to fire on Stonewall Jackson's forces as they moved through a cornfield north of Sharpsburg, Maryland. The shooting was so intense, Hooker later said, that "every stalk of corn in the northern and greater part of the field was cut as closely as could have been done with a knife." With dawn breaking on a clear day, the Confederates fell blind in a storm of corn and fire, then died in rows as neat as the stalks had been. An hour later, the newly reinforced rebel army rallied and the fighting continued, much of it centered on the sunken roadway later called Bloody Lane and the whitewashed pacifist meetinghouse known as the Dunker Church.

The wagon carrying Gardner's gear rolled into view of the battle-scarred chapel at the same hour of the worst fighting two days before. The Dunkers—so called for their preference for full-immersion baptism—were a peaceful people and would be horrified to see their humble house of worship become an icon of such a deadly battle. Its plain walls were pockmarked now; inside, its sanctuary was filled with the wounded, too unstable to be carried away.

Sharpsburg was a day's ride from Washington, where Gardner had for years been the manager of Mathew Brady's thriving photographic studio on Pennsylvania Avenue. With Brady still living in New York, Gardner was an equal partner in all but name, recognition, and profit—though he had done a great deal to expand the business. At the end of the 1850s, when the craze for owning two-by-four-inch portraits known as cartes de visite was about to sweep the nation, it was Gardner who had acquired the four-lens camera that made reproducing such images cheap and easy.

Brady had his own knack for recognizing business opportunities, of course. It was he who had sought the federal government's permission to follow along on the army's Potomac campaign. He had gone uninvited to view the battle at Bull Run —"like the war horse," it was later said, Brady "sniffs the battle from afar"—and had dreamed up the rolling darkrooms that were so strange-looking they had come to be called "whatsit wagons." Recognizing that the war would spread quickly in many directions, he had hired the best photographers available to follow the army's movements. Not just Gardner but James Gibson, George Barnard, and Gardner's frequent collaborator Timothy O'Sullivan were dispatched with an eye toward bringing back as many battlefield images as could be captured. Whatever came of the war, Brady suspected, providing pictures of its prosecution could be lucrative.

Without a doubt, Gardner owed his ongoing employment as a photographer to his employer's genius. Yet still it rankled. When generals and politicos paraded through the gallery eager for images that might be reproduced as engravings in the press, it was Gardner who arranged the backdrop behind them. It was Gardner who posed them beneath the ceiling windows in a sturdy wooden chair. And it was Gardner who captured and finished the images—every one of which was stamped *Portrait by Brady*.

Hard feelings could wait, however. Gardner was a long way from skylights and velvet curtains now. Between the wagon and the church, bodies had been dragged into a tidy cluster beside a two-wheeled ammunition cart, dead horse still attached, straining at its harness as it swelled in the late-summer heat.

The big man clambered down from the rumble seat and unpacked his camera. Slightly more maneuverable than the multiocular beast he used in the gallery, the model he brought with him had two lenses. It was designed for the innovative purpose of taking two images intended to be viewed simultaneously. When seen through a handheld stereoscope, they would be given depth by the mind's own magic, the eyes reconciling the repetition of detail as space through which one might move and explore.

On the battlefield before him, the best opportunity to take full advantage of the dramatic stereoscopic vista would be to use the white church surrounded by dark trees as the background, like a stage set on which the action before it would unfold. The church door had been removed and holes punched by mortar fire at several places in the south-facing wall. On the image these openings would show as pure black invading the luminescence of the structure, a battle between light and dark setting the tone for all within its orbit.

Closer to Gardner there were of course the dead themselves.

Seven of them, all on their backs as if they had been dragged by their suspenders. Partly obscured by the ammunition cart, the horse was not immediately apparent as nonhuman — all the better to require a good long look past the wagon wheels, the spokes of which would draw the eye toward the center of the frame as if to a target.

Even for a master of the form like Gardner, the wet plate process had ten steps that could not be rushed. As the dead awaited his further attention, he would clean a fresh plate with a calcium carbonate mixture known as rottenstone, then wipe away its chalky residue with a cloth. Next he would bathe the glass in a succession of potent chemicals: first a blend of grain alcohol, cadmium, ammonium, potassium, and ether, which allowed an image to adhere; then silver nitrate, the vehicle for the necessary chemical reaction that darkened by degrees when exposed to light.

If he was pleased with how these first steps had been completed, Gardner slid the glass into a coffin-shaped box that protected it from the sun's rays as he carried it to the camera for the crucial moment of exposure. Then it was back again to the whatsit for treatments to develop the image (ferrous sulfate, potassium nitrate, acetic acid) and fix it to prevent fading (potassium cyanide). That the cyanide was pure poison was just one risk among many of the photographer's art. The final steps involved both heating the plate over an open flame and coating it with a highly flammable varnish brewed from grain alcohol, lavender oil, and sandarac, the resin of a cypress tree.

The whatsit would later be compared by some to "a spiritualist's cabinet on wheels." This was mainly due to its odd appearance, but there was also something to the nearly mystical nature of the chemical transformations it concealed. That tiny particles of silver could darken in sunlight and then be prevented from following their natural inclination to return to their prior state was curious enough; that this process could be used to preserve the likenesses of men lying dead in a churchyard seemed nearly miraculous.

After he had developed the images and examined them in the morning light, Gardner saw that they would indeed be powerful stereographs.

Brady would be pleased with how his assistant had successfully brought even this scene to life. The camera had not captured the stench or heat of the place, nor the flies nor the distant anguish of the not-yet-dead inside the church. But it did record the lines of shade and brightness, and the way battered bodies and a wrecked building could regain something of their wholeness by balancing each other on the fulcrum of an ammunition cart's wheel. It also recorded the way distant trees and the grass beneath your feet might reveal themselves as part of a larger organism when arranged by a discerning eye.

Indisputably it was an image of death, but who would argue that it was not also, in its way, beautiful?

———

LIKE ROBERT OWEN before him, Gardner hadn't immediately looked to America as the place to find his utopia. He first set his sights on his hometown. He began to work as a journalist and soon acquired the *Glasgow Sentinel*, the second most popular newspaper in the city. He saw the paper's editorial page as his own personal soapbox. From the start, he was less interested in the daily news than in, he said, "enlightening the public" and "guiding right the popular mind of this country."

It was in this spirit that he traveled to London to report back for *Sentinel* subscribers on the first world's fair, known as the Great Exhibition of the Works of Industry of All Nations. For six months in 1851, six million people had the opportunity to see more than one hundred thousand objects ranging from the latest machinery to the fine arts. It was intended as a spectacle of human progress, allowing visitors to examine up close full-scale steam engines and hydraulic presses, luxury carriages and the most advanced firearms, as well as the works of artisans from around the world, with exhibit spaces for goods from nearby Guernsey and Jersey alongside booths for Malta and Ceylon.

Even before it opened, Karl Marx, who lived in London at the time, denounced the fair as a distraction from impending revolution. "With this exhibition," he wrote, "the world bourgeoisie erects its pantheon in the new Rome, where it places on show the deities it has fabricated."

On the whole, the idealistic Alexander Gardner was similarly dismayed. That such wealth had been spent on a tourist attraction while so many Scots suffered was, he thought, a moral calamity. At a time when society was "half starved by its own toil," he wrote, it pained him to see "some rolling in luxury" while others were "weary and afoot, dusty, hungry, envying and dangerous."

Yet he was not so far removed from his apprenticeship as a jeweler and his scientific education that he did not remain both an artist and a curious soul at heart. He was particularly drawn to the exhibit on "philosophical instruments," a category that included, according to the fair's extensive catalog, "instruments relating to Astronomy, Optics, Light, Heat, Electricity, Magnetism, Acoustics, Meteorology, etc." Within this vast field, his eye was drawn to the same works that most impressed the exhibition's judges. "That photography is yet in its infancy, there can be little doubt," the judges wrote. "By improvements in the camera and the daily increasing practical knowledge of experimenters, we may expect to behold compositions, embodying a degree of reality otherwise beyond our power of attainment."

Of all the nations represented in the photographic exhibit

—Britain, France, Austria, and the United States—the Americans surprised the judges with their skill in capturing that most elusive subject, the human face. In portraiture, they declared, "America stands prominently forward." It alone was notable "for stern development of character; her works, with few exceptions, reject all accessories, present a faithful transcript of the subject, and yield to none in excellence of execution."

And of all the Americans whose work stood out in London, one was singled out for special recognition:

> BRADY (*United States, No. 137*) *has exhibited forty-eight daguerreotypes, uncoloured. These are excellent for beauty of execution. The portraits stand forward in bold relief, upon a plain background* ... *The portraits of General Taylor, Calhoun, General Cass, and James Perry, are strikingly excellent; but all are so good that selection is almost impossible. The Jury awarded the Prize Medal to Mr. Brady.*

Not long after Gardner's return from London, the *Sentinel* began to feature reviews of the booming Glasgow photography scene. "The art of 'sun picturing' seems to be making rapid strides," one review began. "Every time we are called upon to inspect the exhibited specimens of this art we are more struck by its wondrous capabilities."

Among its capabilities, Gardner came to see, was the remarkable power to reorganize the world, to create an idealized simulacrum of society in which the troubles he had so long railed against could be bent to his will. Photography, the Great Exhibition's catalog had said, "opens a fresh field of philosophical inquiry." In the judges' somewhat grandiose opinion, the art "gives to man increased physical knowledge, and may work great changes in his moral destinies."

With his otherwise disappointing visit to the Great Exhibition, a new path became clear. Photography was a moral technology, and, at least as far as its practice concerned viewing and reshaping humanity, its most important developments were occurring in America.

In 1856, at the age of thirty-five, Gardner resolved to rejoin the members of the Clydesdale Company who had gone before him. Along with his mother, his wife, his son, and his newborn daughter, he sailed for the United States. Only upon arriving did he learn that much of the company had succumbed to tuberculosis. The town they had founded was dissolved, its survivors scattering to be absorbed into their new country.

One dream was dead, but another had been born. Gardner went to New York to seek a job with Mathew Brady. He still believed he could put the chaos of the world in order—if not in newsprint or on a farm in Iowa, then perhaps with lines of silver and sunlight etched on glass.

GARDNER POURED THE chemical baths back into their respective jars, then packed his camera into the whatsit wagon. Leaving the Dunker Church behind and the dead men where they lay, he rode in search of other scenes to capture. The clatter of metal and glass announced his progress as the cart moved over the battle-pocked landscape.

His wasn't the only horse-drawn rig in the vicinity. There were of course the carts of the burial details, weighed down with bodies, then emptied, then filled again, like some gruesome streetcar making its way across a city in the early evening. There were also sightseers, rolling out in fine carriages to see for themselves the carnage that would make unbeatable conversation fodder around Washington's better tables.

Along the Hagerstown Pike, where some of the battle's fiercest fighting had ground on for hours two days before—September 17, 1862—a line of Confederates still lay where they fell. They had been surrounded as Union forces advanced on the road from both directions; their only shelter had been a split-rail fence with vertical posts every six feet connected by five horizontal rails. It would have proved more adequate as a defense if shot and shells had not been raining down from both sides.

Gardner positioned his camera so that the fence stretched diagonally across the frame, seeming to disappear into the distance. The bodies, bloated in the heat, stiff with rigor mortis, seemed ready to rise and walk away. One man's arm stretched into the air as if he'd died while reaching for a rope with which to pull himself out of harm's way.

Some photographers might have made the dead the only detail worth noting in the picture. Gardner instead directed the camera's gaze at five sections of posts and split rails. The fence became the perfect focal point for an image ultimately about a nation divided. Though there were bodies scattered around the fields both north and south of the fence, from where Gardner stood it looked as if a destroying angel had stopped short at the split rails, passing over all that lay beyond. The rough timber seemed to confine death to one side of this conflict, and the Confederate soldiers in their mortal disarray left no room for interpretation of which side that was.

Gardner was now years away from the utopian scheme that had brought him to America, and he accepted that the living could never be permanently organized in such a way that the chaos of the world would seem to have a clear meaning. But at least the dead might be.

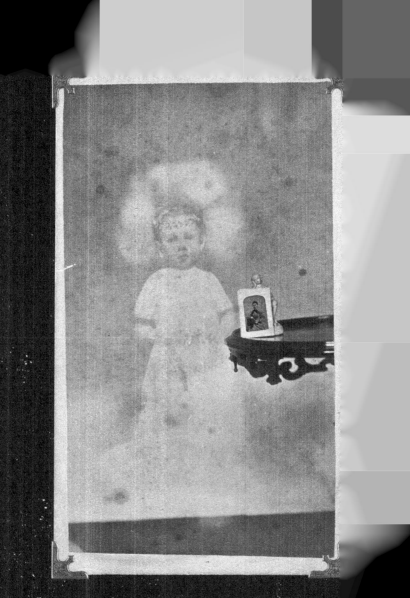

Spirit image of a child beside a photograph of a family men
William Mumler, 1862–1875.

CHAPTER 13

CHAIR AND ALL

"EVER SINCE I have commenced taking these pictures," William Mumler said, "I have been constantly dogged forward and back from my camera to my closet by *investigators,* till I have become sick of the name."

In the beginning of his efforts on behalf of Spiritualism in Boston, Mumler resolved that he would devote just two hours each day to the making of images. Demand alone, he later claimed, had determined that it become a full-time occupation. He shut down the engraving and printing shop he had opened just the year before, and thereafter the studio was his sole place of business. He posed portraits all morning and all afternoon. Only darkness prevented him from taking pictures through the night as well.

In this work he had found his true calling, and had evidently inspired others to follow in his footsteps. Another spirit photographer had been discovered, his work confirmed by no less an authority than Robert Dale Owen — son of the Scottish reformer and a rising politician in his own right, as well as a respected explorer of the paranormal.

To provide solace to the bereaved and confirmation of the afterlife to the spiritually curious, Mumler thought, was undoubtedly a noble use of his time. But the endless requests he received from those who sought only to injure his reputation were becoming too much to bear.

Certainly the attentions of J. W. Black had been flattering. After he had passed the tests of that esteemed man of art and science, it seemed he might be allowed into the rarefied fraternity of the upper echelon of Boston's photographers. That Mumler's name was becoming known beyond Spiritualist circles was evidence that this was surely the case. Granted, much of the coverage was skeptical, but on balance he could be satisfied that he had defenders of sufficient social standing to bring him a higher class of clientele—men and women of means who would not quibble over prices where visions of eternity were concerned. This undoubtedly would be pleasing to Hannah.

And how could he not be pleased as well? No sooner did a dismissive article appear in the press than a more informed opinion arose to make his case better than he might himself. As far away as New York, there was even a respected judge and state senator coming to his defense in print.

"Your article of yesterday in regard to Spiritual Photography professes to solve the mystery, and announced that Appleton's artist can do the same thing, wherever there is a photograph of the dead person," the former New York State prison inspector J. W. Edmonds wrote to the *Evening Post*. "That is not the mystery of this thing," he insisted. "But it is to take a picture containing a likeness of a person who is dead, and of whom there is no photograph or likeness in existence! This is what the Boston operator professes to do, and the question is, Is that so?"

It was a natural question; Mumler could not deny it. Since his first image became known, a parade of alleged experts intent on getting to the bottom of the mystery had proposed to march through the studio with notebooks in hand, recording and inspecting every detail. Skeptics now called on him constantly, some openly scornful, others hiding behind obvious subterfuge, all insisting they follow Mumler step by step from camera to darkroom and beyond, each hoping to be the one to slay the dragon of Spiritualism by exposing him as a fraud.

And not only were nonbelievers out to get him. Among those who should be cheering loudest, his spiritual brothers and sisters who claimed to be open to new discoveries, reticence was rampant—some of which, he no doubt felt, was tinged with jealousy.

From New York, the nation's leading Spiritualist, the Seer of Poughkeepsie, Andrew Jackson Davis, had gone so far as to arrange for another photographer to watch Mumler at work. As the editor of the *Herald of Progress*, which had first publicized the spirit photographer, Davis was now the progenitor of both Mumler's fame and his scrutiny.

The photographer Davis sent to shadow Mumler was a man of roughly Mumler's age, William Guay, who had been born in Germany but had joined the cosmopolitan polyglot community of New Orleans sometime before 1852, when he opened Guay's Photographic Temple of Art on Poydras Street, not far from the belly of the snake made by the Mississippi River as it moved through the city. When the war came, the photographer had joined the Confederate army, though it cannot be said if he did so willingly. In any case, Guay parted company with the Louisiana State Militia within a year.

This was not at all unusual at the time. As the *New York Times* reported on a group of Confederate infantrymen who had abandoned their posts at the first opportunity early in the war, conscripted immigrants in New Orleans were particularly eager to leave behind a war that never seemed theirs to begin with. "They are all Germans," the *Times* reporter noted of the deserters, "and all state that they were picked up by press gangs in New Orleans, gagged, carried to the recruiting offices, and from there in closed wagons to the camp at the racetrack, and forced to take service in the Southern army . . . Their whole company are German, who volunteered under the same circumstances."

Whether or not Guay came to his service so dramatically, he seems to have slipped quietly away sometime after the reoccupation of New Orleans by federal troops in April 1862. Still maintaining ownership of his Temple of Art, Guay made his way north even as the war raged. He soon was an unimaginable psychic distance from the fighting, living and working in a city where ghosts appearing on plates of glass was apparently as exciting as things could get. He quickly involved himself in a range of business pursuits that had nothing to do with soldiering, including applying his knowledge of photography in an unexpected way.

"You can rest assured that I was resolved, if permitted, to allow nothing to slip my utmost scrutiny," Guay wrote of his initial investigation of the spirit photography mystery. "Having been permitted by Mr. Mumler every facility to investigate, I went through the whole of the operation of selecting, cleaning, preparing, coating, silvering, and putting into the shield the glass upon which Mr. M. proposed that a spirit-form and mine should be imparted—never taking off my eyes, and not allowing Mr. M. to touch the glass until it had gone through the whole of the operation."

As part of his investigation, Guay sat for photographs before Mumler's camera on multiple occasions. He could not contain his surprise at what he saw when the images were developed. "The result was," he said, "there came upon the glass a picture of myself, and, to my utter astonishment—having previously examined and scrutinised every crack and corner of the plate holder, camera, box, tube, the inside of the bath, etc—another portrait!"

In one image, the better of the two, he explained, he saw clearly his father's visage, presumably not seen since he had left Germany, or perhaps longer, depending on when Herr Guay had left the world. In the other, far more faintly, he saw his late wife. Mumler had never seen a picture of any of his family members, Guay insisted, so the notion that the photographer worked from existing images was not a possibility.

Guay closed his letter to Andrew Jackson Davis with an unambiguous testimony on behalf of Mumler's work:

> Having since continued, on several occasions, my investigations as described above, and received even more perfect results than on the first trial, I have been obliged to endorse its legitimacy.
>
> Respectfully yours,
> WILLIAM GUAY

Between them, J. W. Black and William Guay claimed thirty years of photographic experience. Mumler hoped the fact that each had made similar findings known would be the end of it. But it was only the beginning.

In Philadelphia, a successful commercial photographer with Spiritualist leanings, Isaac Rehn, had likewise sought a visitation at 258 Washington Street.

Rehn had been trying for years to take pictures proving his belief that "the spirits of those who once dwelt with us do still hold intercourse with mortals." As early as 1848, he had traveled to New York to have a private meeting with the Fox sisters, and since then had joined all the important Spiritualist circles in his city. With his own eyes he had seen undeniable manifestations that a new age of communication with the dead had begun, from mediums speaking for the residents of the eternal place called Summerland, to invisible agents moving furniture across a room. "These movements became unusually violent," he said of one such experience. "Two card-tables, around which the company sat, having been drawn to the centre of the floor, were thrown backward and forward with great force. After moving thus for some minutes, one of the tables started toward some two or three of the company, and pressed heavily against them, causing them to recede until they had reached the wall."

Any photographer who had seen such forces at work naturally would want nothing more than to capture them on glass and share them with the world. That a man like Mumler had succeeded in doing so, though he was not only a metaphysical neophyte but an amateur behind the camera, must have been galling to Rehn. When he asked to see for himself how images like those given to Guay had been attained, Mumler declined. "I have been harassed enough by self-appointed investigators," he said haughtily, "and find there is no end to it."

He made a point of turning all would-be detectives away. From now on, only those like Guay—and perhaps only him —who had seemed genuinely sympathetic to Mumler's mission were to be permitted behind the curtain.

———

IF THE FACT THAT photographers were frequently the most intent on challenging him surprised either of the Mumlers, it would have been William rather than Hannah. While he was still new to picture-making and its particular customs and culture, she had run her studio in the midst of many others on Washington Street for years, and no doubt knew photography to be a cutthroat business. Even photographers who happened to be Spiritualists, those supposedly invested in aiding human progress through bridging the gap between the living and the dead, often seemed willing to climb over corpses for professional advancement.

Take Isaac Rehn, for example. Anyone who kept up with the gossip of the trade surely knew that several years before, the Philadelphia photographer had collaborated with another in developing improvements on the photographic process that had fast became the industry standard. Though Mumler's spiritual achievements lay beyond their grasp, for a time they both reaped the material rewards. Mortal partnerships are always only temporary, however.

Rehn's Boston-based associate, James Ambrose Cutting, held a series of patents on the new and wildly popular photographic process called the ambrotype, which some have said he named for himself, but more likely found its inspiration in the Greek *ambrotos,* "immortal." At the start, Cutting was first among equals in their partnership, with Rehn relegated to serving as witness on the ambrotype's original patent application.

The two men not only worked together but had sat side by side at séances, and in this pursuit it seems it was Rehn who was the more advanced. Once, while Cutting was visiting Philadelphia, the photographers attended a circle with a local medium as part of a mystical coffee klatch known as the Penetralium.

Cutting was a big man, tall and stout, and so it was a remarkable sight when his chair moved suddenly beneath him. All present felt the power in the room palpably. Rehn was more sanguine about such events by then, but Cutting lifted his feet in alarm, like a child sliding on a sled, clutching at the sides, afraid he might fall. The spirits present in the room then hoisted him fully from the floor—"chair and all," Rehn said.

Cutting was childlike in other ways as well. Having come from a more humble station than the trained artist Rehn, Cutting had no experience with money when his patent payments began to come in. His first invention—an improved beehive—had earned him enough to move from rural New Hampshire to Boston, but it was nothing compared to the money his new photographic process would bring him. For a time, he received a license fee or a percentage from every studio in the country taking ambrotypes, which was nearly all of them, given how much time they saved over the patience-taxing daguerreotypes.

For a decade, Cutting and Rehn reaped huge rewards, but eventually many photographers decided they'd had enough. Some made their own small adjustments to the process to avoid the fees; others who paid grudgingly were rankled by a perceived lack of collegiality on the inventors' part, particularly Rehn, who pushed for extensions of the patent's applicability. Though the ambrotype was widely adopted—including by big studios like Brady's in New York—many photographers were nostalgic for the time when they had all seemed to be working toward a common goal, and were eager for the days of the ambrotype to pass.

Cutting responded to these negative feelings by getting out of the business altogether. He used much of the fortune he had so far amassed—$40,000, according to one estimate—to design a boat and have it custom built. Naturally, he called it *Ambrotype*.

At the time, excursion steamers and pleasure yachts constantly plied Boston Harbor and the ocean beyond. They were a useful conveyance between many points in the city, and a fine vessel like *Ambrotype* was an unmistakable marker of social standing. Cutting occasionally used the boat for grand fishing tours, taking a handful of ladies and gentlemen on a twenty-five-mile sail, then baiting hooks and encouraging all to cast into the deep. As one of Cutting's invited guests recalled, "The noble rock cod, haddock, hake, not omitting an occasional sculpin, nibbled most gloriously, and we soon had enough and more than enough for a fry for our supper." An on-board cook prepared and served the meal in grand style.

Cutting did not build *Ambrotype* solely for pleasure, however. Following his specifications, the shipwright had installed an opening in the boat's hull. Much like the windows in a photo studio that looked always up into the sky, this portal looked always down into the abyss. Through it, Cutting was able to track and catch schools of sea life. Along with the fish caught by his guests and fried by his cook, Cutting hauled in lobsters, sharks, eels, and turtles off the New England coast, then ventured farther north and south for more exotic species, including a pair of seal pups.

Using his yacht to gather specimens and his knowledge of glass and metallurgy to design and patent the first aquarium tanks built in the country, Cutting soon opened the Boston Aquarial and Zoological Gardens, located on the very boulevard that had become home to so many menageries of Spiritualists and photographers, Washington Street. To his own Atlantic haul he added alligators from the bayou and porpoises from the Arctic, and he trained his two seal pups until they were star attractions. He named them Ned and Fanny and worked with them from the time they were three months old. Soon they could swim to Cutting on command and perform a variety of tricks. Ned's specialty was playing a hand organ.

Despite this bit of showmanship, Cutting intended his Aquarial Gardens to be a place of science. He was no doubt chuffed when the *New York Tribune* reviewed his holdings and found that "the exhibition has already drawn numerous visitors of the most intelligent people." The interest of those who attend "increases at every visit," the *Tribune* added, noting that such an increase in interest was "the natural consequence of an investigation into the habits of a hitherto unknown class of living creatures."

Just as he had made a bad decision working with Rehn, however, he soon made another business mistake. Perhaps because he knew him through his book, *Aquaria of America*, Cutting partnered in his enterprise with one Henry D. Butler, late of New York, more recently relocated to Boston. While he did have a bona fide interest in fish, Butler was also a longtime associate of P. T. Barnum. He served as manager of the American Museum for a number of years, and for a short time was even the museum's official owner while Barnum sorted out a brief period of financial insolvency.

If Butler provided resources necessary to the Aquarial Gardens' existence, the benefits of this arrangement were counterbalanced by his pronounced Barnumizing influence. In November 1860, Cutting's aquarium began to display not just sea creatures and exotic animals, but humans. The first were "South African aboriginees"; then came "the red men of the forest," including a "Mohawk chief . . . with his wife and family."

The press judged this to be an entertainment one would visit only in "desperation of dullness." Indeed, those drawn by its "flaming advertisement of five real living native savage Africans" were disappointed. Not only were the human exhibits vacant, but many of the undersea specimens Cutting had acquired were also gone. "We went and found the fish tanks drained and deserted, no stickleback building his nest, no soldier-crab going through the broadsword exercise with his eccentric right claw," one of the visitors said. In one tank, "a solitary seal flopped about, occasionally holding up one melancholy flipper as if soliciting sympathy."

If the sad creature described in this tableau was Ned, the sympathy was well deserved. Fanny had not survived the Aquarial Gardens' transition from living naturalist's cabinet to sideshow entertainment.

The cloud lingering over Cutting finally turned to a full-on curse in the first half of 1861. In February, three of the "aboriginees" assaulted Butler. In April, one of them was found hanging by the neck inside the aquarium, an apparent suicide. Whether or not the two incidents were connected, by May, Butler had returned to New York, leaving Cutting in sole control. He made plans for the remaining Africans' exodus from the city, and for the museum's return to serious scientific and intellectual pursuits.

But it was not to be. A few months later, P. T. Barnum himself bought the Aquarial Gardens, taking advantage of Cutting's newly perilous fiscal circumstances. The great showman kept

Cutting around for a short while, largely to feed the fish and carry on his work with Ned, now called "the Learned Seal."

By the fall of 1862 Cutting was out, his name unceremoniously scrubbed from signage and advertising. Now known as Barnum's Aquarial Gardens, the space Cutting had created became a mere satellite of the American Museum. It hosted visits by New York's most popular freak show performers and served as an aquatic way station for the more exotic sea creatures Barnum shipped via Boston to New York. Obviously aggrieved, Cutting was determined to open a new aquarium to compete with Barnum's —which was how, in November of 1862, immediately following his published investigation of Mumler, William Guay entered the aquarium business.

Exactly when and why Guay began his partnership with James Cutting is a sunspot on the historical record. Andrew Jackson Davis had hired Guay; Cutting certainly moved among Spiritualists frequently enough that he knew the Seer of Poughkeepsie; and Davis could have sent Guay Cutting's way. Even if Guay had taken on Davis's assignment with some faint hope that he might cash in, it is difficult to see what he possibly had to gain from entering a partnership whose success would depend on live animals remaining alive with the help of a steam engine pumping 860,000 gallons of water a day.

Still, he seems to have given it his all. Guay soon secured a contract for the popular "Family of Esquimaux" to travel to Boston after their New York engagement, and, apparently working with resources he had at hand, the Confederate deserter assembled an exhibit he called "Rebel Relics from Recent Battlefields."

Against Barnum, however, Cutting and Guay's New Aquarial and Zoological Gardens didn't stand a chance. It remained open less than a month. While Guay found new employment with the Mumlers, Cutting never recovered. Photography abandoned, his finances in ruin, and his latest dream failed, he had one further blow to endure.

Deciding earnest Boston was not the right market for his sensibilities after all, Barnum closed the aquarium he had so recently acquired. He shipped many of the most popular live attractions to the American Museum, including Ned.

Cutting died soon after, in the same lunatic asylum in which the Mumler apparition Isaac Babbitt had seen his last corporeal days.

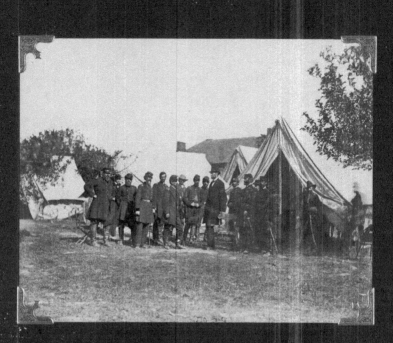

Abraham Lincoln meets Union troops at Antietam.
Alexander Gardner, 1862.

CHAPTER 14

DID YOU EVER DREAM OF
SOME LOST FRIEND?

THREE WEEKS AFTER the Battle of Antietam, as Boston's Spiritualists were conversing with the ghost of Lieutenant William Berry in the *Banner of Light*'s séance room, Mathew Brady opened his New York studio to the public to show images of the carnage Alexander Gardner had captured, bringing the casualties of war home in a different way.

"The living that throng Broadway care little perhaps for the Dead at Antietam," the *New York Times* began its startling review of the exhibit, "but we fancy they would jostle less carelessly down the great thoroughfare, saunter less at their ease, were a few dripping bodies, fresh from the field, laid along the pavement. There would be a gathering up of skirts and a careful picking of the way; conversation would be less lively, and the general air of pedestrians more subdued. As it is, the dead of the battle-field come up to us very rarely, even in dreams."

As an artist, Gardner could only have been pleased by such high-profile notice of his work. To urge the nightmare landscape through which he had walked upon those who would look away had been precisely the point of his labors in Maryland. Not only did the *Times* recognize the significance of his individual images; it suggested that, collectively, they might remake the American public's perception of the war and its costs.

By the fall of 1862, the public for the most part did not even know what it didn't know. Though a roll call of the dead was published regularly in the northern press, printed letters alone could convey only so much. "We see the list in the morning paper at breakfast, but dismiss its recollection with the coffee," the *Times* review continued. "There is a confused mass of names, but they are all strangers; we forget the horrible significance that dwells amid the jumble of type. The roll we read is being called over in Eternity, and pale, trembling lips are answering to it. Shadowy fingers point from the page to a field where even imagination is loth to follow. Each of these little names that the printer struck off so lightly last night, whistling over his work, and that we speak with a clip of the tongue, represents a bleeding, mangled corpse.

"We recognize the battle-field as a reality, but it stands as a remote one. It is like a funeral next door," the unnamed reviewer wrote. "It is very different when the hearse stops at your own door, and the corpse is carried out over your own threshold."

To deliver bodies to the doorways of every willfully ignorant household in America — that was the potential of taking a camera into battle. For a utopian like Gardner, there could be no more powerful tool for working toward the end of human suffering than to show it in all its horrific detail. With his glass plates and chemicals, Gardner had turned the war into art so visceral it could not be ignored. True to those earliest dreams of Daguerre or Morse, he had used photography to close the distance between the living and the dead.

Yet if the first few paragraphs acknowledging this in the exhibit review had pleased the war's most tireless chronicler, the next lines would have stopped him cold:

> Mr. BRADY has done something to bring home to us the terrible reality and earnestness of war. If he has not brought bodies and laid them in our dooryards and along the streets, he has done something very like it. At the door of his gallery hangs a little placard, "The Dead of Antietam." Crowds of people are con-

stantly going up the stairs; follow them, and you find them bending over photographic views of that fearful battle-field, taken immediately after the action.

Of all objects of horror one would think the battle-field should stand preeminent, that it should bear away the palm of repulsiveness. But, on the contrary, there is a terrible fascination about it that draws one near these pictures, and makes him loth to leave them. You will see hushed, reverent groups standing around these weird copies of carnage, bending down to look in the pale faces of the dead, chained by the strange spell that dwells in dead men's eyes.

It seems somewhat singular that the same sun that looked down on the faces of the slain, blistering them, blotting out from the bodies all semblance to humanity, and hastening corruption, should have thus caught their features upon canvas, and given them perpetuity for ever. But so it is.

Gardner had already begun to copyright his own images. As his personal renown as a photographer continued to grow, as it surely would, a separation from his employer ought to have come soon in any case. But this exhibit marked a turning point. A rupture.

It was not only the fact that Gardner's name did not hang above his own creations—that was, after all, an inevitable condition of working for another man. It was also that, as a consequence, Brady had managed to make himself synonymous with a transformation of their shared art. He was already the most famous photographer in the country. His public relations savvy and affinity for figures of popular culture had made him the image maker of choice of every celebrity of the age. Now it seemed Brady would be regarded not just as the most famous, but the most historically significant as well.

Another review:

From these pictures the historian will gather material for his pages; for the embrasures of earthworks and the walls of fortresses will crumble and resolve themselves into dust, while the colors of their photographic counterparts will only have deepened and fastened with time. And here a wonder suggests itself, that the substance should fade and the shadow imperishably remain.

Should the enterprise of Mr. BRADY fail to secure success amid the blare of trumpets and the beat of drums, it will surely be recognized when we shall have smoothed the wrinkles of war from our weary brows, and swept from them the crimson blossoms of battle, to bind them instead with the sweet silver lilies of peace.

The enterprise which begets these battle pictures is worthy of support as well as praise. Appealing as they do to the popular heart, they can scarcely fail of success. In one point of view their value can scarcely be overrated. They present a panorama of the war, faithful as is everything that comes from the studio of the Sun, that impartial artist, whose only study is truth.

Gardner could be forgiven for thinking "truth" was an odd word to apply to one man's earning praise for another man's efforts. He had logged more hours on the battlefield and trekked longer miles in the army's wake than anyone, his employer included. And yet it was Brady now credited with using his camera to summon the muse of history: "Among the many sun-compellers," it was said, "Mr. BRADY deserves honorable recognition as having been the first to make Photography the Clio of the war."

Brady had finally won for himself a spot in the mythology of great Americans on which he had built his career. When it came to the battlefield with which he had secured this position, however, he had not been there at all. But who could have known that from simply viewing the images now hanging on Broadway? The man who had stood among the bodies, who had focused his eye and his instruments on the dead to keep some part of them in the world of the living, Alexander Gardner, was nowhere to be seen.

GARDNER OPENED HIS OWN studio in Washington in November 1862, while his Antietam photographs held New York in thrall. To much less fanfare, he began making and displaying images under his own name in a building at Seventh and D streets, a short walk from the red sandstone of the Smithsonian Institution. On the wooden façade of his new artistic home, he had listed the services he would offer in thick stripes of whitewash, each letter as tall as a child:

GARDNER'S GALLERY
Cartes de Visite, Stereographs, Album cards,
Ambrotypes, Ivorytypes, Hallotypes
Imperial Photographs

He made sure to include all the popular photographic formats of the day, and naturally advertised the high-priced, large portrait style known as the Imperial, a specialty for which Brady's establishments had become known thanks to Gardner's expertise. In smaller letters he added the extra services provided by many photographers, such as the coloring and retouching of images that promised to make every photograph a slight improvement on reality, and the sale of photo cards depicting many of the well-known politicians and cultural luminaries who had lately made Gardner their portrait artist of choice.

Of all the styles and subjects on offer at Gardner's new gallery was one he chose to advertise with the largest letters on the building's outer walls:

VIEWS OF THE WAR

These four words were twice the size of the others, suggesting something of the proprietor's estimation of how popular they would be. With the war more than a year old by then and no resolution in sight, pictures of the ruined country, and ruined bodies scattered across its southern states, continued to be prized.

In order to gain better access to such scenes, Gardner had agreed to serve as the official photographer for the Army of the Potomac. He accepted an honorary commission as a captain from General George McClellan, who put the photographer's skills to use not only chronicling life among the infantry and the aftermath of battles, but making perfect copies of maps and other documents essential to the war effort.

The photographs he took while trailing McClellan's forces were some of the most memorable of the war, and never more so than when he was on hand for Lincoln's arrival in Sharpsburg to personally dress down the general for his failure to pursue Robert E. Lee into Virginia following the Union's slim victory at Antietam. Though it was not the intention of the pictures he made that day, Gardner inadvertently recorded the only known images of the president in mourning.

In February of that year, Lincoln's third son had died before his twelfth birthday. No less than the bloated bodies Gardner had photographed along the Hagerstown Pike, the boy had been a casualty of war. Just outside Washington, Union forces had for months camped beside the Potomac River, polluting the White House's own water supply with their waste. With his oldest son, Robert, away at school, his two younger boys, Thomas and William, took ill with typhoid. Tad recovered; Willie did not.

In the images Gardner made of Lincoln near McClellan's headquarters — a white canvas tent held up by a wooden pole — the president wore a black mourning band on his stovepipe hat, like a ring on the finger of a nation now married to Death. Willie had become for him a personal emblem for the loss so many felt, and though he stood as straight and nearly as tall as the tent pole, Lincoln seemed physically diminished.

If he did not blame himself directly, the press throughout

the rebel states hoped to persuade him to do so. "It is not in the Southern character to rejoice in the afflictions of even a bitter and odious enemy," the *Charleston Courier* wrote of Willie's death, "but we may hope that the lesson will show the despot President in some degree the evils of war."

An artist who had painted Lincoln in happier times, Alban Jasper Conant (no known relation to the medium), remarked that since the boy's death, "ever after there was a new quality in his demeanor—something approaching awe." In 1860, the future president had posed for a portrait that the painter came to call "Smiling Lincoln," but the smooth-faced, bemused fellow he had once been was now impossible to see in the bearded, haggard man he had become just two years later.

It was well known how deeply the boy's death had affected him. Only weeks before he posed for Gardner in Sharpsburg, an aide had happened upon the president perusing a volume of Shakespeare, the lesser-known work *King John,* in which a mother speaks of the possibility of meeting her son in the afterlife. Lincoln's thoughts on heaven veered toward the heretically skeptical, but the passage moved him nonetheless:

> *. . . I have heard you say*
> *That we shall see and know our friends in heaven:*
> *If that be true, I shall see my boy again . . .*
> *But now will canker-sorrow eat my bud*
> *And chase the native beauty from his cheek*
> *And he will look as hollow as a ghost . . .*
> *And so he'll die; and, rising so again,*
> *When I shall meet him in the court of heaven*
> *I shall not know him . . .*

"Did you ever dream of some lost friend," Lincoln had asked his aide, "and feel that you were having a sweet communion with him, and yet have a consciousness that it was not a reality? That is the way I dream of my lost boy Willie."

For Mary Todd Lincoln, the hope of such communion was not just a dream. Long curious about Spiritualism, her interest intensified after Willie's death, sparking rumors of séances convened in the White House.

While the Confederate newspapers danced on the boy's grave, the northern Spiritualist press reported on the progress of his soul into the afterlife, noting the medium Fannie Conant's claims that she had successfully channeled his ghost. As she had with so many of those who had died during the war, she fell into a trance in the *Banner of Light*'s offices and spoke in a voice that answered to his name. In the first lady's estimation, this was not at all far-fetched. "Willie lives," Mrs. Lincoln was known to say. "He comes to me every night and stands at the foot of the bed with the same sweet adorable smile he always has had."

She even made a clandestine pilgrimage to see the spirit photographer who was receiving so much attention. At the time she first visited Mumler, Mrs. Lincoln had also recently learned that her half brother, a soldier in the Confederate army, had been killed in action. She arrived at the Boston studio in disguise and left only half satisfied, carrying an image of herself seated in the foreground and an apparition said to be her fallen brother standing nearby. She no doubt hoped it would be her innocent boy rather than her traitorous sibling who appeared on the glass, but the spirit world, she knew, could no more be controlled than the world of the living. Though he might have profited from such an image, it was later said that Mumler chose not to do so, "out of regard for President Lincoln, who was at that time on the eve of a reelection to his office."

That his wife held such innocent belief in the possibility of bridging the chasm that had opened between parents and child became a further weight on the thoroughly pragmatic president.

"Mr. Lincoln was greatly annoyed by reports that he was interested in Spiritualism," the family's pastor, Dr. Phineas Gurley, later recalled.

It was not that Lincoln failed to understand the longing for connection Spiritualist beliefs offered, however. He understood it perfectly well. Something of that longing showed in his eyes as Gardner prepared one plate after another to record his image on glass.

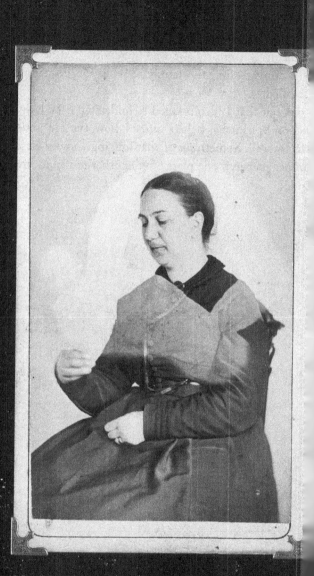

Mrs. H. B. Sawyer, embraced by a spirit she recognized
as her late husband and holding a spirit she believed
to be the child they had lost.
William Mumler, 1862–1875.

CHAPTER 15

WAR AGAINST WRONG

WILLIAM GUAY — former photographic studio owner, former Confederate soldier, former paranormal investigator, and former aquarium manager — soon found yet another occupation: working for the Mumlers at 258 Washington Street. "Superintending improvements in the operating room," as one reporter noted, his job of the third month of 1863 was to streamline the process required to handle the ever-growing number of requests they received.

It was around this time that the Mumlers began advertising a more ambitious service than they had previously felt equipped to offer. When the business began, William had humbly insisted he could never be sure if a spirit image would appear; now he was so certain of his technique, he claimed his clients did not even need to visit his studio. They could simply send information about a departed loved one in the mail, along with seven dollars and fifty cents, and receive photographs of spirits in three weeks' time. "Persons residing at any distance from Boston desirous to obtain Photographs of their departed friends by Mr. W. H. Mumler, will please send for Circular which gives all the particulars," their regular advertisement said.

Requests for mail-order spirit photos poured in. One received from New York was from none other than P. T. Barnum.

As the business continued to prosper, the specter of investigation continually reappeared. A letter published in the Spiritualist press recounted how a gentleman visiting the Mumler gallery had looked with great interest at all the spirit photographs displayed, only to be surprised by the ghostly presence of his own wife, who remained resolutely of this world. Yet there she was hovering as an apparition above a tableau of living figures of no known relation. There was no mistaking it, the man said. Not only had his wife posed at this gallery before all the spirit photograph excitement began; she remembered the sitting distinctly because she had worn a hat that was "so much outre" that she had never liked the picture. Now she would be wearing it forever in someone else's eternity. The writer of the letter addressing this outrage was not unsympathetic to Mumler's beliefs. In fact, he shared them.

"Being an investigator of the spirit-phenomena almost from its first rap, and becoming convinced of its truth very early in its career," he wrote, "I was of course pleased at the new phase of spirit-photography, and hoped to find it proven." But he also recognized that making or embracing false claims could only hurt the cause. "Facts have been, are now, and must continue to be the foundation of the great gospel of Spiritualism," he continued. "The separation of fact from fiction has been, is now, and must also continue to be the only way to establish on an eternal basis the *truth* and ultimate triumph of the fact of inter-communication between the inner and outer life."

As quickly as the Spiritualist press had lined up to praise Mumler, it backed away, publicly retracting earlier endorsements of the man, his technique, and the supposedly objective experts whose testimonies the same papers had not only published, but commissioned. "Early in the progress of the 'spirit photograph' controversy, we published an endorsement of Mr. Wm. Guay, whose testimony with reference to these pictures was positive and important," the editors of the *Herald of Progress* wrote. "At that time, without a long or intimate acquaintance with Mr. G., we felt satisfied of his integrity and reliability as a witness. We are now fully persuaded that our endorsement was premature, if indeed our confidence was not misplaced. Without positively affirming Mr. Guay's deliberate untruthfulness, we do not hesitate to say that he is not strong enough to tell the same story at all times! Our published endorsement of Mr. Guay as a reliable witness on this question is therefore hereby retracted and withdrawn."

In the view of many, however, there still remained cause to believe. "There has as yet been no satisfactory exposé of the methods employed by Mr. Mumler in producing these pictures," the *Herald* continued, "neither have we seen any entirely successful imitations by other artists."

The investigator most doggedly pursuing such an exposé turned out to be another artist-inventor. Like Morse, Cutting, Rehn, Serrell, and indeed Mumler himself, Charles Boyle would soon have a number of patents to his name, particularly as the inventor of a process that allowed photographic images to be printed directly on wood, which had many practical applications and was praised generally by the photographic establishment.

After being repeatedly rebuffed by Mumler in much the same dismissive way Isaac Rehn's request had been treated, Boyle sent a challenge to the *Banner of Light* offices with a request that they print it. "I propose to go to Mr. Mumler's rooms with a committee of disinterested men and an honest reporter, and I will then and there, in the presence of that committee and reporter, discover and exhibit the trick of spiritual photographing as done by said Mumler, if he, Mumler, will grant said committee, reporter, and myself the same privileges that I have heard he has given to Mr. Guay, who has written favorably of his (Mumler's) operations in regard to spirit photographing."

Mumler again refused, arguing variously that owners of studios that did more business than Boyle's had already tested him, and so there was no need for duplicate efforts by lesser photographers, and that the spirits occasionally became so "disgusted" with the mortal need for proof that they refused to have their picture taken at all.

"I wish it distinctly understood that I am not at war with the pure article, should it ever make its appearance," Boyle stressed to the Spiritualists who watched this row. "I simply war against wrong. No one would rejoice with a deeper thankfulness than myself to see proved beyond peradventure that the dead live on and can return so palpably to earth, as to hold their shapes upon its science."

———

ON THE TWELFTH DAY of February, a Spiritualist editor, John Latham of Boston, stood in the offices of the *Banner of Light* and happened to see one of Mumler's photographs displayed on a desk. The picture showed a woman from New York—Mrs. Blossom was her name—who claimed to recognize a ghostly figure in the picture as her own departed mother. Mrs. Blossom had sent this photograph along with a locket containing a smaller likeness of her mother so that the editors of the *Banner* might compare them. A man standing nearby spoke of these two images as the best proof yet that Mumler was legitimate. Yet Latham was not so sure; he felt certain he had seen the ghostly image before.

Some months earlier, Latham's friend Mr. Pollock had shown him a spirit picture taken of his wife in which a very similar sort of ghost had appeared. When the two men compared the images, they found they were right. While they sorted out how best to deal with this apparent ruse, a third friend happened along and was able to provide further information. The ghost in both images was alive and well.

Upon visiting her house and informing her of the use to which Mumler had put her image, she was quite alarmed to discover she had somehow been drawn into such an affair. "To think that they should pretend that I am a spirit," she huffed, "when I am still in the body!"

She excused herself to find her photo album. A moment later she returned with an image of herself identical to the ghost Mr. Pollock now held in his hand. She then turned it over to show the stamp printed on the back:

MRS. STUART'S PHOTOGRAPHIC GALLERY

"If there were a collection of all the pictures made at Mrs. Stuart's, celestial and terrestrial, there would be some funny revelations," the photographer Charles Boyle said. "Many 'spirits' would be found to resemble mortals altogether too much, and many to appear too often; and if truth only would rise again, as the distinguished 'medium' pathetically observes, then 'spirit photography' à la Mr. Mumler sleeps the sleep that knows no waking."

With evidence mounting and negative newspaper reports beginning to pile thick on his desk, Mumler's staunchest supporters abandoned him. Not only did William Guay shake the dust from his feet as he departed a city that had brought him nothing but misadventure and disappointment; even the dean of New England Spiritualism, H. F. Gardner, could no longer ignore his doubts. Mumler quietly withdrew from the public debates over spirit photography, offering not a word of defense as Boyle and other investigators declared victory.

"I have neither the time nor desire to pursue the soulless, heartless, humanityless, tomb-robbing ghoul any further," Boyle soon wrote, washing his hands of the spirit photography business, "but must leave it as I found it, crouching in all its degrading deformity by the graveside, feeding on the memories of the dead."

Hotbed of Spiritualism though it was, Boston was perhaps not the best place for Mumler to introduce spirit photography to the world. The city's zealotry both in support of and opposition to novel spiritual pursuits had made his ghost pictures suspect from all sides. In the end, it was neither the skeptics nor the true believers who harassed him to the point of closing up shop, but a coalition of those with very different reasons to challenge his claims.

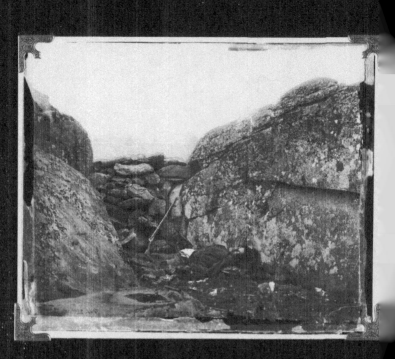

"The Home of a Rebel Sharpshooter." Alexander Gardner studio, attributed to Timothy O'Sullivan, 1863.

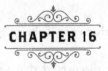

CHAPTER 16

WHOSE BONES LIE BLEACHING

MIDWAY THROUGH THE summer of 1863, with the ninety-seventh anniversary of American independence looming, Confederate troops began massing along the Pennsylvania border, making signs of a possible push into the North to demonstrate the reach of the rebellion. Their aim was to shock northerners into abandoning the war.

As they had done after they heard of the fighting in Sharpsburg, Alexander Gardner and his assistants Timothy O'Sullivan and James Gibson, whom he had hired away from Brady at the first opportunity, loaded up their whatsit wagon and rode out from Washington to the village of Gettysburg. They did not arrive in time to see the battle itself, but the damage it had done to the surrounding farmland was everywhere apparent. Gardner made no notes on his general impressions of Gettysburg or the battlefield for which it would immediately become known, but another past associate of his former employer did.

The landscape the photographers saw before they had unloaded their cameras can be found in an account written by Mathew Brady's old collaborator in phrenology, Eliza Farnham. The former prison matron had spent more than a decade on the West Coast and had recently returned for a speaking tour of Spiritualist meetings in eastern cities. While in Philadelphia, Farnham had heard of the terrible fighting 130 miles away. She left the city immediately to see if she might be of service to the wounded.

Two days later, she discovered that Gettysburg was a place beyond all human help.

"The whole town, about 3000 inhabitants, is one vast hospital," Farnham wrote, "all public and a great many private buildings full of sufferers . . . The road, for long distances, was in many places strewn with dead horses; the human dead having been all removed by this time. The earth in the roads and fields is ploughed to a mire by the army wheels and horses. Houses are occasionally riddled with bullets, cannon or shell, and the straggling wounded line the roads, and rest against the fences."

She wrote a letter to Andrew Jackson Davis's *Herald of Progress* to inform her fellow Spiritualists of what she had seen, and to urgently request donations.

> Gettysburgh, July 7, 1863.
> Dear friends of the Herald, both readers and editors, lend me your ears, hearts, and means for a little while. We want all that you can spare that will minister to the physical comfort of thousands of suffering men, besides papers, pamphlets, and any other reading easy for feeble persons to handle. We want old, clean, soft cloths, whether cotton or linen, sour fruits, jellies, jams, &c. We are going this moment out to the field hospitals of the Second, Third, and Fifth Corps, where, as we understand, the condition is much worse than that we have seen in the hospitals of the town.
>
> In great haste,
> E. W. Farnham.

When she reached the field hospitals, not even the otherworldly certainty of her faith prepared her for what she found. "There are miles of tents and acres of men lying on the open earth beneath the trees," she wrote later that day. "Good God! What those quiet looking tents contained! What spectacles awaited us on the slopes of the rolling hills around us! It is absolutely inconceivable, unless you see it.

"I never could have imagined anything to compare . . . Dead and dying, and wounded, in every condition you can conceive after two days in such a rain of missiles. Old veterans, who have seen all our battles, say that there never has been such firing anywhere for more than half an hour or so, as there was here for the greater part of nine hours. No wonder that men who were rushing upon and through and upon it should be torn to pieces in every way," she wrote. "But the most horrible thing was to see these limbs lying, piled up like offal at the foot of a tree in front of the surgeon's tent."

No amount of jellies and jams, she realized, would do these men any good.

As Farnham worked herself to exhaustion among the tents of the dying, Gardner, Gibson, and O'Sullivan climbed down from their rolling photography studio and began hunting for vistas with which to tell the story of what had happened there. The corpses of Union men had been mostly gathered up, carted away by burial details charged with making a distinction between rebels and those loyal to the nation. In the pitted farmers' fields, this left only Confederates to serve as the photographers' subjects.

Gardner had learned a thing or two since Antietam about how to turn such scenes as Farnham described into stories that would help his images capture a viewer's imagination. He walked the woods and wheat fields with a prop rifle on his shoulder, ready to add it to any tableau that needed an extra telling detail.

He found one such scene far from the cries of the field hospitals. The rocky outcropping at the base of two hills just south of Gettysburg was likely called Devil's Den long before the battle made it hell on earth. A century before, Scotch-Irish and German settlers had told tales of "ghosts and hobgoblins seen there in the still hours of the night," and even before their arrival it was a place the Susquehannock people considered close to the spirit world, not least of all, the archaeological record suggests, because many had fought and died there.

Union forces had held the high ground, firing all but unmolested as the rebels tried to advance. Confederate corpses now crowded the surrounding fields. Gardner took several images, making notes for the stories he would write about each. To a dead horse still attached to a wrecked artillery wagon he gave the caption "Unfit for Service." To a cluster of bloated bodies in an area enclosed by low walls of exposed rock, he attached the label "The Slaughter Pen." When he found a man on his back with his insides torn out, probably gutted by hogs that had escaped their pens during the fighting, he decided the story of this image would be improved if the livestock went unmentioned, leaving it to the viewer's imagination. Because so many of the men had died in summertime farm fields, he described the scene as a whole as a "harvest of death."

Forty yards from the largest boulders of Devil's Den, Gardner saw a young soldier who had somehow retained the glow of youth despite lying in the sun for two days. He painstakingly took the dead man's photograph from several angles. As he moved around the body, he considered it the way a painter might look upon a fruit bowl: an object like any other caught in the play of light and shadow, frozen in time for a still life. He noted that the man's cap and gun were "thrown behind him by the violence of the shock."

Beneath the body, Gardner saw a ragged blanket. He took pains to include this detail in the photo's composition, supposing that it showed how the soldier had settled in here for a long engagement with the northerners. He imagined the rebel at close range with his Union counterpart, each man pulling tricks — a hat on a stick, a false misfire created with a gunpowder flash — to draw the other into fatal view. Gardner placed his prop gun carefully beside the body, angling it just so, to direct the eye of the viewer of the photograph he would make.

After he had completed the image, Gardner composed a short narrative about it. In place of photographers finding the soldier unattended, forgotten by his comrades, he suggested there were others on the scene to take care of the fallen: "A burial party, searching for dead on the borders of the Gettysburg battle-field, found, in a secluded spot, a sharpshooter lying as he fell when struck by the bullet. His cap and gun were evidently thrown behind him by the violence of the shock, and the blanket, partly shown, indicates that he had selected this as a permanent position from which to annoy the enemy. How many skeletons of such men are bleaching to-day in out of the way places no one can tell. Now and then the visitor to a battle-field finds the bones of some man shot as this one was, but there are hundreds that will never be known of, and will moulder into nothingness among the rocks."

For all his efforts, Gardner worried that he hadn't fully captured the spirit of the young man, neither in the images he had made nor in the story he had imagined about the soldier's final moments. Moreover, the setting here was not ideal. The ragged landscape, a mud of halftones, made it difficult to pick out the body amid the other detritus of war.

Gardner prepared to move on to find another body. But then he looked up the slope and noticed Devil's Den looming above. It was unmistakably a much more photogenic setting: a craggy nook with nothing but daylight above. Seen from the right vantage point, the stones arranged around the boy would look at once like a cradle and a grave.

Gardner and his crew dragged the body forty yards uphill —over ravaged crabgrass, fragments of shrapnel, a field plowed under by mortar fire—and began his work again. They positioned the dead boy's youthful features so they fully faced the camera's eye, his head tilted slightly against one wall of rock, his feet tucked up against another slab as if he were the oldest son outgrowing his childhood bed.

Photographing a battlefield was not unlike posing ladies in their finery for a carte de visite: he used the same gentle touch to raise a chin toward the light and took the same care with the composition drawn by a drape of fabric. Only the props were different. To complete his image, Gardner placed his rifle at the scene's focal point, its barrel pointed up toward the white sky, drawing the gaze of whoever saw this dramatic tableau from the blemished earth to the forgiving emptiness of heaven.

With a new view of the same death, Gardner instructed his men to prepare more plates for exposure. Gibson used a two-lens camera ideal for producing highly marketable stereographs. O'Sullivan peered through a box with a single glass eye. The more aesthetically pleasing arrangement they had created inspired in their employer a grander vision of the soldier's final moments, one that joined the indifference of the terrain to a world of love and family to which this soldier would never return. Abandoning the fiction of the burial party, the photographer gave himself a starring role in the drama: "The artist, in passing over the scene of the previous days' engagements, found in a lonely place the covert of a rebel sharpshooter, and photographed the scene presented here," he wrote. "The Confederate soldier had built up between two huge rocks, a stone wall, from the crevices of which he had directed his shots, and, in comparative security, picked off our officers."

Gardner took careful note of the physical details. The stone nearest the boy's feet still seemed to echo with the noise of battle. The vegetation remained shadowed with fire. "The side of the rock on the left shows, by the little white spots, how our sharp-shooters and infantry had endeavored to dislodge him," he wrote. "The trees in the vicinity were splintered, and their branches cut off, while the front of the wall looked as if just recovering from an attack of geological small-pox."

This death could only been seen as a net gain to Gardner's northern audience. But who could look upon a murdered child and not feel some sympathy? Gardner imagined the boy's final moments in such a way that he became every lost son, every death that taught American fathers and mothers the evils of war. "The sharpshooter had evidently been wounded in the head by a fragment of shell which had exploded over him, and had laid down upon his blanket to await death. There was no means of judging how long he had lived after receiving his wound, but the disordered clothing shows that his sufferings must have been intense. Was he delirious with agony, or did death come slowly to his relief, while memories of home grew dearer as the field of carnage faded before him? What visions, of loved ones far away, may have hovered above his stony pillow! What familiar voices may he not have heard, like whispers beneath the roar of battle, as his eyes grew heavy in their long, last sleep!"

GARDNER MADE SIXTY images on the battlefield of Gettysburg. Three quarters of them depicted death. Though it is not known how many he manipulated as he did the image that came to be titled *The Home of a Rebel Sharpshooter*, his desire to make stories of the casualties he found is well documented.

He was not the only one carefully creating images by which the war would be remembered. With his lead battlefield correspondent now taking pictures for himself, Mathew Brady also journeyed to Gettysburg. By the time he arrived, more than a week after the fighting, most of the dead had been carted away.

Brady and his assistants focused some of their work on Culp's Hill, a wooded rise where the trees bore marks of furious shooting. A pockmarked forest could hardly tell a story, however—at least not one that could be captured on glass and sold to a public hungry for images of death.

Finding a particularly alluring spot, a copse of thick oaks standing tall despite the war's brief interference, Brady positioned his camera so that a single fallen tree would haunt the background of the photograph. Taken together, the erect and broken timber might suggest at once a steadfast Union and its sacrifice. He called for an assistant to lie down in front of the fallen tree, providing a human focal point to the image and driving the message home. When the photograph was produced for sale, he included a caption that lacked Gardner's poetry, but perhaps was even more audacious in its regard for what photography could do to the line separating life and death. "In the middle ground a dead soldier," he wrote.

Gardner returned some months later, in time to hear Lincoln deliver his Gettysburg Address. After revisiting the spot where he had dragged a body and posed it like a boy sleeping, he would claim that neither the soldier's bones nor his rifle had been removed. "The musket, rusted by many storms, still leaned against the rock, and the skeleton of the soldier lay undisturbed within the mouldering uniform, as did the cold form of the dead four months before," Gardner later wrote. "None of those who went up and down the fields to bury the fallen, had found him. 'Missing,' was all that could have been known of him at home, and some mother may yet be patiently watching for the return of her boy, whose bones lie bleaching, unrecognized and alone, between the rocks at Gettysburg."

That either human or military remains could be found months after the area became a prime spot for treasure hunters is most unlikely. Yet if there was any truth in this at all — if Gardner did indeed revisit Devil's Den in November — he might have noticed that it was by then even more crowded with the photogenic dead than it had been when he first rolled up in his whatsit wagon.

A local photographer named Peter Weaver had apparently heard how popular images of the fallen of Gettysburg had become. He brought a dozen living Union soldiers with him and arranged them dramatically on the rocks, posing them amid strewn rifles and caps, as if they had all been freshly killed in the battle fought months before—as if this latecomer of a battlefield photographer had learned the tricks of the trade from the master.

When the artist was satisfied that he had captured a few images he could sell to those eager to view death from the comfort of their parlors, the casualties of war populating his photograph rose from the rocks of Devil's Den. They dusted themselves off, straightened their caps, and went off to fight another day.

PART III
HUMBUGGED

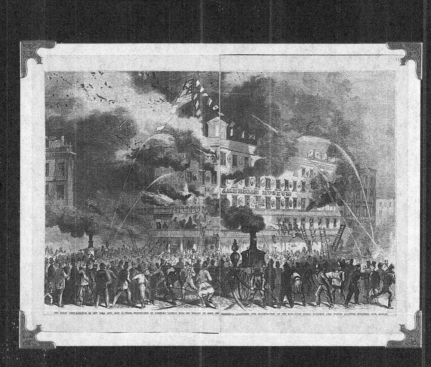

The burning of the American Museum, July 13, 1865.

CHAPTER 17

ALL IS GONE
AND NOTHING SAVED

BY THE SUMMER OF 1865, the fighting had been over for months, but still the war's fog lingered.

Across the South, bodies rose from hastily dug graves and made their way home with the help of Adams Express. In the nation's capital, Alexander Gardner trained his camera on John Wilkes Booth's co-conspirators as they ascended the gallows at Washington's Old Arsenal Prison. With all his experience photographing the dead, he was unprepared for the movements of the condemned as the trapdoors fell and they hung by the neck. The sway of their bodies gave some of his images an unfortunately blurred appearance. Signs of life, as ever, complicated the photographer's art. In the afterlife, too, the battle lines drawn by conflict endured. Judge John Edmonds reported that he had recently been visited by both the president and his assassin. "Lincoln was kind and gentle to him, and manifested only sorrow and compassion for Booth," Edmonds said, while the murderer shrugged off his own responsibility, claiming, "I only enacted my part in the great drama." No matter that surrender and victory had been settled; in Summerland as in the earthly realm, the spirit of animosity hovered like a dark cloud.

Even in Manhattan, usually so quick to move on to the novel and the new, there remained something heavy in the July air. After four years of losses so numerous they would never be fully known, it was a time when more Americans than ever believed their land must be haunted. Grief clung like humidity on the skin. While the mercury flirted with triple digits, the avenues filled with soldiers anxious to shed their blue woolen sack coats. Every day it seemed another regiment passed through the Battery Barracks at the foot of the city, returning from the South by steamship on their way to the rail lines that would take them on the last legs of their journeys home. Those hoping to find slightly less oppressive weather once back on northern soil were sorely disappointed. No matter if they joined the maimed housed by the hundreds in the nuns' hospital at Central Park, or marched miraculously whole of body through Union Square, they arrived in a summer as searing as it had been in the battle-scarred places they had left behind.

Some mornings in the first week of July began near ninety degrees. By afternoon, outdoor workers dropped from sunstroke in the street. Newspapermen, well versed in the art of transforming injury into column inches, carried on with daily casualty reports as if the war were still raging, though now with a new enemy. New York City, the *Herald* said, had become "too torrid for human endurance." Evidence of this mapped the boroughs: at Third Avenue and Eighty-Fourth Street, an Irish laborer was "prostrated" by the heat and transported to Bellevue Hospital. In Brooklyn, a teamster fainted under the midday glare and was crushed by the wheels of his cart as it crossed Myrtle Avenue. In Greenwich Village, a private of the 1st New York Cavalry Regiment died of heat exhaustion barely a week after mustering out.

For relief from all this—from the heat, from the grief, from the malaise both inspired—there was really only one place to go: Barnum's American Museum, which had the undeniable distinction of being a semipublic space in a sweltering city that maintained a tomb-like cool throughout the summer.

The permanent draft moving through five floors of exhibit rooms and performance halls was rare enough that Barnum had made the temperature inside the museum one of his starring attractions. Daily advertisements in the press boasted of a revolutionary new ventilation system that diffused thirty thousand cubic feet of air per minute through its chambers with the force of a steady seaside breeze. The recently installed network of fans and water pipes ensured that the thirteen wax figures of Barnum's life-size *Last Supper* would not go soft, that his mermaid pieced together from a monkey's torso and a fish tail would not wilt and show its stitches, and that the two living white whales imported from the North Atlantic swam in a tank as cool as the waters of home. Ned the Learned Seal leaped out of the water and played his hand organ in delight.

Did anyone paying the twenty-five-cent admission price know what a cubic foot of air might feel like? Never mind—on these hot and somber days when it seemed you could survive a war only to be killed by daylight, thirty thousand of them sounded like just the thing.

Such masterly marketing of air was the most literal expression yet of what Barnum had long called his "puffery," his instinctive understanding of how best to inflate and exploit an audience's collective desires—or, as he put it, the "insatiate want of human nature."

History generally remembers P. T. Barnum as a confidence man more than willing to fleece the gullible public. But he was less interested in playing his patrons for fools than in giving them what they wanted. If they often wanted to be played for fools, well, it was only his duty as a showman to oblige. While he probably never uttered the words most famously attributed to him, "There's a sucker born every minute," he did offer a more interesting assessment of the human condition where perception was concerned. "The American people," he said, "like to be fooled."

After all, to be tricked—"humbugged," in Barnum's English —was in some instances not merely to be lied to. It was to be coaxed from one understanding of reality to another. It was to make the unreal real, if briefly, simply by experiencing it as such. To be humbugged at the American Museum, its proprietor insisted, might even be seen as an elevating experience. It was, in its way, transcendent. In a place where the city's otherwise inescapable heat could be thwarted, the usual rules of living seemed no longer to apply. Perhaps even the terms of life's end were open to negotiation.

NOT FAR INSIDE THE entrance to the American Museum, one of the latest featured attractions made this possibility plain. With his ear ever to the ground to detect far-off rumblings of the new and the strange, Barnum had recently learned of the existence of images purporting to provide proof positive of life after death. He had immediately purchased as many as he could lay his hands on.

The fruits of this effort were now arrayed in a small section of the museum's impressive portrait gallery. The series of framed photographs showed several views of the same bespectacled man with long curly hair and a somewhat quizzical gaze. A few museum patrons might have recognized him as the eccentric New Englander turned gold-mining adventurer William Cornell "Colorado" Jewett, who had recently made a name for himself —and not a particularly good name—as a deluded busybody who had spent the war years insinuating to foreign governments that he had the authority to broker a truce between the Union and the rebel states.

Curious figure though he was, Jewett was not in fact the true subject of Barnum's display. Of far greater interest—both to those who came to see the photographs and to the man who had hung them—were the specters floating within each frame: ghostly faces staring down at the odd-looking fellow from above, each seeming to provide a partial explanation for the other-worldly expression the man wore.

What little Barnum knew in July of 1865 of William Mumler, the photographer who had made these images, was that he then lived in Boston, the spiritual center of Spiritualist America. He knew, too, that Mumler was a man of science, and that he was probably exceedingly shrewd. Barnum judged him to be "ingenious," and noted with evident respect that he was no mere artist or con man but "a scientific chemist."

It was perhaps this that most intrigued Barnum. How could a scientist, a man of reason, be drawn into such an elaborate hoax?

Not that the charms of the photographs were entirely lost on him. He found the images "remarkably ghostlike and supernatural," he later said, and believed that a man like Mumler must have been as amused by them as he was.

As Barnum understood the story of their creation, Mumler had originally made this type of image by accident while teaching himself the photographic process. It was only when prominent Spiritualists learned of the pictures and offered money for them that Mumler had headed down the swindler's path. The "spirit photographer" now sold copies of his pictures for ten dollars apiece. This was many times the going rate for photographs of any kind, but then he wasn't really selling photographs. No, Mumler was selling solace, which any salesman worth his salt would not sell cheap.

Barnum knew such temptations well. One of his most popular publications was called *The Art of Money Getting*. The years spent in devotion to this art had been financially turbulent but ultimately rewarding beyond a scale he never could have imagined. Barnum understood the allure of a fast buck as well as anyone, and he never let himself forget how quickly it could lead even a good man astray. "Money is in some respect like fire," he said, "it is a very excellent servant, but a terrible master."

In any case, the prospect of fortune seemed to be only part of Mumler's motivation. There was also clearly an emotional impulse behind it all. Barnum had heard of grieving mothers who had gone to Mumler desperate for images of children lost. He had heard of widows seeking final visions of their husbands, and of widowers eager for a last glimpse of departed wives. Every story offered a comforting suggestion that the partnerships made in life were not so easily dissolved.

Barnum at the time had been married thirty-five years to a wife he called the "best woman in the world"; they had four daughters together, one of whom died just before her second birthday. Who would not want the solace of a parting glance made permanent, a suggestion—no matter how improbable—that love endured? The years of Mumler's earliest photographic activity had coincided with the steepest decline in population the nation had ever known. Six hundred thousand Americans here and then gone as suddenly and as finally as Barnum's lost daughter. For those convinced of Mumler's powers, ten dollars was never better spent.

The spirit photograph display was not Barnum's only foray into the gray area between life and death. His first promotional triumph, thirty years earlier, had involved an elderly woman named Joice Heth who seemed to have attained immortality because, it was claimed, she had served as George Washington's wet nurse more than a century before. With the nation's origins now beyond living memory, Barnum sensed the American hunger to make direct contact with someone present at its naked and needy infancy. When the huge crowds the supposedly 161-year-old woman had first drawn dwindled, Barnum spread a rumor that Joice Heth was not a living person at all, but a clockwork automaton. He staged this performance until the day she died, and then he sold more than a thousand tickets to her autopsy so the world could judge for itself.

Then just twenty-five years old, Barnum had taken a common type of traveling, carnival-style entertainment popular in the early nineteenth century and, by making it a spectacle fit for the urban press, had expanded its relevance. The questions he encouraged his audience to ask about the death and life of Joice Heth—who, it must be added, was not in fact an automaton but a living woman, and a former slave, estimated by the doctor who performed her autopsy to be in her eighties—were those that blurred the line of science and spirit. Was there some medical explanation for her alleged longevity? Had such intimate contact with the secular saint George Washington granted her immunity from death?

Barnum had become famous with the Joice Heth performances in the 1830s in part because the mechanistic view of the locomotive age fueled audiences' desire to understand the invisible engines that drove all living things. Thirty years later, when the nation was consumed more with grieving than with gadgets, Mumler's images offered visions of ghosts in the machine.

———

THOUGH THEY HUNG IN the American Museum for some time, the spirit pictures of William Mumler were not the photographs most closely associated with Barnum and his world. That distinction belonged to the works of an artist far better known than Mumler would ever be.

Barnum was what we would call today an early adopter. Just as he had sought out the newest and best ventilation system available to cool his museum, he embraced other novel technologies as well. He was likely the first to use illuminated signs in Manhattan, making him the pioneer among those who turned a stretch of Broadway into the Great White Way. He was undoubtedly the first—and probably also the last—to use steam engines to pipe river water into a city building for the purpose of filling a custom-made tank for the trained seal Ned and his newest companions, a pair of beluga whales.

Through his long career, Barnum embraced no technology as naturally as photography. By the 1860s the various methods of permanently affixing images to glass, tin, or paper were no longer so new. They were in fact ubiquitous. Broadway was home to no fewer than two hundred photographic studios. The most famous, that of Mathew Brady, had for many years been located directly across the street from the museum. A sitting before Brady's camera was an essential stop for all those who imagined themselves as players on the world stage. Along with St. Paul's Church and the museum itself, Brady's studio established the corner of Ann Street and Broadway as a crossroads of image-making, a place where one's soul, one's appearance, and one's understanding of the world could be transformed.

Brady had been a Barnum collaborator for years. He had photographed nearly all of the museum's human-oddity performers, providing a never-ending stream of keepsake cartes de visite, which could be purchased in the museum. Brady and Barnum had each reaped the benefits of successive generations of misfits and exiles: men, women, and children who because of physical defects or intentionally altered features had come to call the American Museum home. These were the princes, jesters, and courtesans of King Barnum's court, and Brady was the court's artist, capturing likenesses of them all. The motley assortment gathered into his camera's dark chamber early in his career suggested his true calling was to catalog life's great variety.

But that hot July Barnum had something no photographic studio could boast: images captured by the famous Brady in the same gallery as those concocted by the infamous Mumler.

———

ALL YEAR LONG THE American Museum drew a crowd, but summer mornings were especially good for business. Women in petticoats and men in straw hats flocked to a place so impossibly comfortable it seemed that human ingenuity could confound nature itself.

The museum's patented circulation system was the work of the father of steam heat, Joseph Nason. Not long before Barnum had brought a machine-made chill to the premier tourist attraction in Manhattan, Nason and Company had provided the same service to the U.S. Capitol in Washington. That Barnum would turn to the best in the country for his patrons' comfort surprised no one; his museum was another kind of American capital, the spiritual center of a nation always at the intersection of known and unknown.

Such great comfort came at a cost, however. Its supernaturally pleasant air, the inviolability of its otherworldly sights — all this relied on machines kept carefully out of public view. Coal-fired boilers and steam engines chugged away endlessly underground. Paradise above was made possible only by an inferno below.

Midway through the month, beneath the "always cool and delightful" salons with which Barnum had made his name, something went wrong. To explain his singular success in a snake-oil era when hucksters were everywhere, he once said, "My 'puffing' was more persistent, my advertising more audacious, my posters more glaring, my pictures more exaggerated, my flags more patriotic, and my transparencies more brilliant." These "transparencies" were the massive backlit painted banners that draped the museum's façade, announcing his newest attractions with letters that glowed as if written in fire.

The latest transparency was in its way the most audacious, for it made light even of the war, though it was barely won. The latest would also prove to be the last.

At the time, the papers were full of calls for the head of Jefferson Davis. The former president of the Confederacy had recently been taken into federal custody. Just before his arrest in May of 1865, Davis made a decision that would haunt him. As a Union general reported, he "hastily put on one of his wife's dresses" while attempting to escape.

In fact, he was apprehended wearing not a dress but his wife's raincoat and shawl, which his defenders argued were nearly unisex in the style of the day. To the northern press, however, the story was too good to check. Newspapers and magazines rushed to publish sketches of Davis as a bearded southern belle. "Nobody will attempt to make a hero of such material," one account said. "He will appear in petticoats in history."

Barnum instantly announced that he would pay $500 for Davis's dress, and sent a telegram to his museum manager: "Put outside a picture of Jeff Davis in petticoats, represented as running, exposing his boots." The mere possibility that it would soon be on display at the Manhattan headquarters of Barnum's entertainment empire set the nation abuzz. "If Barnum can get possession of the rig in which Davis was taken," one newspaper predicted, "it will be worth an overflowing oil well to him." The *Brooklyn Daily Eagle* wryly predicted, "Before a month expires, the dress . . . will be in every museum in the country—genuine, of course, in every instance."

Since the actual dress did not exist, Barnum had to improvise. Banners painted with the feminized image of the Confederate leader draped the museum's façade. A song from the war promised to "hang Jeff Davis from a sour apple tree," but Barnum had other plans. Why hang a man once when you could mock him for profit all season long?

Inside the museum, Barnum installed a Davis display he called "The Belle of Richmond." With a wax figure of a man wearing a dress similar to those seen in the sketches that had already made the story notorious, it might have enjoyed an epic run. But the fervor that made it a hit also doomed it from the start.

———

THE FIRE THAT BROKE out at the American Museum on July 13, 1865, was a destructive marvel. Thirty thousand people turned out to watch the conflagration while Barnum's menagerie spilled out onto Broadway. In the midst of this mayhem, Jefferson Davis came tumbling down. As the crowd jeered, a bearded mannequin dressed in women's attire was hurled into the street, its skirt acting briefly as a parachute. "As Jeff made his perilous descent," the *New York Times* reported, "his petticoats again played him false, and as the wind blew them about, the imposture of the figure was exposed." Landing to "cheers and uncontrollable laughter," the statue was then promptly hanged, just as the song suggested.

While the cause of the fire remained a mystery, many assumed arson. "It is suspected," the *Pittsburgh Gazette* reported, "the guilty parties were rebel sympathizers offended by the prominence Barnum has given to the manner of Jeff Davis' capture." A Confederate partisan who witnessed the blaze wrote that the banners painted with Davis's image "gave the flames such an impetus, that they could not be controlled." That diehard Confederates had started the fire made a good story, and Barnum spread it far and wide. He had many other enemies as well, not least of all various Spiritualists, though an attack such as this did not seem their style.

Rumors of arson aside, it is far more likely that the conflagration began within the machinery beneath the museum, in the fires that kept the air cool. The technology that had made the fantasy possible was also its undoing.

The flames had spread from the engine room to the first floor and beyond by the time firefighters arrived. Moving past a Last Supper melted to thirteen pious puddles, the first firemen entering the building charged up the stairs, where they spotted—wonder of wonders in a burning building—a tank full of water. They hacked into the glass with fire axes until a leak sent spray into the air. Then came the deluge. The whales moaned and writhed as the tank drained onto the floorboards; their deaths did little to slow the flames.

Nothing did. The same New York press that had been wringing drama out of heat stroke for a month now had a genuine disaster to contend with. As one reporter noted with a grand statement worthy of Barnum: "All is gone and nothing saved." The museum may have been a transcendent intersection of the known and unknown, but there was no humbug that could save it from burning completely to the ground.

Newspapermen looking for a silver lining announced with relief that a firefighter from Brooklyn had found Ned the seal in the firestorm and carried him out alive.

While the oil-painted transparencies of Jefferson Davis spread the flames out onto Broadway and even blackened the columns of St. Paul's Church, inside the museum the flames found their most potent fuel in the portrait gallery. Mumler's spirit photographs on the wall, Brady's cartes de visite on their sales carts—no matter the different intentions behind them, they all burned with similar ease, vanishing in plumes barely distinguishable from the haze that shrouded the city.

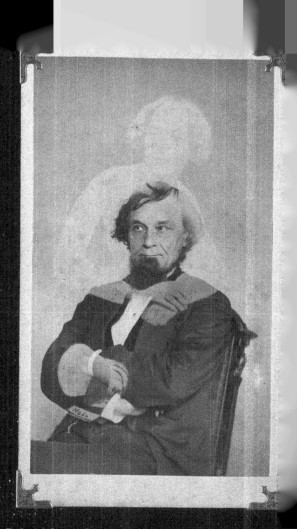

Colonel Amos Cushman of the New York State Mili[...]
with an unidentified female spirit image.
William Mumler, 1862–1875.

CHAPTER 18

A FAVORITE HAUNT
OF APPARITIONS

REPORTS OF THE MUMLERS practicing their art in Boston became scarce after the latest and most damning rounds of investigations, and ceased altogether by the time the war ended in 1865. With the dead still being counted, it might have been a boon season for spirit photography, but Mrs. Stuart's studio stood shuttered on Washington Street. Though its skylights stayed open, the sun filtering through the panes no longer captured images of either the living or the dead.

Not that William Mumler had left the business entirely. For a time, he hoped to reinvent himself as a photographic artist who directed his camera only on the mortal side of the veil that separated this world from the hereafter. Like many an image maker out to cash in on scandal, he occupied himself throughout the summer of 1865 with the production of illustrations of Jefferson Davis in a dress, selling them to delighted northerners who could no longer hope to see the spectacle in person after the American Museum had burned.

The Davis cards Mumler produced showed the disgraced Confederate spliced together with a hand-drawn tableau of two Union soldiers taking the bearded cross-dresser captive at gunpoint. Beneath the comic scene, Mumler wrote with a calligraphic flourish a few words Davis had uttered before meeting his ignoble end: "We are about making a movement that will astonish the world."

Crude though it was by later standards, this kind of art itself was an innovation. The idea of marrying a photograph with a more traditional pen-and-ink drawing would later become common in satirical weeklies that soon proliferated. Mumler might have become a pioneer in that field, creating clever photo manipulations that commented on the news of the day.

But then William Guay returned to town.

With his Boston aquarium liquidated and his services updating the studio no longer required, the Mumlers' erstwhile assistant had gone home for a time to Louisiana, where the stigma of his desertion from the Confederate army had apparently been eclipsed by the bitterness of the war's end. In a place desperate to forget rather than remember, however, photography was no longer as popular as it once was. Guay's Photographic Temple of Art in New Orleans declared bankruptcy in 1868, and its proprietor drifted north again—apparently to encourage his former employers to give spirit photography another try.

Mumler did not take much convincing. He had never gotten over the sting of the public rebuke he had received in the Boston press, and remained convinced that he was a truth teller offering spiritual advancement to a world not yet ready to receive it. "A prophet is not without honor save in his own country," he said, quoting scripture.

This time, the Mumlers would go somewhere they hoped their talents might be appreciated.

———

FROM THE BEGINNING, New York had beckoned to Mumler as the capital of the nation's photographic industry, the only place to go if he was to rebuild his reputation as a serious practitioner of the art. The city still was home to Morse, Brady, and Gurney, and had been the starting point for Alexander Gardner's already legendary career. The fact that Barnum had sought Mumler's work for display surely also contributed to Mumler's sense that he might find a receptive audience.

Just a few blocks from the gallery where Brady had his start, and not far from the recently rebuilt American Museum, Mumler found a new place of business in the photo salon of W. W. Silver, a successful portrait artist with six years' experience. By November of 1868, when the spirit photographer arrived with his family and erstwhile assistant William Guay, he hoped the scandal of his earlier foray before the public had been long forgotten.

Silver's studio at 630 Broadway was a tastefully appointed two-story storefront. Customers waited in the parlor downstairs, then ascended a staircase to the sitting room when the photographer was ready for them. Though Mumler was renting space and equipment and making use of Silver's developing chemicals whenever possible, he immediately made himself at home. He printed cards advertising the services of a "Spirit Photographic Medium," with no mention whatsoever of who the actual proprietor might be.

No Spiritualist himself, W. W. Silver was dismayed to see the address he had spent a half-dozen years establishing as a serious place of business associated with so dubious a pursuit. Mumler's certainty tested his skepticism, however. By the end of his first week providing the newcomer with a studio and a camera, Silver's interest was sufficiently piqued that he agreed to sit before the spirit photographer's lens.

As he had so many times in Boston, Mumler positioned his subject in a chair lit from windows in the ceiling. He placed his hand on the camera, removed the cloth covering the glass, and stood still as the plate was exposed. Silver watched him closely the entire time, so nothing Mumler did with the equipment would escape his notice.

And yet when he looked at the picture Mumler had made of him, Silver saw the face of another sharing the frame. It was the form of a woman—his mother. He had no doubt about it.

He still could not call himself a believer, but from then on Silver allowed Mumler the full use of his property, and by extension, his reputation. Soon enough, he accepted that, despite the sign reading SILVER above the door, most of the customers who crossed the threshold did so looking for the man with the power to peer into the world to come. War widows, bereaved parents, successful businessmen gripped by emptiness that fortunes could not fill—the sorrowful parade that had ended abruptly on Washington Street in Boston several years before recommenced at 630 Broadway.

One day David Hopkins, a well-known wealthy railroad contractor, arrived seeking Mumler's services. An ardent Christian, he thought there must be some trickery at work and hoped to detect it, but he kept his opinions to himself. In the photograph taken of him, Hopkins saw himself seated before a neighbor who had died earlier that year. He at first would not believe his own eyes, but then took the image home to show others who had known the dead woman. Friends and family gathered around and studied it, and all agreed it must be her. Why she had chosen to visit him, he could not say.

On another day, Mumler photographed Lutheria Reeves. A housewife of the city, she was still mourning the loss of her eleven-year-old son when a nephew visiting from Vermont, a scientifically minded young man, announced he was going to investigate the rumors of Spiritualist activity on Broadway. Eager to be distracted from her grief, Mrs. Reeves went along, and soon found herself sitting before Mumler's camera. In two separate sittings she received pictures showing herself and her son. To her relief, the boy appeared healthy in one of the photographs, as if the world to come had healed him at last.

As sorrowful solitaries and in raucous groups of skeptics, they came for months. For a time Mumler's salon seemed to have the same gravitational pull as Morse's studio had a generation before. Now, however, it drew not just photographers but scores of men and women, all haunted by loss. And once again, breathless accounts of ghostly happenings began to appear in the press. "The great commotion of the week with us has been the production of spirit-photographs at a gallery up Broadway," a correspondent wrote in a column that soon was reprinted as far away as San Francisco. "The locale is supposed to be a favorite haunt of apparitions from the 'world to come' who propose to distribute their photos among their friends here. This may be a humbug," the reporter added, "but I am too stupid to discover it myself. I felt it in my boots that the whole thing was a grim joke while I was witnessing the phenomenon, and yet I was helpless to effect a sensible solution to the mystery."

Closer to home, the *New York Sun* noted that Mumler's work had recently come up at the regular meeting of the New York Spiritualist Conference, which proposed that a committee of their choosing should visit the spirit photographer and investigate his claims. When Mumler told them they were welcome to watch him work, but only if they paid for their pictures in advance, they voted on a proclamation that suggested a fierce division in the ranks of the city's believers:

> *Resolved,* That this conference considers that Mr. Mumler does not meet this attempted investigation in such a manner as we should expect from one conscious of having a great truth in his possession, and that while thus refusing to the Committee of this Conference the privilege on fair terms of such an investigation as must necessarily help to confirm his claims if true, he had no right to expect from us as a body the endorsement which some individuals see reason to give him, or any confidence whatever.
>
> *Resolved,* That Mr. Mumler's treatment of the Committee

does not prove pro or con the truth or falsity of spirit photo-graphing; neither does the adoption or rejection of the Commit-tee's report establish one or the other proposition.

If the ambivalence of the city's Spiritualist community trou-bled him, Mumler gave no indication of alarm. Far more of his effort was expended attempting to win over the thriving local photography community, beginning with the meeting of the Photographic Section of the American Institute at the Cooper Union, the same intellectual center that Lincoln had credited with winning him the presidency (with Mathew Brady's help) nine years before. Since that time, New York's elite artists and eager amateur camera enthusiasts had been gathering there regu-larly to make presentations on their craft, its past and its future.

"Too often in the busy life which most of us lead," the Pho-tographic Section's founding president and early Samuel Morse collaborator John William Draper said at the start of one meet-ing, "we are apt to be looking at the future, occupying ourselves with its promises, and neglecting a review of what we have real-ized in the past." Young as photography was, the hundreds now plying the trade in New York recognized they had much to learn from those who had come before, and from each other. As an art form still finding its way, it was collaborative and supportive even as competition among the professionals was fierce. "Experience, they say, is the best of all teachers; but what is experience with-out reflection, without meditation?" Draper asked. "We advance with all the more certainty and with all the more pleasure, if we look back and deliberately weigh what we have accomplished, and examine without any concealment what are to be considered as our shortcomings." Toward this end, the meetings of the Pho-tographic Section followed a format of addressing several cat-egories of inquiry, from "improvements in developing chemicals and lenses" to the "application of the art to astronomy in the obtaining of impressions of the heavenly bodies" to "photographic methods of preventing counterfeiting of bank notes."

Though it might have been ill advised to share his work with a group that had so recently considered the use of photography in detecting fraud, Mumler arranged to exhibit several of his best images for the Photographic Section's March 1869 convocation.

After his photographs had been displayed, he explained that his spirit pictures were best understood not as a religious or metaphysical phenomenon, but as a new application of existing technology that they all would soon come to embrace. He then distributed a booklet he had printed to introduce himself to potential clients. "My object of placing this little pamphlet before the public is to give to those who have not heard a few of the incidents and investigations on the advent of this new and beautiful phase of spiritual manifestations," Mumler's booklet said.

> It is now some eight years since I commenced to take these remarkable pictures, and thousands, embracing as they do scientific men, photographers, judges, lawyers, doctors, ministers, and in fact all grades of society, can bear testimony to the truthful likeness of their spirit friends they have received through my mediumistic power.
>
> What joy to the troubled heart! What balm to the aching breast! What peace and comfort to the weary soul! To know that our friends who have passed away can return and give us unmistakable evidence of a life hereafter — that they are with us, and seize with avidity every opportunity to make themselves known; but alas, in many instances, that old door of sectarianism has closed against them, and prevents their entering once more the portals of their loved ones and be identified.
>
> But, thank God, the old door is fast going to decay; it begins to squeak on its rusty and time worn hinges; its panels are penetrated by the worm holes of many ages, through which the bright, effulgent rays of the spiritual sun begin to shine, and in a short time it will totter and tumble to the earth.

Boston has been the field of my labors most of the time since I commenced taking these wonderful pictures, where I have been visited by people from all parts of the Union; but at the earnest solicitation of many friends, I have concluded to make a tour through the principal cities of the United States, that all may avail themselves of this opportunity to obtain a likeness of their loved ones.

Rather than insist that his powers were unique, Mumler suggested to the Photographic Section that any photographer might similarly take up this new application of the art. And if any were interested, naturally he would be available to provide instruction at a reasonable rate.

———

DESPITE MUMLER'S EARNEST EFFORTS to enlist new apostles of spirit photography, just one attendee of the Cooper Union meeting sought him out to learn more.

Patrick V. Hickey had been born in Dublin and remained in Ireland long enough to complete what a later biographer called "a brilliant collegiate course" before the age of twenty. Within a few years of his emigration he had sufficiently acclimated to his new country that he had risen to the rank of science correspondent of the *New York World*. In an era of unprecedented innovation, it was a coveted beat that kept him constantly moving through a city that at times seemed peopled entirely with inventors. Perfect for an ambitious young journalist out to make a name for himself.

Hickey's employer, a decade-old daily owned and published by the former Confederate sympathizer Manton Marble, had seen its share of controversy, no less so than in 1864 when it had published a forged statement purportedly made by Abraham Lincoln calling for an "immediate and peremptory draft" of 400,000 additional troops at a time when the Union victory seemed to be in sight. Marble had been arrested and the *World* building put under armed guard for undermining the war effort, and ever after the broadsheet had tried to debunk hoaxes rather than be duped by them.

Hickey regularly attended photographic exhibitions, but had never before seen the kinds of pictures Mumler put on display. The spirit photographer was probably not unknown to him, however. The previous month, the *World*'s chief rival, the *New York Sun*, had run an account of the goings-on at 630 Broadway that would have made any self-respecting science correspondent cringe. "What our reporter thinks about it he declines to say," the *Sun* noted. "If there is a trick used, he does not know what it is. He gives us the facts, and we give them to our readers, to think about as they please. The whole thing is a marvel anyway, and deserves to be investigated by scientific men."

To a man of P. V. Hickey's intelligence and aspirations, this was an unignorable challenge. He decided he was just the scientific investigator needed to call Mumler on his ruse. Armed with his nose for a good story, and urged on by his tabloid writer's competitive streak, Hickey made an unannounced visit to the spirit photographer's studio.

At first glance, W. W. Silver's place of business seemed an ordinary photographic gallery. Far more bustling than he had expected, it was, Hickey noted, not a one-man operation, but was staffed by a small team, including a woman who took a special interest in arranging the subjects to be photographed. Others in the studio presented themselves as those who had previously engaged Mumler's services, but in their efforts at conversation they seemed less like clients and more like salesmen. They insisted to Hickey that paying ten dollars for a dozen images made by Mumler was a bargain, even if it was well above the going rate.

"Many persons would gladly give a thousand dollars to obtain the likeness of a deceased friend or relative," an apparently satisfied customer said.

All told, Hickey spent an hour that day observing the comings and goings before Mumler's camera. It did not take nearly that long for the journalist, skeptical to begin with, to be convinced there was something amiss, and likely a story to be told.

Yet if his initial aim had been merely to write an article attacking the spirit photographer's credibility, something about the visit altered his plan. He had entered 630 Broadway as an investigator, and might have reported a fine story of his brief interactions with Mumler's associates and the doubts they raised.

Hickey was not simply a journalist, however. He was also a steadfast Roman Catholic, a man of deep devotion whose faith informed every aspect of his life.

At the time he crossed paths with Mumler, Hickey was beginning a long career as one of the pioneers of Catholic journalism in the United States. He was soon to launch a number of sectarian publications, including the *Catholic Review* and the *Illustrated Catholic American*, that would set the standard for the church's approach to engagement with a country that remained blatantly anti-Catholic despite—or because of—the growing influence of men like himself who were loyal to Rome.

To a devout Catholic, a man like Mumler represented not only a swindler but a spiritual threat. It would be a gross understatement to say that Hickey's faith took a dim view of the beliefs of those who looked for departed loved ones in Mumler's images. The church's position on Spiritualism was that it was nothing less than the "work of the devil, a tangle of blasphemies, of contradictions, of brazen absurdities; frauds accepted by a faithless and credulous people." As an 1866 meeting of Catholic bishops known as the Second Plenary Council of Baltimore had warned, "There is little reason to doubt that some of the phenomena of spiritism are the work of Satan." And as the Roman newspaper *La Civiltà Cattolica* had approvingly noted, "In the United States, the evil consequences on the public and the private morals are so evident that many journals are asking the government to stop this situation."

The great fear of the growing Catholic population in the United States was that even with the influx of immigrants like Hickey, the ranks of the Roman Church were in fact being dramatically outpaced by the Spiritualists. The same Catholic conference that argued that Spiritualism was the work of the devil claimed—hyperbolically—that occult communication with the dead had eleven million adherents in America.

Working for the secular *World*, Hickey was not yet in the position to voice a plainly religious opinion of Mumler and his alleged photographs of the departed. He could, however, follow Rome's counsel by asking the government to stop this situation —not as a journalist, but simply as a New Yorker. Hickey resolved to take his concern about the spiritual crimes being committed at 630 Broadway directly to the newly elected mayor, Abraham Oakey Hall. The new administration made it easy. He had only to go to City Hall and write his concerns in the official complaint book.

On the pages of the *World* he would have had more readers, but in this case he hoped one might be enough.

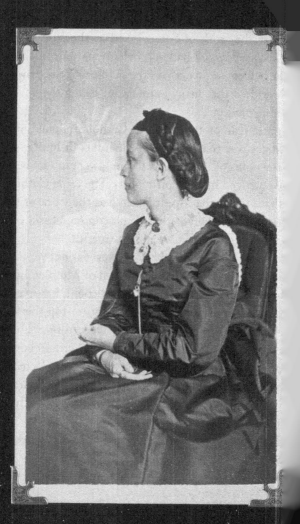

Ella Bonner with the spirit image of a child.
William Mumler, 1862–1875.

CHAPTER 19

THE SPIRITS DO NOT
LIKE A THRONG

CITY MARSHAL Joseph H. Tooker was a native New Yorker, a proud product of Public School 7 on Chrystie Street, son of a sailor based at the South Street Seaport, and grandson of a Jacob Street hide merchant. He had come up on the hardscrabble Lower East Side and seen every crooked scheme that slithered into Manhattan, from the recent counterfeit-watch craze bilking tourists out of $40,000 a week to the "sawdust swindle" that tricked the guileless into buying boxfuls of dust. Mumler's apparitions left him unfazed.

More than being Mayor A. Oakey Hall's confidant and crony, Tooker was, the famously corrupt mayor once said, his "modern Yorick." This description might have derived from the marshal's jovial demeanor, his fondness for pranks, and the theatrical interests he would pursue after he retired from city government, but his resemblance to Shakespeare's poor fellow of infinite jest no doubt also could be found in his bald pate and protruding brow, which gave him an unmistakably skeletal presence. The image evoked of Hamlet with the jester's skull in hand also seemed particularly apt for a man tasked with investigating images from beyond the grave.

By the spring of 1869, Mayor Hall had been in office just four months, and as a former district attorney he continued to take an interest in seemingly minor crimes, especially those that might reflect badly on the metropolis he now led. In all such cases, he turned to Tooker.

The marshal reveled in his proximity to power and long remembered the thrill of wielding outsized authority for the first time. When he was a boy, the blatant Protestant bias in the city's schools was becoming a source of tension between the Public School Society, a Quaker-oriented philanthropy that oversaw the only free schools then available, and the growing ranks of New York Catholics, led by a pugilistic prelate in the person of Archbishop John Hughes—known as "Dagger John" for his aggressive style and the belligerent flourish he put on the small cross every Catholic bishop included as part of his formal signature. When Archbishop Hughes won a minor skirmish in an ongoing theological conflict over student reading materials, school officials deputized a handful of boys to blot out offending passages in classroom texts, including *Hale's History of the United States, Maltebrun's Geography,* and *The English Reader.*

"These books were gathered together," Tooker later recalled, "and a committee of boys was named to open them at the heretical places." Urged on by Dagger John, the Public School Society armed young Joe Tooker and a few other juvenile censors with pads dipped in printer's ink, and the future city marshal reveled in blacking out pages at a time. He already displayed traits of the man he would become: pragmatic and problem-solving, with a strict moral sense, but ultimately less concerned with personal conviction than with getting the job done.

His involvement with the Mumler affair had begun as soon as the name of the spirit photographer appeared in the complaint book kept always open on his desk.

The complaint book—an ever-growing compendium of perceived slights and alleged injustices committed by and against New Yorkers—had in fact been Tooker's idea. First tried briefly a decade before, as a place where citizens might call attention to "any violations of the ordinances and derelictions of duty upon the part of any person holding office under the City Government," the municipal log of residents' grievances as revived by Marshal Tooker quickly filled with outrage over crimes ranging from petty theft to attempted murder. "From 10 to 4 the big space in front of the marshal's desk was daily crowded by a miscellaneous throng," he remembered. "Probably as eighty is to a hundred were the preposterous to the good causes of complaint."

To sift the worthwhile cases from the wastes of time, Tooker oversaw a staff of a dozen ordinance officers who "sometimes were obliged to be rather rough in their efforts to drive away the persistent cranks." Much of the work could not be delegated, however. "One man, a voluble Frenchman, suspected his wife of homicidal intentions," he said, "and in all seriousness begged that I would taste of a plate of butter that he had brought with him, and which he was sure was poisoned."

P. V. Hickey had visited City Hall to make his complaint against Mumler while the details of his investigation remained fresh in mind. Though he might have been dismissed as one of the many cranks Tooker's gatekeepers routinely turned away, or else as a troublemaking busybody—he had not, after all, been a victim of Mumler's swindle himself—his complaint was novel enough and sufficiently indignant to draw the mayor's attention.

It surely did not hurt Hickey's cause that many of Mayor Hall's political enemies, including the well-known editor and politician Horace Greeley, whom Hall had once called "a harlot, a gorilla, and a three fingered Jack," were known Spiritualist sympathizers. Shutting down a man like Mumler might send a message to other supernaturalists that Hall's control of the city would extend even into the world to come. The mayor told his marshal to look into the Mumler matter personally.

Tooker knew something about the photography business. He had sat for pictures in the very earliest days of the daguerreotype, when only Samuel Morse and a few other entrepreneurial artists in New York had hung out their shingles as writers of light. As he had when visiting those earlier studios, Tooker went to 630 Broadway as if he were merely a client desiring an image of himself.

Greeted at the studio door by an associate of Mumler calling himself Mr. Silver, Tooker explained that he was skeptical that the likeness of a deceased person could be made by a photographic process, but asked if it was possible to produce such a likeness.

"Not only is it possible," the man answering as Silver said, "but Mr. Mumler, an operator and spiritualistic medium, actually produces such pictures by supernatural means."

Tooker was by then well known around town, especially among the sorts of grifters he assumed he was dealing with now. He invented a tale of his interest in spiritual phenomena that included the use of a pseudonym — William Wallace — and then inquired if the spirit pictured could be one designated by the living subject of the photograph. If so, he added, he would very much like to have a portrait of his deceased father-in-law.

When the man calling himself Silver told the man calling himself Wallace that the price of these pictures would be ten dollars per dozen, Tooker scoffed. Ten dollars was more than three times the going rate.

"The spirits do not like a throng," the man who claimed he was Silver said. A premium fee was necessary to protect the gentle souls of the departed from the "vulgar multitude."

There was also a woman working in the studio that day, and Tooker came to understand that it was Mrs. Mumler, a pretty woman whose age he found difficult to determine. After ringing a bell, she led him up the stairs to the posing room, where her husband was waiting by his camera.

A few minutes later, Tooker held in his hand a glass plate

showing a likeness of himself sitting beneath the faint outline of a man's face. He studied the plate for a moment and declared that he did not know anyone resembling the indistinct features. Surely, Mumler insisted, it must be the face of Tooker's late father-in-law, as requested. Heading off any possible skepticism, the photographer warned that such visions of the dead could at first be difficult to recognize but then "produced surprising effects," including ladies fainting on the gallery floor. "Think of the matter seriously," Mumler told him, and insisted he come back the next day to pick up photographic prints of the image.

When he returned the following morning, the mayor's chief marshal was presented with a bill reading "one dozen spirit photographs, ten dollars." He collected the pictures, paid the fee, and then, with what he believed to be clear evidence of fraud in hand, Tooker took Mumler into custody. No less than a heretical line in a textbook, the spirit photographer was deemed a threat to the public good and hastily removed from view.

A crowded waiting room watched as the man who captured ghosts was taken to the Tombs.

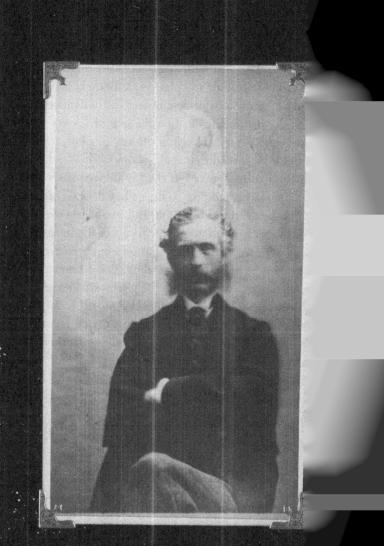

Unidentified man with unidentified female spirit image.
William Mumler, 1862–1875.

CHAPTER 20

THE TENDEREST SYMPATHIES OF HUMAN NATURE

IN HIS SIX years seeing the city's worst from his perch inside the Tombs police court, Judge Joseph Dowling had gained a reputation for ruthless efficiency. It was said that he plunged through cases with a swiftness that kept the human sewer of the justice system blockage-free. "He has a hard class of people to deal with," a report said of Dowling shortly before Mumler arrived before his bench, "and this has made him not a little sharp in his manner." Even his critics noted that the "penetrating power" of his glance was legendary for striking fear in the hearts of those who thought they might deceive him. He directed the full searching force of that gaze now at Mumler, whose trial was about to begin.

Naturally, all other eyes in the room likewise fell on the spectacle of the lumpen, rumpled figure who had once again become the center of so much attention. Studying the accused from a few feet away, a young prosecutor by the name of Elbridge Gerry already saw that this was a case with which he might make his reputation. Mayor Hall himself had taken a special interest, and Gerry, equipped with both wisdom and a mustache well beyond his years, wondered how he might turn this open-and-shut case to his long-term advantage. Closer still to the man at the center of the proceedings, the attorneys for the defense appeared resigned to their lot, remaining as silent as would any lawyers whose client's future seemed to rest on spectral evidence.

In the two weeks since Mumler's arrest and preliminary appearance at the Tombs, lawyers for and against him had gathered a motley assortment of Spiritualists and photographers, scoffers and true believers, sideshow hucksters and members of the fourth estate. The questions they sought to answer concerned not only the possibility of otherwise invisible figures being captured through methods the likes of Daguerre and Morse had brought into the world, but the very nature of the soul and the religious commitments of the country.

"What is this modern Spiritualism?" prosecutor Gerry asked the court. "Only a form of infidelity in a new dress.

"The truths of the Christian religion, as asserted in the Bible, have always been acknowledged by the people of this nation," he continued. "That religion is the basis of all human law, and constitutes the vital essence of our legal system. It was for this reason that in our own state the court held that blasphemy against God, and contumelious reproach and profane ridicule of Christ or the Holy Scriptures, were offenses punishable at the common law."

To help him make this grand case out of such a small-time affair, the first to be heard in the proceedings against William Mumler was the man who had started the spirit photographer's troubles in New York.

Though the prosecutor was from an esteemed patrician family and his opening witness was an immigrant only a few years off the boat, the lawyer shared with Patrick Hickey a visceral dislike of the spiritual threat Mumler represented. The grandson and namesake of a signer of the Declaration of Independence and a Revolutionary War hero, Elbridge Gerry was not one for revolutions himself, but was an ardent defender of orthodoxy. From the moment he took charge of the case against Mumler, it was clear this would not be a simple prosecution for fraud.

As Hickey explained to the court, he had met Mumler some six weeks before the start of the trial. It was then that, as part of his "duty to procure scientific news" for the *World*, he had attended a meeting of the Photographic Section of the American Institute at the Cooper Union. "At that meeting," Hickey testified, "pictures were exhibited having thereon an image which was said to be of a living person and an indistinct or shadowy outline of a person in the background." These images, he continued, "were stated to be specimens of cards taken by a person named Mumler, doing business as a photographer at number 630 Broadway. Mumler and his agents represented such cards to be produced by supernatural causes. In other words, that the shadowy face was the likeness of a spirit present at the time."

Before the Cooper Union meeting adjourned, Hickey had requested one of Mumler's booklets, but was told there were no more available. The photographer had given Hickey his business card instead, and Gerry now submitted it as evidence to Judge Dowling's court:

> **WILLIAM H. MUMLER**
> *Spirit Photographic Medium*
> *No. 630 Broadway, N.Y.*
> *N.B. —All are respectfully invited to call*
> *and see the specimens, and get a pamphlet*
> *giving full information.*

In the interest of science, and perhaps for the chance to pass a test of deduction his peers had failed, Hickey had taken Mumler up on this invitation the very next day. On visiting the address provided, he discovered that the studio to which he had been directed was not operating in Mumler's name. The sign above the door indicated the establishment was owned by a W. W. Silver. Once inside, he was told that this was indeed the place to find Mumler.

With Gerry's questions walking him through his visit, Hickey reported that after leaving the studio that day, he discovered that

Mumler "had practiced similar deceptions in Boston until he could no longer remain there." With a believer's ardor and an immigrant's zeal to protect his new home, he had resolved to take his concern about the spiritual crimes being committed at 630 Broadway directly to the highest office in the city.

———

THOUGH MAYOR HALL HAD considered attending the proceedings, and briefly thought he should prosecute the case himself, he apparently thought better of it. His modern Yorick, Marshal Tooker, appeared in his place.

"What led you to enter upon the prosecution of inquiries into this matter," Gerry asked as soon as the marshal took the stand, "and what was your motive of proceeding to the photographic gallery of the defendant here?"

Tooker explained to the crowded courtroom that the mayor had told him to look into the Mumler business personally.

"For what purposes were you so directed?" Gerry asked.

"A complaint had been made before Mayor Hall relative to certain photographs issuing from the premises of 630 Broadway," Tooker said.

"And you repaired to the premises so designated?"

"Yes, sir."

"What did you expect to get there, if anything?"

"I expected to have my portrait taken."

As he had when visiting the city's first daguerreotype studios years before, Tooker had gone to 630 Broadway as if he were merely a client desiring an image of himself. This time, however, he did so with a clear sense from Hickey's complaint that this was not only a place where pictures were made, but one where "the tenderest sympathies of human nature were daily outraged."

"Did you, as you expected, have your portrait taken?" Gerry asked.

"Yes, sir."

"Did you notice any trick or deception practiced by the photographer on that occasion?"

"Yes, sir."

"What was it?"

"Well, when I went into the room certain representations were made to me which were not afterwards carried out as promised. Mr. Mumler promised to give me a picture of a relative or of someone deceased near in sympathy to me, this he failed to do, and I therefore consider that was a trick and a deception practiced on me."

Gerry finished his questions there and returned to the prosecution's table. The case was straightforward as far as he was concerned. Since it was manifestly impossible that the spirit photographer had done what he claimed, Gerry needed only to present the details of the swindle to the court.

The facts, he believed, would speak best for themselves.

———

LEADING MUMLER'S DEFENSE, John D. Townsend was a lawyer comfortable with lost causes and unpopular defendants. Until now, his specialty had been helping men get away with murder. Of the forty-five accused killers he had represented, only one was executed, and he, having committed a crime the press called "infamously brutal," had certainly had it coming. During his ten years in practice, Townsend's vigorous efforts on behalf of the city's most dangerous had earned him the sobriquet of "The Fighting Lawyer."

With the fight for Mumler now begun, however, he chose not to enter the ring. When the self-satisfied Gerry turned his star witness over for cross-examination, Townsend stayed in his chair, allowing his assistant to continue the questioning.

Like Townsend, Albert Day had served ten years in the New

York bar. Though he had developed a reputation for "marked ability, moral integrity and fair success," he had not endured the scrutiny of high-profile cases as the lead defense attorney had. Townsend likely instructed him to handle the interrogation of the early witnesses less for his trial experience than for his experience in spiritual matters. Some of this was personal—Day's wife, Olive, was a woman known to delight in "recondite themes of mental contemplation, scientific, philosophic, metaphysical and mystical, even to astrology"—but it was professional as well. Day had more than once in his career found himself putting his sensitivity to theological issues in service of the law. When a client's will was challenged on the basis that he had lost his senses by claiming to hear divine voices, Day successfully argued that men in biblical times did much the same, and few would question their sanity today.

Faced now with the imposing Marshal Tooker, Day similarly sought to call into question assumptions made about truth and falsehood and the contexts in which both are employed.

"Have you, Mr. Tooker, any other name that you are known by besides your proper name of Tooker?" Day asked.

"No, sir, no name that I am known by."

"Did you ever, for any purpose lately, assume the name William H. Wallace?"

"Yes, I did, sir."

"Wallace is not your real name?"

"No, sir."

"Why did you assume that name?"

"I assumed it for the purpose of prosecuting inquiries into the spirit photography business."

Tooker had hoped to avoid any complications to his investigation that offering his own well-known name to Mumler might create, so his use of a pseudonym was perhaps understandable. Indeed, it was not the first time he had done so. He had been a journalist before his turn toward the law, and in that capacity he had written under several noms de plume—going by the name "Bolivar" when he wrote for the *Boston Saturday Evening Gazette* and "Walton" when his work appeared in the *Sunday Atlas*. From time to time he even signed his articles "The Widow Rogers." Hiding his identity to write "incisive but never rancorous political articles," he was no stranger to bending the truth—perhaps not as drastically as he alleged Mumler had done, but enough to raise doubts about his credibility.

Returning to the subject of promises Tooker claimed Mumler had made when he visited 630 Broadway, Day asked him to be specific.

"What promise did he make to you?"

"He promised or undertook to give me a spiritual photograph of a deceased relative, or of someone in close sympathy with me at the time," Tooker said, "and this he failed to do."

"He failed to do that, did he?" Day asked.

"Yes, sir."

Tooker's testimony might have been damning. He was a well-respected man acting on the authority of the highest office in the city, and he seemed to have common sense on his side. But one further detail worked against him: he had in fact never seen his father-in-law when he was alive.

How, then, Judge Dowling wanted to know, could he be certain the image Mumler showed him was not the man in question?

To those who saw spirit photography as an obvious fraud, the question was absurd, but the doubt it created lingered in the air of the court. The prosecution had planned to rest its case after Tooker's testimony. It had not proven the knockout punch Gerry had expected, however. The defendant's lawyer spoke with renewed confidence, now certain the case would not be as open and shut as Mumler's doubters supposed.

"That will do, Mr. Tooker," Day said. "You can go."

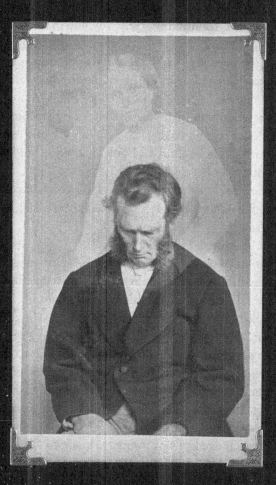

The medium Bronson Murray with the spirit image of Ella Bonner.
William Mumler, 1872.

CHAPTER 21

WEEP, WEEP, MY EYES

HAVING HEARD HIS name invoked more than once during the proceedings, W. W. Silver at last raised his voice above the courtroom din.

"I have nothing to do with the establishment!"

Other than the obvious fact that his name appeared on the door where the alleged crimes had been committed, he expressed bafflement over why he had been compelled to be there at all.

Judge Dowling peered down at the shouting man with bafflement of his own, until Marshal Tooker spoke up from the gallery, where he remained to watch the proceedings even though he would give no further testimony.

"That's not the Mr. Silver I saw at 630 Broadway," the marshal said. Mumler did indeed have an accomplice, he indicated, but this was not the man.

"You had better find that stray piece of silver, and the quicker the better," Judge Dowling said. "This one is probably counterfeit."

When William Guay reluctantly took the stand, he made no explanation or excuse for leading an officer of the law to believe he was not Mumler's longtime partner and accomplice but W. W. Silver, the previous owner of the studio. Instead, he insisted that in fact he remembered very little of the day the marshal had come calling.

"Were you present on the occasion which Mr. Tooker visited

the premises of 630 Broadway, relative to the spirit photograph business?" Day asked.

"I don't know Mr. Tooker," Guay answered.

At Judge Dowling's direction, the marshal stood to identify himself, but still Guay professed ignorance.

"I don't recollect his appearance from being there," he said.

"Do you know whether Marshal Tooker had any interview with Mr. Mumler?" Day asked.

"I don't know," the witness said again. "But I have reason to believe that he had. I think the gentleman to whom you refer went upstairs to see Mr. Mumler.

"As well as I can recollect," Guay added carefully, "the gentleman you refer to came into the room and inquired about spirit photographs. He then expressed a desire to have spirit photographs taken. I told him what were the necessary conditions in order that he may have a picture taken as he desired. I told him that he must pay ten dollars in advance; he at once pleaded that he did not have that amount on him. I told him he must make some deposit to guarantee his return; he said he was willing to give two dollars as a deposit. I said that was quite sufficient for a guarantee. He made the deposit, and I gave him my card accordingly, and directed him to go upstairs. That is all the interview I had with him."

"What do you know yourself about these spirit photographs?"

"All that I know is that I tried to find out how they were done."

"Have you examined the process?"

"Yes, about eight years ago," Guay said. "I was specially delegated by Andrew Jackson Davis to investigate the subject. I then spent three weeks with Mr. Mumler in Boston, visiting his place every day, and during that time making the most minute examination in endeavoring to discover how these photographs were taken by him, and I confess I failed." As the Seer of Poughkeepsie had paid him well for his efforts, he suggested, he had nothing to gain by allowing any trickery on Mumler's part to go unnoticed.

"During your examination of his process," the lawyer continued, "did you notice anything out of the ordinary course of procedure, or anything beyond the usual mechanical requirements for taking pictures?"

"I remarked nothing unusual in his action," Guay said. "Though I tested the process by every means I could devise, I could find no trick or device, and became convinced that the spectral pictures appearing on photographs of living persons were actually and truly likenesses of those departed, and were produced by means other than those known by artists. I know of two or three methods of producing ghost-like figures similar to these: one by placing a person behind the sitter, another by a peculiar arrangement of reflectors, and the third by chemical means." None of these, Guay insisted, had been used in Mumler's gallery.

When prosecutor Gerry rose for his cross-examination, he was less concerned with photography than with belief.

"Are you a Spiritualist or do you believe in the existence of spirits?" he asked.

"I cannot answer," Guay said.

"Are you a believer of incorporeal presence?"

"That I cannot answer."

"Are you a disciple of Andrew Jackson Davis, or a believer in his philosophy?"

"Yes, I am," Guay finally admitted.

How he had gone from serving as Davis's investigator to becoming Mumler's partner, he was not inclined to say.

FROM THE OPENING OF the inquiry in Judge Dowling's court, the presence of another man who preferred to be addressed as Judge had complicated the proceedings.

When the man on the bench asked the defense if it was ready to proceed, it was often Judge John W. Edmonds, the ardent Spiritualist and former state prison inspector, who answered. When a shout of *Objection!* rang through the Tombs, it was as often as not Judge Edmonds's voice that could be heard.

One of the most respected figures of New York's legal community, the jurist and social reformer Edmonds stood close by Mumler's defense team. Though technically present as a witness, he appeared ready to jump into the legal fray, and Judge Dowling, erring on the side of collegiality, appeared willing to indulge him. Edmonds had followed the spirit photographer's career for years, and saw clearly what the images he made might mean.

When called to the stand, Edmonds admitted that though he had heard of Mumler's experiments with spirit photography in Boston years before, he had only recently met the accused.

"I have known Mr. Mumler some two or three weeks," he said. "On the occasion of my becoming acquainted with him I had gone to his gallery."

He had sat for two pictures, he explained, which he now showed the court.

"These are the photographs. In one, I assumed a position which allowed only the taking of my side-face. In the other, I faced the camera."

On each image, he indicated, a spirit form shadowed his own. It was a different form each time, but both were clearly female. As a reporter present later noted, both also were "charmingly pretty."

"One of these pictures is a face which I think I recognize," he said of the ghosts floating in the upper right corner of the photographs. "The other is unknown to me."

Edmonds himself, in profile and frontal poses, appeared in

the images as distinguished and distinct as he did while seated in the witness chair.

Judge Edmonds was now a man of seventy, nearing the end of a long and tumultuous career in service of the public and the law. Born in 1799, he was roughly as old as the century, and had counted himself part of the country's transformation from struggling new republic to rising global power. As a young lawyer he had worked in the Albany law office of Martin Van Buren and from there had climbed steadily up the ladder of New York politics. At the age of thirty-three he was elected to the state senate, and at forty-four he became the state prison inspector, a role in which he became known as "a man full of sympathy for the unfortunate and erring." He distinguished himself through reforms—including abolishing the whip and hiring the woman for whom Mathew Brady made his phrenological portraits on Blackwell's Island—and soon won the spot in the judiciary that earned him the title by which he would ever after be known.

Prior to his fiftieth year, he had enjoyed the kind of worldly success that made inquiries into the world to come seem inconsequential. He had no interest in questions of what kind of existence there might be beyond life on earth. In the autumn of 1850, however, his wife died suddenly. They had been married thirty years, and he was, it was said at the time, "warmly attached to her." In the months following her death, Judge Edmonds was often seen standing by her grave, speaking aloud as if in deep conversation. On the monument he faced during these visits, he'd had inscribed lines from Pierre Corneille's play *Le Cid*:

Pleurez, pleurez, mes yeux, et fondez-vous en eau!
La moitié de ma vie a mis l'autre au tombeau.

(Weep, weep, my eyes, and melt into water!
One half of my life has sent the other to the grave.)

Just three years before, Edmonds had been elevated to the state supreme court; his life following his wife's untimely death became an unending round of days spent hearing the troubles of others, and nights spent in private desolation. "I was at the time withdrawn from general society," he later recalled. "I was labouring under great depression of spirits. I was occupying all my leisure in reading on the subject of death, and man's existence afterward. I had in the course of my life read and heard from the pulpit so many contradictory and conflicting doctrines on the subject, that I hardly knew what to believe, and was anxiously seeking to know if, after death, we should again meet with those whom we had loved here, and under what circumstances."

Late one night while he was reading an investigation of the subject, he thought he heard his wife. She spoke clearly, a full sentence addressed to him. Far from filling him with love or longing, he felt as though he had been shot. He lit lamps throughout the house and searched the rooms for any sign of a source for the voice he had heard. When he found nothing, he attempted to sleep, convincing himself that his lingering grief had created a powerful delusion.

As fate would have it, however, this all came to pass at the very height of the Fox sisters' revelations.

"I was invited by a friend to witness the Rochester Knockings," Judge Edmonds later remembered. "I complied, more to oblige her and to while away a tedious hour. I thought a good deal on what I witnessed, and determined to investigate the matter, and find out what it was. If it was a deception or delusion, I thought that I could detect it. For about four months I devoted at least two evenings in a week, and sometimes more, to witnessing the phenomenon in all its phases.

"I kept careful records of all I witnessed, and from time to time compared them with each other, to detect inconsistencies and contradictions. I went from place to place, surveying different mediums, meeting with different parties of persons, often with persons whom I had never seen before, and sometimes where I was myself entirely unknown—sometimes in the dark, and sometimes in the light—often with inveterate unbelievers, and more frequently with zealous believers."

Eventually he became one of the latter. "There is in Spiritualism that which comforts the mourner, and binds up the broken-hearted," he said, "that which smoothes the passage to the grave, and robs death of its terrors."

Despite the personal solace he found in these newly born beliefs, he knew his public life might be impaired by his conversion. When word began to spread that a justice of the Supreme Court of the State of New York spoke to the dead, he resigned from the bench and published a book that both defended his legacy and evangelized for his nascent faith. He was allowed to keep his title as a matter of respect for past service.

His support for Mumler now, he told the court, was not merely about his own experiences. "I know a great many persons who have visited Mumler, some of whom have met with astonishing success in procuring spirit pictures of departed friends. Mr. Livermore of Wall Street has been peculiarly successful."

Edmonds's longtime friend Charles Livermore was perhaps the second most respected Spiritualist in the city. After making his fortune, he devoted himself to spiritual pursuits. For a time, he had hired one of the Fox sisters to be his private medium, hosting regular séances in his home.

Edmonds produced an image of his friend for the court. It showed a man with sideburns as thick as paintbrushes and with his eyes cast downward. A spectral woman floating above him seemed to cradle his head in her arms. With her body behind Livermore's shoulders and her hands clearly evident on the lapels of his jacket, the image briefly caused an uproar among the photographic practitioners seated in the courtroom. "This is the most remarkable of the photographs exhibited in court," a reporter noted, "from the fact that the photographers present declared that by no means known to them, other than the bodily presence of some one behind the chair, could the picture of the lady's hand be produced."

When asked how such an image might come about, Edmonds did not claim to understand. "Spiritualists reason that these photographs are actual pictures of disembodied spirits, but they do not know," he said. "I am myself not prepared to express a definite opinion. I believe, however, that in time the truth or falsity of spiritual photography will be demonstrated, as Spiritualism itself has been demonstrated, and I therefore say that it would be best to wait and see. The art is as yet in its infancy."

After the defense had finished, prosecutor Gerry pressed for answers on questions Edmonds could more conclusively provide.

"How much were you charged?" he asked.

"They charged me $10 for the first sitting, and $5 for each of the others. I watched the operator closely while he was taking the picture, but could detect no fraud; of course, with my limited knowledge of the photographic art, I would not have been able to tell if he had used fraudulent means to effect his end. I have no definite opinion as to these pictures, having many years ago made up my mind never to form an opinion without knowledge; invariably, when I have done so, I have made an ass of myself."

But was he a believer, Gerry wanted to know, or was he not?

"I believe that the camera can take a photograph of a spirit, and I believe also that spirits have materiality—not that gross materiality that mortals possess, but still they are material enough to be visible to the human eye, for I have seen them.

"Only a few days since I was in a court in Brooklyn, when a suit against a life assurance company for the amount claimed to be due on a certain policy was being heard. Looking toward that part of the court-room occupied by the jury, I saw the spirit of the man whose death was the basis of the suit. The spirit told me the circumstances connected with the death; he said that the suit was groundless, that the claimant was not entitled to recover from the company, and said that he (the man whose spirit was speaking) had committed suicide under certain circumstances. I drew a diagram of the place at which his death occurred, and on showing it to the counsel, was told that it was exact in every particular. I had never seen the place nor the man, nor had I ever heard his name until I entered that courtroom; the appearance of the spirit was shadowy and transparent; I could see material objects through it."

Prosecutor Gerry had shown Judge Edmonds all due deference, but he could not resist pressing him for details on this fantastic story, no matter that it did not have immediate bearing on the trial at hand.

"How do spirits dress?" he asked. "Or do they dress?"

"I have seen spirits clothed in their everyday dress and in their grave clothing," Edmonds replied, "but never saw one without clothing."

"Are you able to define the meaning of the word 'hallucination'?" Gerry asked.

"It is a word difficult to define excepting by illustration. About as fair a case as I can give is that of Othello, who laboured under an idea that his wife was unfaithful to him. Hallucination is a phase of insanity. It arises from some imaginary or erroneous idea." His own communications with the dead, he insisted, were quite different. They had arisen not from error, he believed, but out of love.

Though Gerry had attempted to make Edmonds look foolish by lingering on the subject of the kinds of garments spirits might wear, his testimony was on the whole persuasive to those who heard it. Even Marshal Tooker, who had arrested Mumler and bore no sympathy for Spiritualism, could not help but feel fondness for the aging judge.

"I was impressed by the appearance in the case and the testimony of Judge Edmonds," Tooker later said. "He was an able jurist, and, even with his idiosyncrasies, commanded the respect of the Bar and the people . . . I suppose that there are many other prominent men who give a friendly consideration to the claims of Spiritualism, but we don't suspect them, because they secretly fondle their belief. Once in a while one is honest enough or brave enough to declare himself. Others would do so, but they shrink from probable ridicule."

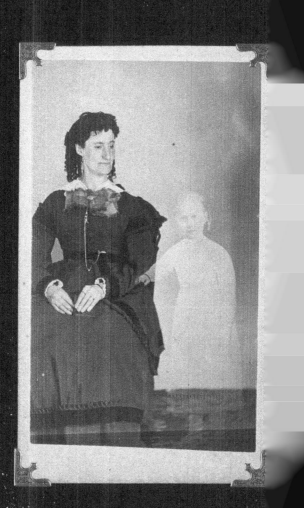

Mrs. Tinkham with a spirit she recognized as her ch
William Mumler, 1862–1875.

CHAPTER 22

ARE YOU A SPIRITUALIST
IN ANY DEGREE?

THE FIRST EXPERT witness for the defense, William Slee, had traveled from Poughkeepsie to speak as an authority on the photographic process. He was one of a pair of brothers operating a respected studio in the small city a half day's journey north of Manhattan, and had been in business for more than a decade — long enough, Mumler's lawyers said, to speak conclusively about the technical aspects of photography and to demonstrate that they had not been manipulated at 630 Broadway.

Throughout the 1860s, Slee Brothers Photography had attempted to popularize porcelaintypes and ivorytypes, novelty items that involved applying images on materials other than glass. In this effort they met with limited success, but the Slees had prospered in Poughkeepsie in part thanks to Vassar Female College, established not long after the brothers opened their doors. They regularly made pictures of the college's founder, the wealthy former brewer Matthew Vassar, as well as official images of faculty members, both male and female, and many buildings on the growing campus. This ongoing association was an inspiration to some at the school, which soon began suggesting photography as a practical use of artistic talent.

"Women have long printed photographs, retouched negatives, and colored vignettes with an excellent finish," noted a college miscellany published during Slee Brothers' heyday in Poughkeepsie, "and now — here I expect to shock the nerves of the sensitive—some are taking charge of photographic galleries. 'A lady photographer!' it is exclaimed, 'may the fates deliver us!' Yes, it is a pity to change . . . It will require time, but photography promises to be one of the most appropriate occupations for women."

William Slee was not opposed to such inevitable social changes, nor to innovative uses of his art. He had been moved to investigate Mumler much as Tooker and Hickey had, though for reasons of professional curiosity rather than civic duty or theological pique.

"Have you had any experience with regard to this so-called spirit photography?" Mumler's attorney Albert Day asked.

"Yes, sir," Slee said. "I visited Mr. Mumler's gallery to see what I might learn with regard to it. I went to the premises of 630 Broadway on invitation of Mumler, and also for the purpose of thoroughly examining the process of taking spiritual photographs as closely and minutely as I possibly could. Mr. Mumler sat me three different times, and each time I watched him very closely, and also closely scrutinized the process of taking the photograph. I did not notice anything unusual or different from the regular process in the operation, with the exception that I remarked that he put his hand on the camera, that was the only unusual thing I noticed. On a subsequent occasion, Mr Mumler visited me at my gallery in Poughkeepsie, and then I told Mr. Mumler that I was anxious to see—"

"Objection," prosecutor Gerry said. Anything that transpired in Poughkeepsie, he insisted, should be inadmissible. The complaint against Mumler had concerned only his actions in New York City.

"I have no objection to allow the widest possible latitude to the elucidation of this singular case," Judge Dowling responded, "and for the purpose of getting out all the facts connected with it."

But Gerry persisted: "The question of what transpired at the witness's gallery at Poughkeepsie is totally irrelevant to the issue before the court," he said. "The question now under discussion is as to what transpired at the defendant's gallery at Broadway."

"The only way of getting at all the facts," Dowling repeated with some impatience, "is to allow the fullest latitude at this investigation."

His opponent duly chastened, Day resumed his line of questioning.

"What occurred on the occasion of Mr. Mumler's visit to your place of business in Poughkeepsie?"

"Mr. Mumler called on me at my gallery," Slee said, "and used my materials during the process of the sittings that ensued from beginning to end, including my camera, chemicals, glass, and all other appliances necessary to the production of photographs. During his subsequent operations I watched him intensely, and the only unusual circumstances that I observed was his placing his hands on the camera, as I had before observed in New York, and the spirit photographs were produced."

When Day had finished with his expert witness, Gerry rose to ask questions of his own, which at first had little to do with photography.

"Are you a believer in the existence of spirits in the popular sense of the term?"

"Objection," Day said. "The question and answer are not material for the inquiry."

"Oh, I know spirits are not material." Gerry laughed. "Material or immaterial as spirits may be, I submit my question is material and bears upon the issue."

Dowling agreed to admit the question.

"I don't believe in anything I don't see evidence of," Slee answered.

"Do you believe in the existence of spirits?" Gerry asked again.

"Do you mean ardent or liquor spirits?"

"Come, sir. You understand what spirits I mean. I don't mean alcoholic spirits, nor spirits from the vasty deep that won't come. Answer the question."

"Witness," the judge interjected, "the question has nothing to do with the popular beverage known as ardent spirits. You are asked if you believe in the existence of spirits in the popular use of the term."

"That's what puzzles me, your honor," Slee said. "More people, to my mind, believe in alcoholic spirits that in any other kind of spirits. But if counsel means spirits from the other world, I answer I do not fully believe in Spiritualism."

"Are you a Spiritualist, sir?" Gerry asked. "Yes or no. Answer."

"I hardly know in what degree of Spiritualism you mean."

"Are you a Spiritualist in any degree?"

"I am. I believe in the spiritual manifestations I have seen."

"Do you believe in spirit photography?"

"Yes, I do."

"What else in the way of spirits do you believe?"

"Well, that is again pretty general. There are a great many kinds of spirits."

"I speak of spirit manifestations."

Slee now spoke slowly, measuring his words. "Well, spirits, as a general thing, operate differently on individuals. I have seen spirit manifestations produced by some power beyond the control of human agency."

"How long have you been a believer in this spiritual power or agency that you allude to?"

"Several years."

"Prior to the date when you called upon Mr. Mumler, had you ever attempted to take spiritual photographs yourself?"

"No."

"After you went to see Mumler experiment on these spirit

photographs, did you go into a darkroom and see the collodion put on the plates?"

"Yes."

"And did you examine the collodion put on the plates?"

"Yes."

"Did you examine the plates before the collodion was poured?"

"I saw him clean the plates."

"Did you examine the plates in the light?"

"I saw him prepare the plates."

"But you did not examine the plates yourself?"

"No."

Gerry walked Slee through the entire elaborate process, demanding to know which side of the glass plates had been submerged in the cyanide bath, how they were placed in the camera's plate holder, and how long each image was exposed.

"How long was the glass allowed to remain in the camera?" Gerry asked.

"I think twenty-five seconds," Slee said.

"And is that not five seconds longer than the usual time?"

"No. I think from twenty to forty seconds is the average time."

Then the prosecutor changed course. He produced a photograph showing an image much like the ones Mumler had made: a clear seated figure in the foreground, shadowed by a ghostly shape lingering behind and above.

"Look at that," Gerry demanded, "and say if that can be produced by mechanical means."

"Objection," Albert Day said. The photograph was not one of Mumler's, yet now it was being examined as if it were a crucial piece of evidence.

"The witness was placed on the stand as an expert," Gerry said, "and as an expert his opinion is admissible on this point."

"Overruled," Judge Dowling said.

For a long moment, Slee studied the photograph in his hands.

The scientific processes to which he had devoted the past decade of his life were almost limitless in the effects they could achieve. In their studio in Poughkeepsie he and his brother had mastered the craft of affixing perfect images to any smooth surface. For the college's astronomy department he had even begun taking pictures of the sun, a task requiring just the right composition, calculations, and talent to produce an image no frail human eye could otherwise look upon. A skilled operator could create any image desired; was that not a testimony to his art's potential?

"Look at that," Gerry said again, "and state if such a picture could be produced by chemical means."

"It would be difficult," Slee admitted, "but I think it could."

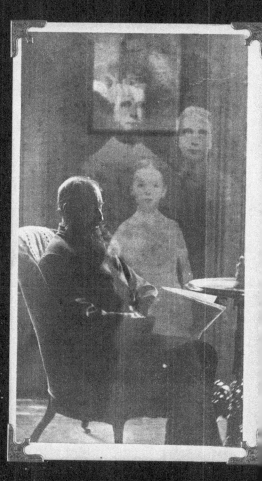

Unidentified man with three spirit images of childr[...]
William Mumler, 1862–1875.

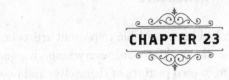

CHAPTER 23

AN OLD, MOTH-EATEN CLOAK

THOUGH CALLED AS a witness to speak on William Mumler's behalf, miniature artist Samuel Fanshaw had ample reason to dislike the accused. To Fanshaw, a man like Mumler might have represented not only the demise of his profession, but a mockery of even more personal pain. Yet the artist had become a believer in the powers of the photographer seated before Judge Dowling.

Before the rise of studio photography in the middle of the century, and particularly of the inexpensive, playing-card-size cartes de visite, only Americans of means could afford to commission images of themselves and their loved ones. They did so mainly through the services of miniature portrait painters like Fanshaw, artists whose skill was the compression of detail onto surfaces a quarter or a tenth the size of the subject, and often considerably smaller.

For decades, miniatures were hugely popular among the upper crust, but most of the practitioners of the art had taken it up solely as a practical matter. As an early-twentieth-century history of New York put it, "Lack of appreciation of art for its own sake" had "restricted painters to the field of portraiture." Artists lucky enough to find themselves in the picturesque northern portions of the state might aspire to create the grand, light-filled landscapes of the Hudson River School. Closer to the city, the choice painters faced was either to act as a mirror to the rich, or to starve among the poor.

At least that choice had been available to portrait artists before photography came along. Afterward, everything changed about those who wanted to own pictures of themselves and how they went about getting them. For a time, miniature artists attempted to mimic the sharp features of the daguerreotype in hopes of competing, but this was a lost cause. "The miniature in the presence of the photograph was like a bird before a snake," one art historian said; "it was fascinated—even to the fatal point of imitation—then it was swallowed."

A dapper man of fifty-five from Westchester County, Fanshaw looked if not swallowed, then certainly stricken. He wore a look of loss about him, but modeled it with an aesthete's easy grace. According to a biographical note in an overview of the New York art world written shortly after his death, "In his earlier professional life, he was a prominent member of the group of clever artists which included Shumway, White, Officer, Cummings, Newcombe and others"—the cream of the city's painting scene in the 1840s. Prospering for a time, he had "successfully practiced the then favourable and fashionable art of Miniature Painting." Through the middle decades of the century, "many graceful portraits from his facile pencil" had been displayed in exhibitions throughout the city.

But then the world turned. Even his formidable skill was no match for the fine detail and endless reproducibility of images made by a camera. "Upon the decline and practical extinction of his charming art through the advent of the Photograph," his biographer noted, "he, like others in his special walk, adapted himself to the altered demands of the age." He became a colorist peddling "improved photographs," resigned to a life spent dabbing tinted ink on images made by others.

Obsolete though his talents now were, he had been called to testify in court precisely for his expertise in making images uncanny in their resemblance to reality.

"I am a miniature and portrait painter," he said in response to defense attorney Day's first question, "and have been such for thirty-five years."

During this long career, one of the most popular services miniature painters offered was the memorial portrait: small keepsake images often set in brooches and worn as jewelry as a form of decorative mourning. A gifted painter could capture the spirit of a deceased relative so completely that the portrait would serve as a tool not only of remembrance but of genuine solace. With rumors of the possibilities of spirit photography spreading through the city, even this niche seemed to be closing.

Like others before him, Fanshaw had gone to the gallery at 630 Broadway to investigate, specifically to see if the images in question could have been created through some clever combination of painting and photography. But he did not detect a miniature artist's hand in Mumler's ghosts. "A picture copied from a picture would not be blurred like those of Mr. Mumler's spirit, but distinct, though faint," he said.

Nor did he see evidence of any mechanical manipulation. "I sat for my picture, watching Mumler's operations carefully," he explained. Most of the spirit photographs he had seen showed subjects facing the camera full on, but he suspected doing so might allow hidden props to be moved into view behind him by means of levers or pulleys operating without his knowledge. Fanshaw insisted his photograph should be taken in profile, so that he could keep one eye trained in each direction.

"I looked all round the room," he added, "but detected no machinery."

After the sitting, Mumler presented Fanshaw with the glass plate, which showed a form other than his own.

And did he recognize the image put before him? Day asked.

"I recognized it as my mother, and my sisters have recognized it in the printed picture. She was sixty-five when she died," he said. "Dead twenty-eight years."

He knew her face well, not only as a son, but as an artist. A posthumous portrait he had painted of her hung in his studio; he looked at it every day. But it was not possible, he insisted, that the photographer had made use of this other image. "The spirit picture is in a different position," he said, and it represented his mother during her last illness, rather than the more youthful portrait he had made from memory.

Mr. Gerry for the prosecution rose to press the witness on the pictures in question, which Fanshaw then displayed for the court. One showed himself in the foreground with the figure of a frail, gray-haired woman floating behind him. The other showed the same profile view of the miniature artist, but now accompanied by a less distinct image—less a human form than a blur of light.

With images he found plainly preposterous on view, Gerry asked the witness about the beliefs that might have inspired his credulity. Was he, too, a Spiritualist, like so many others willing to speak on Mumler's behalf?

"I am not a Spiritualist," Fanshaw insisted. "I believe what the Bible teaches concerning spirits."

This, too, Gerry found to strain the bounds of reason. Scripture says a great many things about communication with the dead, most of it far from positive. The book of Deuteronomy makes it plain: "There shall not be found among you any one," it says, "that useth divination, or an observer of times, or an enchanter, or a witch, or a charmer, or a consulter with familiar spirits, or a wizard, or a necromancer. For all that do these things are an abomination unto the Lord."

By any interpretation of this passage, Mumler seemed to qualify as an abomination best to be avoided. But another biblical teaching on spirits—the one Fanshaw likely had in mind

—came from the First Book of Samuel, in which Saul, the first king of Israel, visits a medium to call forth the spirit of a dead prophet and receive his blessing. Saul himself had outlawed the practice, but even so, he knew that spirits could be "brought up" at times of great need, such as occasions when battles threatened to shatter nations or destroy the land.

"Mumler took another picture," Fanshaw said, indicating the second image he had shown to the court, "on which came a likeness of my son killed in the war."

Fanshaw's son, called Sammie by friends and family, had joined the 6th New York Cavalry in the summer of 1862 along with his friend and his sister's fiancé, Gilbert Wood. The night before he died, Sammie had written home to his father about conditions so dire his boots had fallen off his feet. He had been able to carry on only by taking another pair from a dead soldier.

No sooner had Fanshaw read the note from his son than two others arrived. The first came from Sammie's commander—"In the front rank and with his noble face to the foe, Corporal Fanshaw has fallen," he wrote—the next from a comrade who had found him. "Every one who knew him mourns his loss as they would a brother," the second letter said. "Many have said with a sigh 'Poor Fanshaw! He was a man to be relied upon and he was one worthy of the name of soldier!' But now he is gone. Alas! Alas! The consequences of a cruel, cruel war."

Fanshaw would carry these letters with him through the rest of his days. Others in his family were similarly undone. His daughter Julia had been a teenager when her brother enlisted, and she carried with her a child's memory of a lost sibling for the rest of her life. She became an accomplished poet and recalled in verse what it felt like to happen upon some unexpected reminder of the man her brother had been.

If, looking through an old forgotten store
Of bygone relics, you had chanced to find
An old, moth-eaten cloak a soldier wore,
Would you, I wonder, with your eyes half blind
With tears, have knelt there on the oaken floor,
And cried and cried if you had chanced to find
An old, moth-eaten cloak a soldier wore?

If to your eyes a picture it had brought
Of a young soldier — oh! so young and brave —
Who, loving country, for that country fought,
Till at the last for her his life he gave,
I think, perhaps, like me you would have caught
It to your heart — caressed it o're and o're —
That old, moth-eaten cloak a soldier wore.

Faced with a picture of his boy not just created by his mind's eye through memory but captured and developed in Mumler's studio, how could he not believe? "Though it is not so plain as. my mother's," Fanshaw told the court, he "fully recognized" the image of his son.

Unlike the case of the photograph of the witness's long-dead mother, the prosecutor did not press the grieving man on the image associated with this still fresh wound. Gerry asked not a single question about it, letting the miniature artist rise and exit the courtroom with his sorrow and his certainty intact.

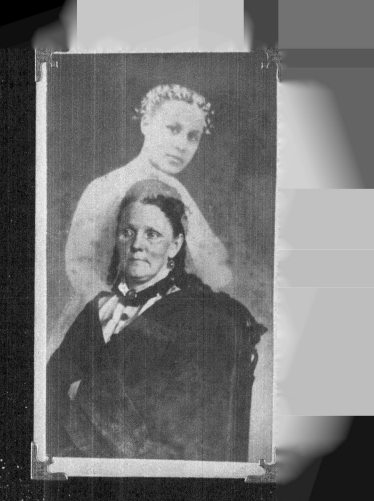

Unidentified woman with an unidentified female spirit.
William Mumler, 1862–1875.

CHAPTER 24

BY SUPERNATURAL MEANS

TESTIMONY OF DAVID A. HOPKINS

Q: Please state your occupation for the court.

A: I am a manufacturer of railway machinery.

Q: How do you know the defendant?

A: I first became acquainted with him at his gallery in Broadway; I went there for the purpose of getting a photograph taken.

Q: Did he see you right away?

A: I waited a while. Another one was having his picture taken, and then I saw Mumler. I asked him if a person sitting for a photograph had any certainty of obtaining a spirit representation.

Q: How did the defendant answer?

A: He said the matter was entirely beyond his control. Sometimes the parties got them, and sometimes they did not. He thought it probable that I would have the picture, but there was no certainty in it. I thought Mumler— before I went there— was a cheat. I then sat down and got a picture of a lady on it. I recognized the person as one who has been dead about eight months. I looked to see if there was any figure about, and I watched Mr. Mumler just as carefully as I could, but could find nothing.

Q: You did not give your name?

A: No.

Q: What was your idea in so doing?

A: I did not want to give him any clue. I must further state that to satisfy myself that I had recognized the picture, I showed it to my family and they immediately recognized it. I then showed it to the neighbors of the deceased person, and they recognized it too, and no one suggested that it might be anybody else.

Q: Do you believe in Spiritualism?

A: I have been sworn upon the Bible, and it is full of Spiritualism. If I did not believe in it, I would have to throw the Bible away.

TESTIMONY OF MRS. LUTHERIA C. REEVES

Q: Do you know the defendant?

A: I know Mr. Mumler; saw him at his gallery, 630 Broadway.

Q: Under what circumstances did you see him?

A: Mr. Charles Welling, a nephew of mine, from Vermont, went to him to investigate this matter and I went with him. The effect on him was very great. A boy of mine, who had passed away, was brought on the picture along with him.

Q: Was it recognized by you at the time?

A: The form of my deceased child appeared on the picture. It was never manipulated. I went there for a sitting myself about the end of March of the present year; it was about the middle of January I had gone with my nephew.

Q: What result was obtained at your sitting?

A: I had two sittings at the time. The form of another boy was on the picture. My boy was nearly eleven when he died.

Q: Was there any picture of your boy in existence at the time he passed away?

A: There had not been one taken for about a year and half or two years. He was very ill. He had not passed away quite a year when I went to Mumler's.

Q: Was the picture you received as representing him upon the glass at the time of the sitting with Mumler a picture of him during health or at the time he passed away?

A: He showed himself to me as he looked in health, and in the picture of my nephew he looked as at the time he died.

Q: They were distinct in appearance?

A: Yes, sir.

Q: State what occurred when you first went to that gallery?

A: There were a great many people when we first went in the room. The arrangement was made with Mrs. Mumler. I think my nephew paid her. We first saw and conversed with Mrs. Mumler; she was the one waiting on these matters. I did not state to her what I went there for. My nephew said he wanted a sitting, she entered his name on the book.

Mrs. Mumler was present at the time I was in the operation room; she came up and held her hand on the camera. Mr. Mumler came out of a side room and came with us upstairs. He then went to his closet and prepared for the sitting, there was no one else there; the sitting was done in a few minutes.

Q: How long after you had been sitting did you have an opportunity of looking at the negative?

A: He came out in a few minutes and showed the negative; I noticed no difference between the taking of pictures at Mumler's and other establishments except her putting her hand on the camera.

Q: Whereabouts on the camera did Mrs. Mumler put her hand?

A: About midway on the edge.

Q: Did she stand looking at you?

A: No, she stood looking at the floor. I remember this because I distinctly heard raps on the floor.

Q: You looked down to see where the raps were?

A: Well, I was rather curious, I suppose.

Q: How many raps did you hear?

A: I did not count them.

Q: Did they come in rapid succession?

A: I do not know what they did.

Q: Did they come slowly?

A: I could not tell; I heard them distinctly. My nephew was sitting at the time for his picture.

Q: Is your nephew a believer in spirits?

A: I can't answer for that.

Q: Are you?

A: I can't answer that question.

Q: Do you believe disembodied spirits return to revisit their relatives?

A: No, I think that is impossible. But it may be so, as long as I recognize these pictures.

Q: Were these pictures the means of converting you to that belief?

A: They are very convincing.

TESTIMONY OF WILLIAM W. SILVER

Q: Please state your occupation.

A: I was a photographer six years in the city of New York. Prior to March, I had the gallery at 630 Broadway, the same place where Mr. Mumler carries on his business.

Q: When did you become acquainted with the defendant?

A: I first saw Mr. Mumler at No. 630 about the 1st November last; he called there for the purpose of making arrangements with me for the place to take spirit-pictures. At the time of calling there I was not a Spiritualist; I rented the place to him at that time, and I sold out to him finally about the 1st March last, since which time I have not been engaged there. I had a sitting for a picture some time in November; I sat to see what I could get, as a skeptic.

Q: What effect was produced at this sitting?

A: I had a form on the plate—a female form—which I recognized as my mother. I am not now a Spiritualist; Mumler did not bring any materials with him to my gallery, but purchased mine; the camera he is now using belonged to me before I finally sold out; I used to purchase all the materials, and prepared everything; I had no manifestations upon my pictures prior to his coming; when he first came he took the picture I refer to. During the time intervening between the first interview and the coming of Mr. Mumler (something about a week) he had no opportunity of manipulating the instrument; he had not been in the place; I have been present when he took other pictures several times, and have watched the process he went through as closely as I could; I have seen him coat the plate with collodion, put it into the bath, and put it into the camera; I also saw him take the plate from the camera, and followed him into the dark room and saw him develop it; I saw the whole manipulation, from the beginning to the end.

Q: Did you detect at any time anything that looked like fraud or deception on his part?

A: No.

Q: Have you ever known of pictures through that camera having been made with a form upon them when you have done the entire manipulation?

A: Yes. Pictures were formed on the plates when I went through the whole manipulation, though Mumler exposed the plate. I mean by "exposing it" that he removed the cloth from the camera.

Q: What particular act did he do while you were manipulating it?

A: He simply removed the cloth from the camera.

Q: Have you ever seen Mumler by the camera at the time these forms were exposed when he did not have his hand on the camera?

A: Yes.

Q: I will ask you, Mr. Silver, whether you can solemnly swear that there was no fraud or collusion in any way between you and Mumler in any of these performances?

A: Yes, I can. On another occasion a picture was taken at the suggestion of Mumler, who was trying the collodion, which I was fixing. I was sat down, Mumler removed the cloth and walked away from it, and told me to take the plate into the dark room and develop it. I did so, and a spirit form came on the plate; I was not a Spiritualist at the time nor am I now.

Q: You did not become a convert to Spiritualism, not withstanding these so-called spirit-pictures?

A: No.

Q: You do not believe altogether in the existence of spirits?

A: Well, only in these pictures. I believe in these spirit pictures certainly.

Q: You believe the impressions produced are impressions produced by supernatural means?

A: Yes.

Q: You swear to this distinctly?

A: Yes. I believe that to be the case.

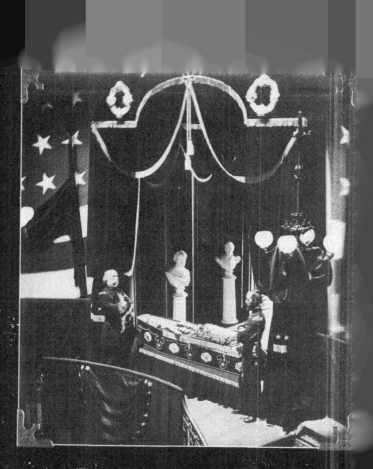

The last photograph of Abraham Lincoln.
Jeremiah Gurney, 1865.

CHAPTER 25

FIGURA VAPOROSA

TWENTY-FIVE YEARS AFTER Samuel Morse demonstrated the telegraph's ability to send messages instantly across hundreds of miles, his invention had transformed nearly every aspect of American life, and perhaps none more so than the press. In May of 1844, Morse himself had begun using his code of electromagnetic dots and dashes to send news items from Washington to a Baltimore paper within a day of demonstrating that it might be possible. A decade later, journalists transmitting stories to their editors, and newspapers sharing stories across state lines, accounted for half of all telegraphic traffic. In 1861, a transcontinental cable was completed. In 1866, the first telegraphic messages were sent across the Atlantic. This early networking of the world came at just the right time for headlines concerning the trial of William Mumler to spread around the globe, even as the spirit photographer sat in Judge Dowling's court.

In New York, a city of ten thousand con men perpetually on the make, the proceedings in the Tombs were reported largely as a tale of a crook and his likely comeuppance. The local narrative was simply that the new mayor, A. Oakey Hall, had wanted to crack down on petty crime, and had personally charged his marshal Joseph Tooker to make an example of a man whose swindle could not be more apparent. Mumler was often portrayed as dark of complexion and somewhat greasy in appearance. He and his coreligionists, according to the Manhattan papers, were vaguely foreign-seeming elements troubling the religiously homogeneous waters of polite society.

Stories about Mumler transmitted by telegraph told a different story, however. "The Mumler spirit-photography case is increasing in interest," the *Fort Wayne Daily Gazette* reported. "When a well known photographer comes up and swears that Mumler walked into his gallery without any chance for previous preparation, and then and there using an apparatus he had never before touched, produced on the spot a likeness of his deceased mother, it argues either marvelous deception on Mumler's part, marvelous lying on the part of the witness, or something of a supernatural nature in the operation. When a dozen others testify to having procured correct images of their deceased friends of Mr. Mumler, one must have considerable faith in material things to think the whole thing a humbug. We will venture to say that the jury is considerably bothered."

In South Carolina, too, the court of public opinion was proving to be considerably lenient. "A very deep interest is felt in the result of the trial of Mumler, the spirit photographer of New York," the *Charleston Daily News* noted. "The testimony taken thus far goes to show the genuineness of the pictures and to entirely exculpate the defendant from the charge of fraud. Wm. W. Silver, a photographer of six years' standing, testified on Friday that Mumler came to his gallery in November last, and that at the time he (Silver) did not believe in the spirit photographs: 'I sat to him, as a skeptic, to see what he could do; he used my apparatus and materials, and there came on the plate a form which I recognized as that of my mother. Mumler had no chance to make any preparation; have since frequently watched his processes without detecting any trick; spirit pictures have been produced when I performed all the manipulations, except that Mumler removed the cloth from the camera; have seen produced once when he did not touch the camera at all; we were trying some collodion, and he walked away from the camera after taking off the cloth; solemnly swear there was no collusion between us; I developed the plate myself and spirit picture came. I believe that these spirit photographs are produced by supernatural means.' A large number of witnesses substantiated Mr. Silver's testimony, asserting that they had received likenesses of their deceased relatives and friends."

"It is certainly very strange, and the mystery baffles all unraveling," it was reported in Wisconsin. "Eminent photographers have explored Mumler's gallery and laboratory, watched his way of producing pictures from beginning to end, and have declared that the result is unexplainable."

With the telegraph's help, papers around the country became an extension of the courtroom. The testimonies of Samuel Fanshaw and Lutheria Reeves were recounted in detail in Cleveland, while William Slee, wishing to say more than he had been given opportunity on the witness stand, wrote a letter to the *New York Tribune* that was picked up and reprinted far and wide. "I will pay $100 to any expert who will come to my rooms, and, under the same circumstances that Mr. Mumler's pictures were produced there, do the same by natural means without detection. If he succeeds, and can give a satisfactory explanation of the matter, I will promptly acknowledge the fact to the world, and thank him for the solution of a mystery beyond my comprehension."

Mumler's name soon became known in the press in England, France, Australia, and Spain, where tales of the photographer's "figura vaporosa" were treated far more credulously than closer to home.

IN THE COURTROOM ITSELF, ghostly figures began to materialize from photography's past.

By the time he appeared before Judge Dowling's bench,

Jeremiah Gurney was no longer the commanding figure he once had been. Through the 1850s, he had been the rival of Mathew Brady for the mantle of preeminent photographer in New York. Not only had he lost that fight by the end of the following decade, but the loss had apparently so unmoored him that he broke ranks with the city's photographic elite to serve as a witness called by Mumler's defense.

With Gurney's own studio at 707 Broadway, it was but a short walk downtown to visit Mumler, to watch the spirit photographer at work, which he did at the request of a wealthy Spiritualist shortly before the trial began. "I have been a photographer for twenty-eight years," Gurney testified. "I have witnessed Mumler's process, and although I went prepared to scrutinize everything, I could find nothing which savoured of fraud or trickery."

Gurney had been brought in as an expert on photographic technique; he did not mention that he had also lately acquired expertise as a photographer of death. He didn't need to say a word about it, however. A picture he had taken of a corpse four years earlier was among the most sought after in the country, even though no one had ever seen it.

As a lifelong New Yorker, Gurney had not had occasion during the war to bring his camera to the battlefield. Unlike Brady and Gardner, he had no studio in Washington that might have put him closer to the action. He was also a fifty-year-old survivor of mercury poisoning by the time other, younger photographers began rolling their wheeled developing labs to the front. Yet he had of course not failed to notice the acclaim that views of the hostilities had brought his rivals. And so when the war came home, he was ready.

His big moment arrived shortly after the assassination of Abraham Lincoln in April 1865. The president's death had sent photographers scrambling for images that might be used to tell the story, and Gurney had an idea that was sure to set his studio apart.

But he faced stiff competition. In the race to record events related to a national tragedy, and to reap the monetary rewards such pictures were sure to yield, Alexander Gardner's connections in the capital had given him a clear advantage.

The Scotsman was the first on the scene at Ford's Theatre to photograph the building in which John Wilkes Booth shot the president. With its windows draped in black mourning cloth and armed sentries posted before the door, the theater's façade as captured by Gardner was itself a promising memorial image, but it was not nearly so moving as the picture he made inside: the empty theater box where the night's guests of honor had sat enjoying a performance of *Our American Cousin* when the assassin put his pistol to the back of Lincoln's head.

Soon after, Gardner was asked to copy images of Booth for the War Department's Wanted poster. Then, following the shooter's death at the hands of a sergeant from the 16th New York Cavalry, he was the lone photographer allowed to enter the autopsy room. While Gardner now had privileged access to such singular scenes, his former employer Brady had to content himself with making photographs of Lincoln's funeral procession, first in Washington and then in New York. Each was a grand spectacle of grief, but neither offered the kind of picture Brady had come to strive for: the isolated instant somehow reflecting the nation as a whole. The only possible image that might do so was perhaps of Lincoln himself, but the president's lifeless body was kept under such close guard that not even Gardner had been able to secure a picture.

Gurney found his opportunity on April 24, nine days after the president's death. Lincoln's body was scheduled to lie in state in the rotunda of New York City Hall, where it would be seen by more than a hundred thousand people before it continued on to Albany and ultimately to Illinois for burial.

The face seen by so many that day was nothing like the ambitious, youthful man depicted by Mathew Brady in 1860, or even the gaunt, mournful one recorded by Gardner in 1862. "The color is leaden, almost brown," the *New York Times* reported on Lincoln's posthumous appearance. "The forehead recedes sharp and is clearly marked; the eyes deep sunk and close held upon the socket. The cheek bones, always high, are unusually prominent; the cheeks hollowed and deep pitted; the unnaturally thin lips shut tight and firm as if glued together; and the small chin covered with a slight beard, seemed pointed and sharp."

To photograph such a face—the well-known features of Abraham Lincoln turned as utterly unrecognizable as parts of the nation had become—would be to display the ultimate cost of the war as no other photographer had managed. And it was Jeremiah Gurney alone who was there to take the picture.

Given special permission to enter the rotunda before the doors were opened to the public, Gurney arranged his camera twenty feet above the body and forty feet away. Far from a close-up, the only image he could make from this distance would show the somber pageantry of the president lying in a darkened hall. Busts of Andrew Jackson and Daniel Webster peered down on the scene. On the floor, arrangements of scarlet azaleas, nasturtiums, japonicas, and orange blossoms formed a shield and a cross made entirely of flowers. At the foot of Lincoln's casket stood General Edward D. Townsend; at the head, Admiral Charles H. Davis, both men with their arms crossed as if uncertain they had made the right decision to allow a photographer to disturb this sacred moment.

Gurney worked for half an hour. He then packed up his camera and returned to 707 Broadway with a photographic prize like no other.

Word of this coup spread quickly. Late in the evening of the next day, Secretary of War Edwin M. Stanton sent an angry telegram.

WAR DEPARTMENT
Washington City
April 25, 1865 — 11.40 p.m.
Brigadier-General Townsend:

I see by the New York papers this evening that a photograph of the corpse of President Lincoln was allowed to be taken yesterday in New York. I cannot sufficiently express my surprise and disapproval of such an act while the body was in your charge. You will report what officers of the funeral escort were or ought to have been on duty at the time this was done, and immediately relieve them and order them to Washington. You will also direct the provost-marshal to go to the photographer, seize and destroy the plates and any pictures or engravings that may have been made, and consider yourself responsible if the offense is repeated.

EDWIN M. STANTON
Secretary of War

Townsend took full responsibility. "The photograph was taken while I was present, Admiral Davis being the officer immediately in charge, but it would have been my part to stop the proceedings," he wrote in response. "I regret your disapproval, but it did not strike me as objectionable under the circumstances as it was done."

Despite Gurney's protests, 707 Broadway was raided by army officers, who seized the negatives and prints for destruction. Their official justification was that Gurney had not sought approval from those with authority to grant it, and that circulating such pictures might cause distress to Mrs. Lincoln. Alternate theories immediately filled the press. "The reason assigned for this action is, that the pictures were surreptitiously obtained, no permission having been given by the War Department," the *New*

York Express noted. "No other photographers obtained pictures, and it is alleged that the seizure was brought about by disappointed rivals."

There is no evidence that either Gardner, who had recently come into Stanton's favor, or Brady, who had known Stanton for years, personally prevailed upon the secretary of war to suppress Gurney's images of Lincoln. Yet for two men then engaged in a contest to be remembered as the photographer who most fully documented the war, it would not do to have another man record one of the most significant images of the era.

For Brady especially, exerting such pressure would not have been out of the question. Considering the lengths to which he would go to remind Gurney who now ruled their profession, doing so would have been in keeping with his approach to business.

Two years later, in a last-gasp effort to reestablish his reputation, Gurney had secured for himself what he hoped would be another game-changing photograph. A quarter century after his first visit to America, Charles Dickens announced he would make a grand return to New York and Boston. On his previous visit, he had made headlines by touring the prison where Brady had his first photographic assignment, and his fame had only grown. His fans waited hours in line for tickets to every U.S. reading he had scheduled. Sensing an opportunity, Gurney had contracted with Dickens's agent, George Dolby, for the exclusive right to take and sell pictures of the celebrated author. As the *Brooklyn Eagle* reported, this did not go as planned:

DICKENS, GURNEY, AND BRADY

A few days since, the Gurneys announced with a grand flourish of trumpets a series of superb pictures of the lion of the day, accompanying the same with a card from the doughty Dolby, which said that Dickens would sit at no other establishment. Of course everybody who wanted a picture rushed to Gurney's to get it.

> What was the astonishment of the trade and the public, when the bold Brady announced with another flourish of trumpets that he too had secured superb pictures of Dickens. This made Gurney mad, Dolby faint, and Dickens irate.

Learning that Dickens's agent had struck a deal with Gurney, Brady had simply manipulated an older photograph to make it look new. He had painted in a different shirt, smoothed the author's unruly hair, and generally given a years-old image a gloss that made it seem fresh from the camera. Gurney threatened legal action, but feared the damage could not be undone. "In justification of our mercantile honor," he wrote in an open letter, "which has been assailed by the publication of editorial articles in different Metropolitan journals, which, if true would tend to place us before the public as impostors, we beg to assert thus publicly, that Mr. Charles Dickens has not, and will not sit to any other Photographers but ourselves in the United States: that any pictures of Mr. Dickens, either exposed to view or offered for sale, and not having our imprint are COPIES of pictures taken in Europe, and that any attempt to advertise them, either by payment or editorial notice, as originals, is a fraud and imposition on the public."

Though he was careful to name no names in his complaint, anyone keeping track of the growing animosity between the city's two best-known photographers would surely have grasped his implication: Mathew Brady was as phony as any other camera-wielding con man trying to pass off an image as something it was not.

THE ALLEGATIONS MADE against Brady never made it to a courtroom, but if they had, Gurney surely would have decried the use of mechanical and chemical means to alter a photograph for the purpose of fooling the public. On the whole, those who purchased images from the many photographers now hawking their services along Broadway remained unsophisticated when it came to viewing them. Given the claims of perfectly rendered detail that had attended the art since the days of Daguerre and Morse, the notion that photographs were not objective reflections of reality was difficult for many to grasp. Had he been able to face Brady in court, Gurney likely would have tried to make all of this clear.

His testimony in the Mumler affair had the opposite effect. Though he was particularly attuned to the ways in which the photographic process could be used to present fiction as if it were fact, he had found nothing amiss when he shadowed the spirit photographer in his labors. "It was the usual process of preparing a plate for taking a photograph," Gurney said. "The only thing out of the usual routine being the fact that the operator kept his hand on the camera. I have no belief as to the spiritual emanation of these photographs; on the contrary, I believe, although I cannot assert positively, that they are produced by purely natural means."

To determine just what these natural means might be, the prosecution called a parade of photographers to the stand to suggest possible methods Mumler might have used. Representing the American Photographic Society, two veteran practitioners of the art, Oscar Mason and Charles Hull, testified that they themselves could produce ghostly images through means far from otherworldly.

Mason, the secretary of the Photographic Section of the American Institute at the Cooper Union, displayed an example depicting a female apparition and described his method. "The effect was produced," he said, "by taking the negative of a lady and making a positive of it. This was subsequently used in making a spirit picture on a photograph. It is very easy to deceive almost anyone."

Hull, a soap manufacturer by trade who had made photography his avocation for eleven years, explaining that he had written many scientific articles on the subject, offered several possible explanations. For example, he said, "a veiled figure seated behind the sitter for an instant might produce the same effect."

Despite his assertion that he would have no more to do with the ghoul or his art, Charles Boyle, Mumler's most tireless investigator in Boston, also returned to speak out against him. Between them, the prosecution's photographic experts proposed seven ways that spirit photographs might be made:

1. The photographer might take an image on one glass plate, then keep it hidden in his camera to produce a secondary image on a new plate when it is exposed.

2. The photographer might direct an accomplice dressed in white to pose for an instant behind the sitter, obscuring himself before being detected.

3. The photographer might insert a translucent miniature image of a spirit inside the camera directly behind the lens. When light passed through the aperture, the miniature image would sufficiently distort the light to leave a "ghost" on the exposure.

4. After the photograph has been taken, while the glass plate is still sensitive, the photographer could place a spirit image behind it while re-exposing it to light.

5. The photographer might impose a blurred image on the slide while the plate is in the silver nitrate bath by means of a secret light.

6. The photographer might print the spirit image onto

paper, and then reuse that paper to print a new image of the sitter on top of it.

7. A glass plate used to take the image of one person may simply be prepared and used again without sufficiently washing off the pre-existing image.

To all of these explanations, Mumler's defense team listened patiently. Attorney Townsend then calmly pointed out that they never argued that spirit photographs could not be produced by such means. The fact remained, however, that as Jeremiah Gurney's testimony indicated, the prosecution had not proven that Mumler had used any of them.

As the *New York Tribune* summed up the trial's proceedings: "The actual developments of the case, thus far, may be briefly stated. It is shown that the so-called spirit photographs *can* be produced by ordinary photographic appliances, and that this may be accomplished by experts so dexterously as to defy detection. It is shown that several such experts have produced such pictures. It is shown that Mumler did produce some, years ago, which were almost if not quite admitted by the parties concerned to be deceptions. But it is *not* shown that the pictures in question are not genuine portraits of spirits."

The prosecution was not done, however. As if in personal rebuke to Gurney both for siding with Mumler and for making images of Lincoln's corpse years before, prosecutor Elbridge Gerry next called the photographer Abraham Bogardus to the stand.

Bogardus had operated a studio on Broadway as long as Gurney himself, and like the other experts testified that he had been able to produce a photograph nearly identical to those now at the center of the controversy. Entered into evidence, Bogardus's picture showed none other than the famous showman P. T. Barnum with a faint image of the late president floating above his head. The incongruous combination, with its implication that the spirit of the man whose memory was already held sacred would visit a known huckster like Barnum, filled the courtroom with raucous laughter, which Judge Dowling did his best to quell.

The impression created by Bogardus's image that spirit photographs were necessarily irreverent was a genuine problem for the defense. It suggested that Mumler held the beliefs of the majority of his countrymen in contempt, and created his blasphemous photographs for spite as well as profit. Townsend set to work turning this assumption on its head.

Knowing Bogardus to be an ardent Christian, he wondered whether there was much of a difference between the beliefs supporting Mumler's work and the photographer's own.

"Are you a believer in the Bible?" Townsend asked.

"Yes, I am thoroughly," the photographer answered.

"Allow me to read from 1 Samuel 28, third verse to the seventeenth verse."

Before Judge Dowling or opposing counsel could question its relevance, Townsend opened a Bible and began to recite a lengthy passage of scripture. He had previously alluded to the story, but now declaimed it as if it provided irrefutable evidence supporting his client's claims.

> Now Samuel was dead, and all Israel had lamented him and buried him in Ramah, his own city. And Saul had removed from the land those who were mediums and spiritists. So the Philistines gathered together and came and camped in Shunem; and Saul gathered all Israel together and they camped in Gilboa. When Saul saw the camp of the Philistines, he was afraid and his heart trembled greatly. When Saul inquired of the Lord, the Lord did not answer him, either by dreams or by Urim or by prophets. Then Saul said to his servants, "Seek for me a woman who is a medium, that I may go to her and inquire of her." And his servants said to him, "Behold, there is a woman who is a medium at Endor."

Then Saul disguised himself by putting on other clothes, and went, he and two men with him, and they came to the woman by night; and he said, "Conjure up for me, please, and bring up for me whom I shall name to you." But the woman said to him, "Behold, you know what Saul has done, how he has cut off those who are mediums and spiritists from the land. Why are you then laying a snare for my life to bring about my death?" Saul vowed to her by the Lord, saying, "As the Lord lives, no punishment shall come upon you for this thing." Then the woman said, "Whom shall I bring up for you?" And he said, "Bring up Samuel for me." When the woman saw Samuel, she cried out with a loud voice; and the woman spoke to Saul, saying, "Why have you deceived me? For you are Saul." The king said to her, "Do not be afraid; but what do you see?" And the woman said to Saul, "I see a divine being coming up out of the earth." He said to her, "What is his form?" And she said, "An old man is coming up, and he is wrapped with a robe." And Saul knew that it was Samuel, and he bowed with his face to the ground and did homage.

Then Samuel said to Saul, "Why have you disturbed me by bringing me up?"

"Now, sir," Townsend continued, "that spirit, or whatever it was, if it was true, had language and appearance, had it not?"

From the prosecutor's desk, Gerry called out, "I object to the question. I do not oppose my learned friend reading from the Bible in court, because there is as much good to be learned from it by a lawyer conducting a case or in the privacy of one's closet. But when it goes to the purpose of confounding a witness, and for the purpose of putting theological questions, a witness not skilled might render an answer which would not be proper. I defy him to produce a precedent for such a course."

Judge Dowling considered the objection. "The Bible has been read as an authority before the jury," he said, "but I have never known it to be brought up before a witness on the stand, and I do not intend to permit it."

"I have not asked a question yet," Townsend complained.

"You ask him his belief," Judge Dowling answered.

"I have not asked any question touching his theological knowledge," Townsend said. "I ask him only as a photographer."

"He need not answer."

"I put the question, and take the exception."

"What is the question?"

"The question is, if in the reading of that, if the spirit appeared with form and language, would there lie anything remarkable if photography had been introduced and had taken the image?"

Prosecutor Gerry laughed. "What an absurd theory! Every well-read man—"

"I have overruled it," the judge said.

But Townsend pressed on. "Now, I propose to offer particular texts at once, to save time, so that it may appear upon the record, so that—"

Dowling cut him off. "You can offer the whole Bible and I will accept it."

Undeterred, Townsend referred to his notes and suggested a litany of scriptural references he claimed would support his case.

"I offer these: the sixteenth chapter of Genesis, as showing appearances in the form of spirits; also the nineteenth chapter of Genesis, first verse; the twenty-first chapter of Genesis, verses 17–19; the twenty-second chapter of Genesis, 10–19; the twenty-second chapter of Numbers, 21–35; the fifth chapter of Joshua, 13–15; the sixth chapter of Judges, 11–23; the thirteenth chapter of Judges, 2–22; the twenty-eighth chapter of 1 Samuel, 3–17; the nineteenth chapter of 1 Kings, 5–8; the first chapter of Ezekiel, 4–6; the seventeenth chapter of Saint Matthew, 1–4; the twenty-seventh chapter of Saint Matthew, 53–54; the twenty-eighth chapter of Saint Matthew, 1–8; the first chapter of the Acts of the Apostles, 9–11; the fifth chapter of Acts, 18–21; the tenth chapter of Acts, 1–5 and 15; and 1 Corinthians, forty-fourth verse."

Mumler's lawyer had held forth on the Bible for far longer

than anyone could have expected. Doing so, he not only put the question before the court of what exactly Christians should find so objectionable about the beliefs to which Mumler's photographs attested, but hinted at a concern no one had dared to mention: why had belief become the focus of this trial?

"That is all I desire to ask," he said.

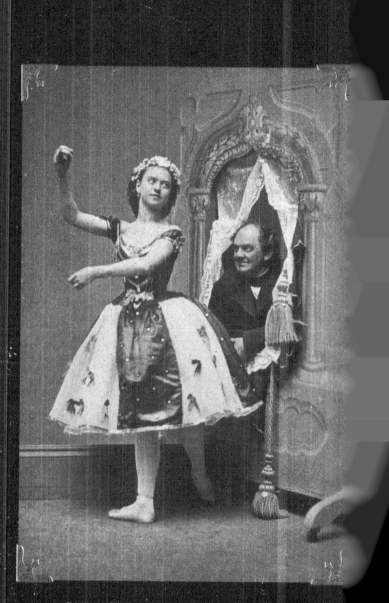

Phineas T. Barnum and Ernestine de Faiber.
Mathew Brady, 1864.

CHAPTER 26

THEY PAID THEIR MONEY,
AND THEY HAD THEIR CHOICE

"DO YOU BELIEVE in spooks?"

The prosecutor's question had been asked and answered in a variety of ways throughout the trial, but posed to P. T. Barnum—expert on all manner of frauds and the people who create them—it finally laid bare the stakes of the proceedings. If the dead truly could make contact with the living, then Mumler's claims were in the realm of the possible; if they could not, then all the experiences of those who had spoken on his behalf were either delusions or lies.

Barrel-chested, avuncular, and flashing an impish grin, Barnum weighed the question, then said simply, "I do."

It was surely not the answer expected from the state's surprise star witness. He let it linger only a moment before complicating his response. Reluctant to lose any of the audience that now sat in rapt attention, Barnum added for the benefit of skeptics a winking suggestion of his awareness of the obvious childishness of the idea.

"It is very easy to see them, if you only believe in them," he said. "When I was a boy I believed in them, and saw lots of them."

The testimony that followed danced around the question he had just implied: which comes first, the seeing or the believing? On this point, the showman would not be pinned down. He had made his career blurring the lines between perception and reality, and he wasn't about to play it straight now.

Despite his coy performance in Judge Dowling's court, Barnum was no Spiritualist. Far from it; a few years earlier, he had written a great deal against such beliefs. During the war years, the nation's apparent need to commune with the dead had become so intense that he was moved to comment on it at length. As a result of his provocations, he was now Spiritualism's Public Enemy Number One. Many adherents had become "much exercised in their minds by my letters about them," Barnum lamented with tongue-in-cheek chagrin. "Some of them fly out at me very much as bumble-bees do at one who stirs up their nest."

The Spiritualists had caused him trouble, but he couldn't help himself when it came to debunking their claims. He regarded table rappers and behind-the-curtain whisperers with the disdain of a master cabinetmaker confronted with a cobbled together scrap-wood box. The amateurish execution of most Spiritualist performances was to Barnum an insult to the humbugger's craft. "I have devoted a portion of my life to the detection of humbugs," he explained when prosecutor Gerry asked how he first became aware of the spirit photography phenomenon. "I have never had a personal interview with Mr. Mumler. I have known him by reputation for seven years. I had some correspondence with him. I do not know where the letters are now, but I think perhaps they burned in the museum."

Barnum had followed the rise of Spiritualism closely for more than a decade, and took particular note when one of the owners of the jewelry firm where Mumler once worked, Bigelow Brothers & Kennard, had told him that a former employee had left engraving behind for the more lucrative art of photographing ghosts.

"I wrote to Mumler saying that I wished to expose all the humbugs of the world. He sent me a lot of photographs," Barnum said, "and I paid him about ten dollars apiece."

Though he had displayed these images proudly in the Ameri-

can Museum, he did not think much of them. They were not singular works of a genius of flimflam, but rather easily reproducible
by anyone who knew his way around a darkroom.

"I went to Mr. Bogardus yesterday and asked him to take my
photograph with a spirit on it," Barnum said. As the respected
photographer had testified, he had done so without difficulty. Yet
for a layman like himself, as for most of those who purchased
Mumler's works, how the trick was done was not immediately
apparent. "I could detect no fraud on his part, although I watched
him closely," he said of his time in Bogardus's studio. But nor was
he tempted to believe there was anything remotely supernatural
involved. "The spirit on my photograph was that of the departed
Abraham Lincoln," he said as the courtroom filled with laughter.
"I didn't feel any spiritual presence."

When the defense's turn to question Barnum came, Townsend
wasted no time. He asked why Barnum ought to be trusted when
he had said himself that he was in the humbug business. His
greatest successes as a showman—such as the Feejee Mermaid
and Joice Heth, the unfortunate enslaved woman represented as
George Washington's nursemaid—had been clear deceptions.
How could the stories he told about Mumler be trusted now?

"I have never been in the humbug business," Barnum pro-
tested. "I have always given the people the worth for their money.

"The mermaid was represented to me to be what I represented it to be to the public, and I have never been disabused of
the idea," he said. "I have never taken money for things I misrep-
resented. I may have draped one or two of my curiosities slightly.
The nurse of General Washington was bona fide. I paid $1,000
for her. I believed in her at first, but subsequently *may* have had
a little doubt about her. I never put myself out of the way to dis-
abuse the public, even after I began to doubt the genuineness of
the old lady."

His role as an entertainer, he explained, was only to present phenomena that might require his audience to reconsider their understanding of the world. "They paid their money, and they had their choice. I never showed anything that did not give the people their money's worth four times over. These pictures that I exhibited, I did so as a humbug, and not as a reality—not like this man who takes ten dollars from people."

Unrepentant charlatan though he was, Barnum had a clear sense of when a moral line had been crossed in the making of claims that beggared belief. "If people declare that they privately communicate with or are influenced to write or speak by invisible spirits, I cannot prove that they are deceived or are attempting to deceive me," he said of Mumler's work. "But when they pretend to give me communications from departed spirits, I pronounce all such pretensions ridiculous."

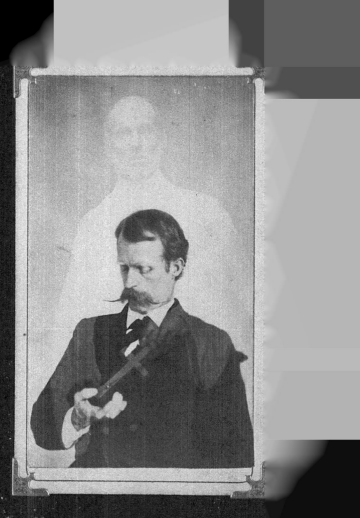

The medium Harry Gordon with a spirit image handing h
William H. Mumler, 1862–1875.

CHAPTER 27

THOSE MORTALS GIFTED
WITH THE POWER OF SEEING

THE THIRD OF MAY was a fine spring Monday in Manhattan, the kind of day one might see sunlight brighten the trunks of the newly green sweetgums in Central Park, or even the faux Egyptian columns of the downtown courthouse, and wonder how it had ever been winter. There could be a sense of certainty on such mornings, despite all experience, that the lingering darkness of the colder months would never return.

Judge Joseph Dowling awoke that morning with such a sense of certainty. He had first set eyes on William Mumler three weeks before, and since then his courtroom had been the subject of dozens of newspaper stories, few of them presenting Dowling's handling of the trial in a positive light. Despite years on the bench dispensing hard justice to the city's worst criminals, it now seemed as if he would be remembered not as a respected police magistrate but as the grand marshal of a Halloween parade.

More than a month after the spirit photographer's gambit had made its debut in the press, journalists were still finding ways to peddle his story—perhaps profiting more from the ruse than Mumler himself.

Far more than he could have anticipated, Dowling had put himself at the center of this drama. For weeks now, he had been on the receiving end of complaints of all kinds. One woman wrote to him greatly agitated that the case was "the first time our belief has been made the subject of a judicial determination." In her estimation, the judge himself would be responsible for the resulting implications for her faith.

This sort of thing came with the territory for a man in Dowling's position. You could not wield the authority to send men to Sing Sing or Blackwell's Island without being subject to accusations and threats now and then. Yet it was not often he was told that the dead would be watching.

"Let me say to you that a great responsibility rests upon you," the woman's letter continued. "Your decision, which will no doubt be given after a careful consideration of the subject, will be looked after by the 'spiritual world' with more than ordinary anxiety."

Of course, he had brought this upon himself by agreeing to hear Mumler's case, but now Dowling was done with ghost stories. His city had talked long enough of death. When he called court to order at ten that Monday morning, he instructed the attorneys for both sides to deliver their concluding remarks. As soon as they had finished, he would offer judgment.

As protocol dictated, John Townsend rose first to speak for the defense. He began by asking why a relatively minor crime had come to receive such outsized attention. "The case under investigation is one that has excited more than ordinary interest," he said. "Not only because of its intrinsic merit, but because of the grave charges in which it involved my client. Public attention was not, however, exclusively directed to the prisoner. The interest in the case has spread itself among those who have religious views differing materially from those entertained by the community generally.

"I will, therefore, direct the mind of the court, in the first place, to the legal aspect of the case, and subsequently will touch upon the belief popularly known as Spiritualism. I am compelled to do this because the question as to what is the belief of Spiritualists has been introduced into this examination, and I should do it, too, for the purpose of showing that there is nothing in the Spiritualistic doctrine that should tend in any way to throw doubt or suspicion on the testimony adduced for the defense.

"Mumler may be wrong in saying he can give a spirit picture," Townsend said, "but that does not constitute a crime, unless he knew he could not give one." The charge against Mumler, the lawyer continued, rested on the accusation that the city marshal Tooker had been defrauded by the photographer because he had paid for a spirit photograph and did not receive one. "When Tooker visited the gallery, he asked if a spirit picture would be guaranteed him, and he was told it would not. Tooker himself expressly swears, on the stand, that Mumler would not and did not guarantee any such thing.

"Mumler is charged with fraud because the prosecution cannot understand how the spirit form was produced; and owing to the fact that Tooker and those who testify on the part of the People are unable to account for the appearance of these shadowy forms, therefore it is sought to hunt down the prisoner, and fix on him the brand of cheat and humbug.

"Suppose, when Morse was struggling to put before the world the great fact that by means of electricity communication might be had on the instant between persons hundreds of miles apart, some skeptic should have asked to have a message sent from New York to Boston; that Mr. Morse, confident of the truth of his discovery, should attempt to send the message, but that owing to some cause not clearly known to him, the continuity should be broken, and the attempt to transmit the message should fail. Would such a failure be counted as a fraud by any court in Christendom?

"And yet Mumler is charged with fraud because the spirit figure which appeared on Tooker's photograph is not recognized by Tooker as being the representation of any person known to him. Then, again, when these forms are recognized, the recognition is attributed to insanity, or something approaching thereto, which is said to characterize Spiritualists. Now, we have the authoritative statement of the Catholic Council which not long since assembled in Baltimore, called by a mandate of the Pope, that although the Christian denominations in the United States number about ten million members, there are eleven million Spiritualists in the country. Can it be alleged that all these Spiritualists are insane?

"It is singular that Mr. Mumler, if he be the man represented by the prosecution, was able to produce in his defense such unimpeachable witnesses as have testified on his behalf," Townsend argued. "Five hundred persons could have given similar testimony to those who had been called for the defense. Mr. Mumler has been here but a few months, and it is wonderful that so many respectable people would come without demand. He obtained pictures of persons dead, who had no pictures taken during life. He took these pictures sometimes without even touching the camera. There is no evidence that Mumler pretended to do what he knew to be false, and consequently the whole element of the crime is wanting.

"Whether considered in regard to the honesty with which it was given, or as the embodiment of facts that the prosecution has failed to controvert, the testimony of the defense calls for the acquittal of the prisoner.

"Now let us look at this countervailing evidence. It is proved that shadowy, ghost-like pictures can be produced by other photographers. Everybody acquainted with photography knows that to be so; it has never been denied by us.

"The experts who gave evidence for the prosecution followed the beaten track in which they had trod for so many years. Science has taught them certain facts, and they are unwilling that anyone should declare anything not fully within their comprehension. They don't believe that science can improve. Men like these would have hanged Galileo, had he lived in their day.

"If the spiritual belief is true, then we must admit that there is nothing in Mumler's works to justify the charge brought against him. Spiritualists found their belief on the Bible. If we believe in the Bible, we cannot fail to believe that spirits do appear, at times, and are palpable to the sight of those mortals gifted with the power of seeing them.

"As far as I've seen," Townsend said, "I never knew a class of people to lead more upright lives, or die happier deaths than professed Spiritualists. Spiritualism came in time to fill a gap in the religious world. People were drifting rapidly toward total neglect or unbelief when Spiritualism appeared and woke them up to the importance of the great hereafter. It was required by the necessities of the times, and if it convinced only one single person of the immortality of the soul it has served a good purpose.

"It is spreading everywhere," Townsend added in closing. "All the Barnums in existence are unable to destroy the faith of those who believe in and adhere to it."

AS TOWNSEND TOOK HIS place again beside Mumler at the defense table, Elbridge Gerry prepared himself to speak.

"May it please the court," the prosecutor began. "I have listened with great pleasure to the remarks of the learned counsel for the defense. If legal acuteness and professional ability alone would suffice to extricate this client from the consequences of his crime, they certainly have not been spared in the presentment of his cause. But while I am compelled to admire the subtlety of the argument, I shall endeavor to expose its fallacies.

"This is no private prosecution. One of the gentlemen connected with a public journal of this city—well called the *World*, from the universality of its topics—had his attention called to these so-called spirit photographs. Satisfied that a huge swindle was being perpetrated, he brought the matter to the attention of the chief magistrate of this city, who at once directed his right-hand man, his Chief Marshal, Mr. Tooker, to investigate it personally. And he did so. I insist therefore that any assertion that private malice instigated these charges is wholly without foundation.

"The prisoner at the bar, William H. Mumler, stands charged by the People with the commission of three distinct offenses; two of the grade of felony, and one of misdemeanor. First: Upon the complaint of Joseph H. Tooker, with having in the month of March 1869, designedly and by false pretenses defrauded and cheated him out of, and obtained from him, the sum of ten dollars, lawful money of the United States of America. Second: Upon further complaint of Joseph H. Tooker, with a concurrent complaint of P. V. Hickey, with having designedly, and with intent to defraud, obtained from said Tooker the sum of ten dollars, by means of gross frauds and cheats which were practiced by the prisoner habitually upon the public for the purpose of obtaining, and with the result of obtaining, sums of money from many credulous persons; and that the prisoner was therefore indictable as a cheat at common law, within the meaning of the statute. Third: Upon the complaint of Joseph H. Tooker, with concurrent complaints of P. V. Hickey, with stealing, taking, and carrying away by trick or device the sum aforesaid from Tooker, and other similar sums from other persons. This brings within the statute of larceny.

"The prisoner took the remarkable position—always a last resort in a desperate case—that the charges made against him were ostensibly true, that he did obtain money from these so-called spirit photographs, but that they were not the result of mechanics, artifices, or other means. Admitting the pretenses, admitting the receipt of money upon the credit of these pretenses, and admitting that the pretenses were made for the purpose of obtaining the money, he traversed the falsity of the pretenses. In other words, he asserts that these so-called spirit forms are produced by means wholly beyond his control, for which he cannot account, and that those means are unknown, and not human. And then, by way of logical sequence, he insists — as his learned counsel has insisted in his argument — that he is not to be punished, because he has not used deceit, or mechanism, or sleight of hand, to produce these so-called spirit pictures.

"Now, the law does not deal with the supernatural," Gerry continued. "Nor recognize it as an element in its dealing with facts. It never attributes to unusual causes results which may be accounted for by the employment of ordinary means to produce them. And hence, when, as here, an averment is made of the existence of things, knowledge of which cannot be had by means of the exercise of the physical senses, the party making the averment must prove it as made. The onus, in other words, rests on him who asserts that unnatural means did produce a natural result.

"Our law interferes with and constrains no man in the exercise of his religious belief. But it does restrain men of every opinion and creed from acts which interfere with Christian worship or which tend to revile religion and bring it into contempt. The law places the Bible in the hands of every convict in our state prisons, and it punished the use of profane or blasphemous language as a misdemeanor. And the law does not recognize any individual belief as an excuse for infringing its provisions made for the safety of the whole community. It does not exempt the Mormon who chooses to marry two wives in this state from punishment for bigamy because he is a Mormon. Nor on the other hand, if any persons believing in human sacrifices as part of their religion should attempt to sacrifice human life in that way, would they be excluded from punishment for murder upon the ground that their religious belief justified or required the act.

"When therefore, as here, a man is shown to have obtained

the money or property of others by means which the law pro-scribes as criminal, it does not permit him to plead as an excuse his religious views or belief, except so far as such a plea amounts to that of insanity.

"I do not assail nor ridicule the belief of any that the spir-its of the departed still hover around the living. But when, as here, it is gravely asserted as an existing fact that such spirits do manifest themselves visibly and audibly to the living, I insist that something more than visions seen and voices heard by only single individuals at a time must be proven to show that such vi-sions and voices are not what medical science has demonstrated them to be, the phantasms of daydreams—the rooted fancy of mind diseased.

"There is no proof of any spiritual agency, only evidence that certain persons believe it exists. Man is naturally superstitious, and in all ages of the world, impostors and cheats have taken advantage of credulity to impose on their fellows less sharp than themselves.

"A word in conclusion," Gerry said. "This case is simply one of many where an adroit criminal is attempting to evade the hand of justice, and to practice, untrammeled by fear of human con-sequences, a most wicked fraud as his livelihood. The law is not only for the protection of the strong and the prudent. It grants no license to the cunning man to deceive the simple by artifices, which he proportions to the mental strength of those with whom he had to deal just as the poisoner proportions his drugs to the bodily strength of his victims.

"The Chief Magistrate of this city, with an energy that does him honor, has determined to put a stop, if possible, to these wholesale swindles. The arm of the law should be liberally ex-tended to aid him in his efforts. And I submit to your Honor, with entire confidence, that probable cause has been shown in this case, to amply warrant the commitment here asked for."

———

BETWEEN THEM, THE ATTORNEYS working for and against Mumler had spoken for hours. Following a brief deliberation, Judge Dowling offered the final word on the spirit photographer in less than a minute. "After careful attention to the case," he said, "I have come to the conclusion that the prisoner should be discharged."

Though the crowded gallery filled with muttering gasps, Dowling pressed on through the increasing din of the courtroom, hoping to be done quickly with the unpleasant task of delivering a ruling that seemed not only to fly in the face of common sense, but to put him on the side of the odd characters who had filled the Tombs court for nearly a month. "However I might believe that trick and deception has been practiced by the prisoner, as I sit here in my capacity of magistrate, I am compelled to decide," he added with a note of resignation, "that the prosecution has failed to prove the case."

To the joy of some of the living and presumably all of the restless dead, William Mumler was free to go.

PART IV
IMAGE AND AFTERLIFE

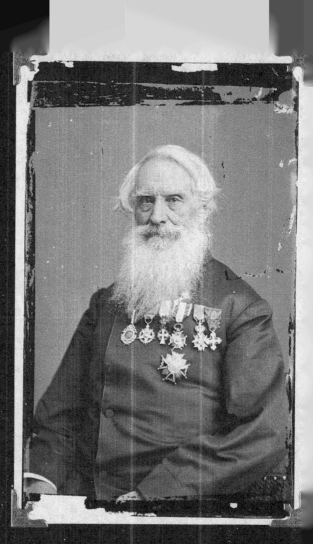

Last portrait of Samuel F. B. Morse.
Mathew Brady, 1866.

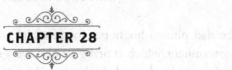

CHAPTER 28

CALM ASSURANCE
OF A HAPPY FUTURE

ON THE ROSTER of prominent photographers who appeared at the proceedings of William Mumler in the spring of 1869, several of the most famous names were conspicuously absent.

If attorneys for either the prosecution or the defense had asked him to testify, Mathew Brady may have had little interest in damaging his good reputation through association with a freak show—at least one consisting of freaks other than those he had so frequently photographed for Barnum. Or perhaps the accusations of fraud he had endured a few years before made the Mumler affair feel a bit too familiar. More likely, he stayed away simply because he was facing a trial of his own at the time.

Though he had seen far less of battle than many of the field photographers in his employ, Brady had taken on nearly all the financial risk of making a visual record of the Civil War. Outside the predictable confines of a studio with darkroom supplies readily at hand, photography could be an expensive business—so much so that by the war's end, Brady was deeply in debt.

He hoped the nation that had sung his praises as an unequaled chronicler of history might now assume some of the cost. In February, just as the press was beginning to notice Mumler's new operation on Broadway, the man whose name was synonymous with photography in the city began appealing to Congress to purchase his vast archive of plates and prints. After a similar proposal to the New-York Historical Society was rejected in 1866, he had pinned his hopes for financial salvation on the federal government, which at first gave him every indication of a positive outcome ahead. On February 13, 1869, Senator Henry Wilson of Massachusetts submitted a resolution in his behalf: "Resolved, That the Committee on the Library be instructed to inquire into the expediency of securing for preservation by the government the collection of war views and incidents photographed by Mr. M. B. Brady."

Despite assurances from Brady's many friends in government, the sale stalled repeatedly. By the time it was finalized six years later, Henry Wilson had moved on to become Ulysses S. Grant's vice president, and Brady, without a champion on Capitol Hill, received for his photographic archive a fraction of its value. His investment in the equipment and personnel required to photograph the war had totaled over $100,000; ultimately, he received only $25,000.

Enduring multiple bankruptcies and eyesight that continued to deteriorate, Brady carried on in failing health and straitened circumstances for another quarter century. Like his teacher Samuel Morse decades before, he soon lost his wife to illness, and it shook him to the core. Unlike Morse, however, Brady was by then too old to find solace in his work.

He might have taken some comfort in the myth-making stories already being told about his exploits, however. More than forty years after he made photographs for phrenologists at a lunatic asylum, and twenty years after he envisioned the possibilities of carting cameras into battle, the press began to lionize Brady as "the pioneer of the photographic art in this country." As he hoped he might be, he was remembered primarily for his efforts during the fight to save the Union. "His pictures of war views are invaluable, and during the rebellion he accompanied the armies and took photographs of their battles and the leading men in them," the *New York World* noted nine years before his death in 1896. "He has done more for history in his way than any man in the world."

Though he lived in New York throughout the Mumler trial, Samuel Morse likewise kept away from the proceedings. There is no question that they would have piqued his interest. Late in life he became obsessed with making connections between science and religion, and left a sizable sum to Union Theological Seminary to fund an annual lecture on "the relation of the Bible to any of the sciences" and "the vindication of the authenticity of the Bible against attacks made on scientific grounds." In one of the last photographs of the great inventor, Brady posed his mentor with his long white beard draped over a chestful of medals: Austria's Great Gold Medal of Science and Arts, France's Order of the Legion of Honor, a diamond-studded medallion given by the sultan of Turkey, and a half dozen other international decorations. The man who had dreamed of erasing distance succeeded in becoming known across the globe, and despite his interest in matters of the spirit, he probably would have found the Mumler affair beneath him.

Lacking Morse's laurels, Brady's former employee Alexander Gardner had left the East Coast soon after the war for another photographic adventure, taking his mobile developing studio out to the frontier to capture the American West. He was no longer drawn to pictures of mayhem, but in chronicling the rapidly contracting borders of Native American cultures, he photographed death of another sort. When he'd had enough of it, he left his camera and chemicals behind to become the president of a life insurance company.

Still a tireless worker, Gardner also learned to value leisure. On weekends, he liked to accompany a local Sunday school class on jaunts into a countryside similar to those where he had made his most famous images. The fields beside the dusty roads bloomed with thistle flowers that reminded him of the Scottish Lowlands where he had been born and raised. One day as he rambled with the children and his thoughts, a small girl appeared by his side. She held a spiky purple bloom in her hand, its stem freshly torn.

"Here's your flower!" she cried.

"Thank you, thank you, my bonnie lassie," Gardner said. "It does a Scotchman proud to his very heart."

The same flowers bloomed every fall at Antietam, but if they also reminded him of battlefields, he kept it to himself, content to have found a humble kind of utopia at last.

Other associates of Brady had not fared as well. Eliza Farnham, the Spiritualist prison matron who had given him his first job and later aspired to serve as an angel of the battlefield, found the scale and horror of death in wartime too much to bear. Shortly after leaving Gettysburg, she fell into an illness from which she did not recover. "From all who visited her during her illness," it was said, "but one testimony was given—that she rested in calm assurance of a happy future. Her faith as a Spiritualist sustained her in sickness, as it had done in health; and regarding death as a friend, and not as an enemy, she awaited the change with joyful expectancy, asking only patience to meet the delay."

Still active on the Spiritualist speaking circuit, J. W. Edmonds delivered Farnham's eulogy. Soon thereafter he began channeling the spirit George Washington, whose guidance, the judge said, was gravely needed if the nation was to rise again.

Like Brady, Jeremiah Gurney continued to take pictures almost into the new century. During life, his reputation never recovered from the business defeats he had suffered at Brady's hands, but decades later his work did find some vindication. One of the photographs he had made of the corpse of President Lincoln—long thought destroyed on the orders of Secretary of War Edwin Stanton—was discovered eighty-seven years after it was seized. Published in *Life* magazine, which then had a circulation in the millions, it instantly became the most reproduced photograph of the Civil War. Though he had never bested Brady while the two were competing to become the biggest photographer on Broadway, in death—thanks to *Life*—Gurney had finally come out on top.

Many of those caught up in the orbit of the Mumler trial were similarly transformed. Not long after his testimony in the Tombs, Marshal Joseph Tooker left law enforcement behind. He dabbled long enough in maritime shipping to earn the title Commodore, and, perhaps influenced by the remarkable drama of the spirit photographer, became a top show-business promoter. As the *New York Times* reported in 1882, "What Barnum was to the circus, Commodore Tooker was to the theater."

Barnum himself rebuilt his museum, only to see it burn again, and then ascended to unexpected respectability. He served in the Connecticut legislature and politely declined when some in the Republican Party asked him to consider running for president.

P. V. Hickey, whose complaint had set Tooker on Mumler's trail, gave up science reporting in the 1870s and devoted himself full time to publishing some of America's first Catholic magazines, as well as a series of books known as the Vatican Library. For these efforts on behalf of his faith, he was repeatedly singled out for praise by bishops throughout the United States and as far as Rome. "To further mark appreciation of these varied and continuous services," it was said in 1888, "the Holy Father was pleased to invest Chevalier Hickey with the dignity of Knight Commander of the Order of St. Gregory the Great, one of the most exalted degrees of knighthood in the gift of the Holy See."

This honor was not without irony. Saint Gregory, who was pope in the sixth century, spoke at length about spirits and drew distinctions between those with bodies and those without, and perhaps—who knows?—would have been far more convinced by Mumler's images than Hickey was. To the journalist's chagrin, similar interpretations of religious tradition also accounted for the most unexpected legacy of the fame Mumler had earned through a trial in which scripture played a central role. Seeing a marketing possibility in the uproar around spirit pictures, an enterprising American publisher soon produced an edition of the Bible with "photographic portraits of Abraham, Moses, David, Jesus Christ, and the Apostles," all attained with techniques as mysterious as Mumler's own.

Mumler's accomplice William Guay seems to have left photography behind after the charges against his employer were dropped. Though it cannot be known with certainty what became of Guay, several years later a bank clerk sharing his name in Halifax, Nova Scotia, was arrested for attempting to leave stacks of blank paper in the vault in place of cash. Given the trajectory of both his wanderings and his career, it seems likely to be the same man.

Of the legal minds who worked to determine the spirit photographer's fate for three weeks in 1869, the lead attorneys for the defense and the prosecution both went on to distinguish themselves with apparently no ill effects of having defended a swindler or lost an open-and-shut case.

In 1874, Elbridge Gerry founded the New York Society for the Prevention of Cruelty to Children, also known as the Gerry Society, which promised "to rescue little children from the cruelty and demoralization which neglect, abandonment and improper treatment engender" and "to aid by all lawful means in the enforcement of the laws intended for their protection and benefit." Those tasked with enforcing such laws, which often included rounding up truants playing in the streets, were known as "Gerrymen" and became infamous among the city's tenement dwellers as child snatchers, figures of fear rather than salvation.

Gerry's other efforts at social reform had similarly ambiguous results, and returned him for a time to lengthy discussions of death. From 1886 to 1888, he led a committee of prominent

New Yorkers to reconsider capital punishment. After looking into thirty-four methods of execution (discussed alphabetically in their published report: *dismemberment, drawing and quartering, drowning, exposure to wild beasts, flaying alive, flogging . . .*), Gerry and his colleagues determined that the current preferred means, hanging, was a medieval practice best abandoned. Much as Mumler had been inspired by science in his visions of the afterlife, Gerry turned to technology for a solution. Consulting with Thomas Edison, the Gerry Commission adopted a plan to build the first electric chair. The gallows kept ever at the ready would no longer trouble defendants brought to the Tombs.

Defense attorney John Townsend could not claim similarly broad social influence, but he did continue to build on his reputation as the Fighting Lawyer. Shortly after winning Mumler's freedom, Townsend turned his attention to corruption in the courts. His efforts ultimately brought the downfall of three members of the state judiciary and eight police magistrates, including Judge Dowling.

Among the Spiritualists, opinion regarding Mumler's legacy remained divided, but the battle lines shifted over time. In New York, the early supporter Andrew Jackson Davis eventually renounced spirit photography as a fraud, while in Boston, the formerly reticent medium Fannie Conant reconsidered.

At the *Banner of Light* offices, Conant carried on with her work of channeling the dead, including the spirit of her longtime collaborator Lieutenant William Berry, who returned just once more to her séance circle to tell his Spiritualist friends why he had not reported back from the Summerland as often as many had wished he would. It had been eight years since he had last appeared among them, and the medium hoped a final word delivered through the Message Department might help them keep from losing faith.

"At the urgent solicitations of many of my friends, I presume to occupy this place for a few moments," Conant said in the trance voice she used for Berry. "They want to know why it is that I have not returned, manifesting through the *Banner of Light*. They expected it long ago, they said. They expected much of me. They are disappointed. They thought I would bring them news that would perhaps eclipse all that they had ever obtained. They thought I was so well posted on spiritual matters here, that I should be able to do much for them." Yet despite what one might think of being dead, the afterlife could keep a man busy. "I have been largely occupied in the spirit-world being the publisher of a daily journal very much larger than the dear old *Banner*," the medium's Berry voice said. "I have an able corps of assistants ... Notwithstanding all their assistance, I have enough to do, and have found it much more profitable to stay behind the scenes."

His hectic schedule aside, Conant added, the real reason Berry had stayed away might be difficult for his mortal audience to hear: the more he had learned of the realm of the living from his privileged position outside it, the less inclined he was to help them. "I am afraid, seeing all I am able to see of their prejudices," the supposed spirit of William Berry said, "that if I were to stand too near I would be likely to use the mallet instead of moral suasion. Instead of going on month after month, and year after year, trying to prove the immortality of the soul, and the power of the soul to return after death, I should speedily open those blockheads and let the soul out where it would fly higher and see clearer. And as we spirits are largely possessed of power over matter, I might be tempted to make a bad use of it."

Berry was not heard from again in Fannie Conant's circle, but she continued giving séances until her death in 1875. Shortly before then, she had sufficiently overcome her uncertainty about Mumler's abilities to sit before his camera a number of times. There is no evidence that, upon leaving her physical body behind, she returned for the purpose of haunting his photographs.

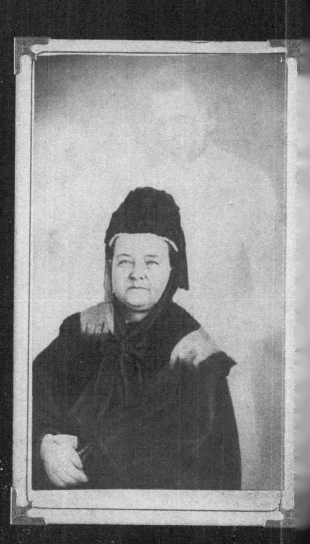

Mary Todd Lincoln with the spirit image of
her husband. William Mumler, 1872.

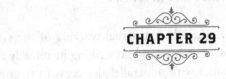

CHAPTER 29

THE MUMLER PROCESS

AFTER THE END of his ordeal in the Tombs, William Mumler seemed on course toward the same bleak financial future as Mathew Brady. He had been cleared of the charges of fraud and larceny, but his reputation was so tarnished in New York that he knew he could not remain.

He moved back to the place where it all began, Boston, and soon recommended taking spirit photographs, though now with far less fanfare. The trial had made him sufficiently well known that he could advertise his services in newspapers throughout the country and sell spirit photographs by mail, without the risks inherent in letting too many people peek behind the darkroom curtain.

As Spiritualism itself waned, the Mumlers made an effort to spread the word of Hannah's ongoing work as a healer. Updating her husband's cure for dyspepsia, Hannah began to manufacture and sell a product she called Mesmerine, "a clairvoyant remedy" that "acts on the blood through the digestive organs." In time, she had enough patients that even the mainstream press took notice.

"One of the most powerful imparters of the Life Principal (animal magnetism) is Mrs. Dr. H. F. Mumler, of this city," the *Boston Globe* reported. "By simply placing her hands upon the head of the patient, the Vital Element is felt coursing through every nerve and tissue of the body, displacing disease and imparting renewed health and vigor to the invalid. When Dr. Mumler is mesmerized, she sees the whole Internal working of the system, detecting the disease at once and prescribing its remedy ... Mrs. Dr. Mumler has met with unparalleled success in treating every form of disease, both chronic and acute, which statement is supported by the testimony and affidavits of many of our best and well-known citizens, both in public and private life."

As Hannah's star ascended in the world of healers, Mumler continued to take the occasional spirit photograph, but his interests began to wander further into the technical side of his art.

Despite the best efforts of so many investigators, no one was able to solve the riddle of exactly how Mumler had created his apparitions. One reason for this mystery was perhaps that Mumler had found new ways to control the chemical reactions on which all photography at the time depended. The ultimate fruit of his mastery of manipulation was a method of printing images directly from photographs to newsprint. The "Mumler process," as it was known, allowed printers to forgo the usual step of having a photographic plate copied by hand by an illustrator or wood engraver, revolutionizing the ability to reproduce images by the thousands.

The illustrated magazine *American Punch*, the U.S. answer to the London journal of humor and satire with a similar name, is generally regarded as a precursor to such publications as *Time* and *Life*. Though he was just the sort of character who might have received a skewering in its pages, Mumler played a role in making such publications possible. "'Punch' depends upon what is known as the 'Mumler' process of photo-engraving, and comes from the establishment of the Photo-electrotype Company of Boston," according to an 1879 description of the magazine. "This process offers numerous advantages, which, to the wood-engraver, are wholly unknown."

The editors of the publication *Facts* likewise credited him with making their work possible. "Nearly all the pictures which have been published in the *Facts* magazine during the last four years have been made by the Photo-Electrotype Company of Boston, of which Mr. Mumler was the originator and treasurer. Other companies who have the right to use Mr. Mumler's patents are doing similar business in other cities. The process makes it possible to obtain a facsimile of handwriting or any line drawing desired, at much less cost than it could be done by wood engraving. The illustrations of the daily papers are many of them made by this process in a few hours."

Mumler helped usher in a new era in which the news, until then mostly reliant on text, entered the picture business. Not only did photographs become ubiquitous, they emerged as the standard of proof for whether or not something had actually happened. Barnum would have enjoyed the irony: a likely falsifier of images played a pivotal role in the creation of the image-obsessed culture that still defines the nation.

By the time Mumler died in 1884, fifteen years after he walked free from the Tombs, he had accomplished enough that spirit photography appeared only as an afterthought in the obituary provided by the *Photographic Times:*

MR. WILLIAM H. MUMLER, a well-known inventor and treasurer of the Photo-Electrotype Company, died at his residence in Boston. He was born in Hanover Street, Boston, in 1832, and if he had lived a few days longer would have reached his fifty-second year.

He first began business as an engraver, and in the twenty years in which he followed that profession attained considerable prominence, but becoming much interested in photography, he entered that business and succeeded in securing a wide reputation as a photograph publisher. He had much inventive genius and a taste for experiment, which finally resulted in the discovery of what is known as the Mumler process, by which photo-electrotype plates are produced and as readily printed from as wood-cuts on an ordinary printing-press, and at great saving of expense. A company was formed about seven years ago, and he had been treasurer of it ever since.

He had lately been further experimenting upon improvements in dry plates for instantaneous photography, and the mental and physical strain brought on a disease which became fatal in about two weeks. The deceased at one time gained considerable notoriety in connection with spirit photographs.

It was without a doubt his "considerable notoriety" that caused his most famous subject to return to his studio.

When Mary Todd Lincoln arrived at Mumler's salon in 1872, it was the second time the former first lady had sought out the spirit photographer's services. If she had followed the court proceedings against him—which, given her interest in Spiritualism, she almost certainly had—she was apparently not put off by the impression given by many newspaper accounts that he was a grifter out to swindle the foolish or the vulnerable.

Dressed entirely in black, wearing a bonnet with a bow that obscured her face, Mrs. Lincoln clearly did not want to be recognized. The Mumlers would later claim that Hannah saw that the spirit of the martyred president had come with her, however, and so they knew immediately who she must be.

Mumler seated and posed this unexpected guest as any photographer would, folding her hands one over the other just as Mathew Brady had done for her a decade earlier, when she was bound for the White House and neither her family nor her country had known the great losses to come.

The picture she left with that day would become the most famous spirit photograph of all. It shows the former first lady sitting in the lower left corner of the frame, a faint outline of her husband seeming to comfort her from behind. He cradles her shoulders as if he is helping her on with her cloak.

To some, the photograph—the last of Mary Lincoln's life—

is evidence of either her gullibility or her madness. To others, it suggests not just the psychological damage done to one woman, but the suffering of the nation that she represents in her grief. To her, it was simply the kind of comfort that made all other meanings irrelevant.

ACKNOWLEDGMENTS

THIS BOOK WOULD not have been possible without the support and encouragement of the MacDowell Colony, which provided me with space to work and think in the early stages of writing.

I am grateful also to the Baltimore photographer John Milliker for initiating me into the mysteries of the wet-plate collodion process, and for answering many questions about the chemicals, the risks, and the art involved in making images in the nineteenth century.

The editorial team at Houghton Mifflin Harcourt, particularly Bruce Nichols, Nicole Angelero, and Larry Cooper, helped this book take shape from initial inspiration to the final draft, while throughout the process my longtime agent, Kathleen Anderson, has been as encouraging and supportive as ever.

All remaining thanks are due to my family—my wife, Gwen, and my daughters, Annick and Jeannette—for accompanying me on explorations of Civil War battlefields, indulging my interest in ghosts, and believing me when I said it was all part of the same story.

NOTES AND SOURCES

Though *The Apparitionists* is the first attempt to consider William Mumler's story in the context of early-American daguerreotypists and the photographers of the Civil War, I have relied on many books on these and other subjects to stitch together several historical strands into a single narrative.

The secondary sources to which I have turned for inspiration, leads, and understanding of the times in which Mumler lived include D. Mark Katz, *Witness to an Era: The Life and Photographs of Alexander Gardner* (Nashville: Thomas Nelson, 1999); Bob Zeller, *The Civil War in Depth* (New York: Chronicle Books, 1997); Robert Wilson, *Mathew Brady: Portraits of a Nation* (New York: Bloomsbury, 2013); Roy Meredith, *Mr. Lincoln's Camera Man: Mathew B. Brady* (New York: Scribner, 1946; Dover reprint, 1974); James W. Cook, *The Arts of Deception: Playing with Fraud in the Age of Barnum* (Cambridge: Harvard University Press, 2001); Geoffrey Batchen, *Burning with Desire: The Conception of Photography* (Cambridge: MIT Press, 1997); Martyn Jolly, *Faces of the Living Dead: The Belief in Spirit Photography* (London: British Library Board, 2006); Clément Chéroux et al., eds., *The Perfect Medium: Photography and the Occult* (New Haven: Yale University Press, 2004); Molly McGarry, *Ghosts of Futures Past* (Berkeley: University of California Press, 2012); and Louis Kaplan's collection of Mumler-related documents, *The Strange Case of William Mumler* (Minneapolis: University of Minnesota Press, 2008).

I am also indebted to other researchers on nineteenth-century Spiritualism, including Marc Demarest, whose blog *Chasing Down Emma: Resolving the Contradictions of, and Filling in the Gaps in, the Life, Work and World of Emma Hardinge Britten* (http://ehbritten .blogspot.com/) is a treasure trove of information about Spiritualists, their beliefs, and their communities. My work was also made much easier by the International Association for the Preservation of Spiritualist and Occult Periodicals (http://www.iapsop.com/), whose digitized collection of nineteenth-century newspapers served as a primary research portal for this book.

PROLOGUE

page

1 *"gray, begrimned," "the tomb of purity, order, peace, and law":* Junius Henri Browne, *The Great Metropolis: a Mirror of New York* (Hartford: American Publishing Company, 1869), 528.

2 *"fraud," "felony," "larceny": New York Tribune,* May 4, 1869.

 "The Tombs has a history": Browne, 530.

3 *"He belongs to the heavy order of the Spiritualists": Emporia Weekly News* (Kansas), May 14, 1869.

 "athletic" or "robust": "Spirit Photographs: A New and Interesting Development," *Journal of the Photographic Society of London,* January 15, 1863.

4 *"hardened and degraded creatures":* Browne, 529.

6 *"The history of all pioneers of new truths is relatively the same":* William Mumler, "The Personal Experiences of William Mumler in Spirit Photography, Part 1," reprinted in *Banner of Light* 36, no. 15 (January 9, 1875), 1.

 "every fibre of his body rebelled": "Topics of Today," *Brooklyn Daily Eagle,* April 13, 1869.

 "Spiritualism is the future church": "Spiritualism," *Brooklyn Daily Eagle,* April 13, 1869.

7 *"What is it you've got to say": New York Herald,* April 13, 1869.

8 *"The intensity of the interest":* "Spiritualism in Court," *New York Daily Tribune,* April 24, 1869.

 "The case of the people against William H. Mumler": Harper's Weekly 13, no. 645 (May 4, 1869), 289.

 "The accused does not know": "Spiritual Photography," *The Illustrated Photographer,* May 28, 1869.

1. PROCURE THE REMEDY AT ONCE AND BE WELL

14 *"A rather portly man":* Earl Marble, "The Round Table," *Folio,* September 1884, 94.

"Those desirous of making purchases": Edward Hepple Hall, *Appletons' Hand-Book of American Travel* (New York: D. Appelton & Co., 1869), 90.

"Although a self-made man": *Annual Report of the Perkins School for the Blind* (Boston: Commonwealth of Massachusetts, 1904).

15 *"I had the reputation"*: Mumler, "The Personal Experiences . . . Part 1," 1.

"being the first to introduce": Reading (Pennsylvania) *Times,* May 13, 1869.

"I am an engraver": Mumler advertisement, 1860s, reproduced by Marc Demarest in *Chasing Down Emma: Resolving the Contradictions of, and Filling in the Gaps in, the Life, Work and World of Emma Hardinge Britten,* http://ehbritten.blogspot.com/2015_03_01_archive.html.

16 *"For the cause of suffering humanity"*: Ibid.

17 *"After a man has passed"*: William Mumler, "The Personal Experiences of William Mumler in Spirit Photography, Part 2," reprinted in *Banner of Light* 36, no. 16 (January 16, 1875), 1.

"magnetism": William Mumler, "The Personal Experiences of William Mumler in Spirit Photography, Part 5," reprinted in *Banner of Light* 36, no. 22 (February 27, 1875), 3.

18 *A. M. Stuart*: Henry Augustus Willis, *The Fifty-Third Regiment Massachusetts Volunteers* (Fitchburg, MA: Press of Blanchard & Brown, 1889), 247.

"Hair braided to order": *Brooklyn Daily Eagle,* March 30, 1848.

19 *"natural clairvoyant"*: Mumler, "The Personal Experiences . . . Part 5," 3.

"What is electricity?": Ibid.

20 *"I have seen men faint"*: Ibid.

2. LOVE AND PAINTING ARE QUARRELSOME COMPANIONS

24 *"I can imagine mama wishing"*: Samuel Finley Breese Morse, *Samuel F. B. Morse, His Letters and Journals,* Vol. 1 (Boston: Houghton Mifflin, 1914), 41.

25 *"There has a ghost"*: Ibid.

"at least seven hundred dollars": Ibid., 260.

26 *"The only thing I fear"*: Ibid.

"spread perpetual sunshine": Samuel Irenæus Prime, *The Life of Samuel F. B. Morse, LL. D.: Inventor of the Electro-Magnetic Recording Telegraph* (New York: D. Appelton, 1875), 146.

"Love and painting are quarrelsome companions": Morse, *Letters and Journals*, 180.

"The more I know of her": Ibid., 240.

"I wish to see the young lady": Ibid., 207.

28 *"He is so harassed"*: Ibid., 264.

"My Dearest Wife": Samuel Morse to Lucretia Morse, Feburary 9, 1825, digital image available at https://www.loc.gov/resource/mmorse.009001/?sp=181.

"There never was a more perfect example": Morse, *Letters and Journals*, 262.

"This is Mr. Morse, the painter": Ibid., 264.

29 *"My affectionately beloved Son"*: Ibid., 265.

30 *"The confusion and derangement"*: Ibid., 268.

"Oh! What a blow!": Ibid.

31 *"I am ready almost to give up"*: Ibid., 269.

3. TIES WHICH DEATH ITSELF COULD NOT LOOSE

33 *"It sounded like someone knocking"*: "Certificate of Mrs. Margaret Fox, Wife of John D. Fox, the Occupant of the House," in Ann Leah Underhill, *The Missing Link in Modern Spiritualism* (New York: Thomas R. Knox & Company, 1885), 4.

34 *"The noises were heard"*: Ibid.

"I do not know of any way": Ibid., 10.

"unhappy, restless spirit": Ibid., 6.

35 *"There must have been a score"*: Ibid., 49.

"that disembodied human": "Modern Spiritualism," *Spiritual Magazine*, September 1869, 386.

"As for the future": Samuel Byron Brittan, lecture delivered at the Stuyvesant Institute in New York City, November 1850, http://www.iapsop.com/spirithistory/first_public_lecture_on_spiritualism.html.

36 *"I soon received letters"*: Underhill, *The Missing Link*, 49.

"I well remember the time": William Mumler, "The Personal Experiences of William Mumler in Spirit Photography, Part 4," reprinted in *Banner of Light* 36, no. 20 (February 13, 1875), 3.

38 *"in all its varied phases"*: *Banner of Light*, 1, no. 3 (April 25, 1857), 4.

39 *"Who are you talking with, mother?"*: Theodore Parker (Spirit) and John W. Day, *Biography of Mrs. J. H. Conant, the World's Medium of the Nineteenth Century* (Boston: Banner of Light, 1873), 19.

"She has been the channel": Ibid., 4.

40 *"It is a simple, straight-forward narrative"*: Ibid., 3.

"SPIRIT RAPPING AND NECROMANCY": *Baltimore Sun*, May 12, 1853.

41 *"Spiritual phenomena"*: *Household Words: A Weekly Journal*, June 5, 1853, 582.

43 *"an impressionable state"*: *Banner of Light*, quoted in Molly McGarry, *Ghosts of Futures Past: Spiritualism and the Cultural Politics of Nineteenth-Century America* (Berkeley: University of California Press, 2008), 50.

"Never in any period," "Tendrils of love have bound them": Emma Hardinge, *Modern American Spiritualism: A Twenty Years' Record of the Communion Between Earth and the World of Spirits* (New York: printed by author, 1870), 509.

4. A PALACE FOR THE SUN

45 *"One of Mr. D.'s plates"*: Prime, *Life of Samuel F. B. Morse*, 26.

"The next word you may write": Ibid., 389.

"In a view up the street": Ibid., 401.

46 *"Objects moving are not impressed"*: Ibid.

   "I specially conversed with him": Ibid., 403.

47 *"I don't know if you recollect"*: Morse, *Letters and Journals*, 129.

   "They are full-length portraits": Ibid., 145.

49 *"bewildered astonishment"*: "Street Saunterings," unsigned column in *Charleston Courier*, May 15, 1847.

   "abortive efforts": Ibid.

   "Soon after, we commenced": Ibid., 146.

50 *"As the Daguerreotype was not patented"*: Prime, *Life of Samuel F. B. Morse*, 408.

   "I learn, with equal astonishment": Ibid.

   "mirror with a memory": Oliver Wendell Holmes, "The Stereoscope and the Stereograph," *Atlantic*, June 1859.

5. I THOUGHT NOBODY WOULD BE DAMAGED MUCH

53 *"Not at that time being inclined"*: Mumler, "The Personal Experiences . . . Part 1," 1.

54 *"being acquainted with"*: Ibid.

   "The outline of the upper portion": "Spirit Photographs: A New and Interesting Development."

55 *"unaccountable," "the negative was taken"*: Mumler, "The Personal Experiences . . . Part 1," 1.

   "portrait of a spirit": *Daily Constitutionalist* (Atlanta), March 5, 1869, 2.

   "The picture was, to say the least": Mumler, "The Personal Experiences . . . Part 1," 1.

   "to have a little fun": Ibid.

56 *"This photograph was taken of myself"*: Ibid.

   "I felt, on reading this statement": Ibid.

57 *"It not only gave the description"*: Ibid.

"mischief": Ibid.

"Here comes Mr. Mumler!": Ibid.

6. A LOUNGING, LISTLESS MADHOUSE

60 *"It is the startling realism"*: Daniel O'Connell Townley, "A Head of Christ," *Old and New* 4, no. 1 (July 1871), 487.

"a series of experiments": *Congressional Globe: Containing Sketches of the Debates and Proceedings of the Third Session of the Twenty-Seventh Congress* 12 (1843), 324.

61 *"it would require a scientific analysis"*: Ibid.

"Every object in it": "Editor's Drawer," *Harper's Magazine* 38, no. 227 (April 1869), 715.

"You will have an artist for a neighbor": Ibid.

62 *"jewelry, miniature, and surgical case manufacturer"*: *The New York City Directory* (New York: John Doggett, 1844), 47.

63 *"a lounging, listless, madhouse air"*: Charles Dickens, *American Notes for General Circulation* (Boston: Ticknor and Fields, 1867), 51.

"The moping idiot": Ibid.

64 *"sufficiently contiguous to each"*: *Documents of the Board of Aldermen of the City of New York* (New York: Childs and Devoe, 1836), doc. 113, 600.

"Make the rain pour down": Dickens, *American Notes*, 52.

"The scenery upon it": *Documents of the Board of Aldermen*, 599.

65 *"Violent battles are frequent"*: Prison Association of New York, *Second Report of the New York Prison Association* (New York: The Association, 1846), 37.

"a handsome building": Enoch Cobb Wines and Theodore Dwight, *Report on the Prisons and Reformatories of the United States and Canada Made to the Legislature of New York, January 1867* (Albany: Van Benthuysen & Sons, 1867), 107.

"The gag has sometimes been applied": Dorothea Lynde Dix, *Remarks on Prisons and Prison Discipline in the United States* (Philadelphia: Joseph Kite & Co., 1845), 14.

7. MY GOD! IS IT POSSIBLE?

70 For a brief account of J. W. Black's experiments in aerial photography, see *Wilmington* (North Carolina) *Daily Herald,* October 19, 1860.

   "The cow pasture character": *Daily Patriot and Union* (Boston), October 18, 1860.

71 *"Boston looks very much":* Ibid.

72 *"Love at First Sight":* *Eastern Carolina Republican* (New Bern, North Carolina), January 12, 1848.

73 *"Puritan of the most exalted type":* Osborne Perry Anderson, *A Voice from Harper's Ferry: A Narrative of Events at Harper's Ferry* (Boston: printed by author, 1861), 9.

74 *"peculiar medium":* *Spiritual Magazine* 4 (January 1863).

   "It behooves us as Spiritualists": "Boston Spiritual Conference," *Banner of Light* 12, no. 11 (December 6, 1862), 5.

75 *"mechanical contrivance":* Mumler, "Personal Experiences . . . Part 1," 1.

   "All I can say to Mr. Black," and dialogue following: Ibid.

8. SHE REALLY IS A WONDERFUL WHISTLER

81 *"bumpology":* See, for example, *Brooklyn Evening Post,* July 8, 1842, 2: "Dr George W. Ellis . . . Professor of Phrenology . . . undertook to hold forth on bumpology 'in all its various branches.'"

82 *"moral insanity":* Marmaduke Sampson, *Rationale of Crime, and Its Appropriate Treatment: Being a Treatise on Criminal Jurisprudence Considered in Relation to Cerebral Organization. Considerably enlarged by Eliza Farnham with her extensive notes and with 19 engraved portraits from daguerreotypes made by Mathew Brady for this publication* (New York: D. Appleton, 1846), 21.

   "The form of head possessed": Ibid., 7.

83 *"No. 1 is the head of a very depraved person":* Ibid., 8.

   "some of the most daring burglaries": Ibid., 9.

84 *"except a little bread":* *Fayetteville Weekly Observer,* November 3, 1856.

"An old Pole": "A Hero's Fate," *Poughkeepsie Journal,* February 17, 1844.

85 *"The Blackwell's Island ferry":* Osage County Chronicle, October 15, 1882.

"Dressed in a striped uniform": Dickens, *American Notes,* 77.

"the officers of the Penitentiary": Sampson and Farnham, *Rationale of Crime,* xx.

86 *"examining the heads":* New York Evening Post, August 23, 1837.

"a man of great determination": Sampson and Farnham, *Rationale of Crime,* 156.

87 *"Before his mind became deranged":* Ibid., 157.

"a half-breed Indian": Ibid., 158.

88 *"A Jewess of German birth":* Ibid., 160.

89 *"quackery"* and *"humbug":* New York Observer, November 7, 1846. Also quoted in Madeleine B. Stern, "Mathew Brady and the Rationale of Crime: A Discovery in Daguerreotypes," *Quarterly Journal of the Library of Congress* 31, no. 3 (July 1974), 132.

"THE PHRENOLOGICAL CABINET": New York Times, September 18, 1851, 3.

90 *"use of improper books":* Prison Association of New York, *Report of the Prison Association of New York,* Vol. 3 (New York: The Association, 1847), 50.

9. NO SHADOW OF TRICKERY

93 *"He says he cannot see":* The Liberator (Boston), November 21, 1862.

"Do you see any spirits present?": "Hon. Moses Dow," *Facts* 1, no. 4 (December 1882), 420.

94 *"I have seen several pictures":* The Liberator, November 21, 1862.

"One of the most frequently repeated": William Mumler, "The Personal Experiences of William Mumler in Spirit Photography, Part 7," reprinted in *Banner of Light* 36, no. 26 (March 27, 1875), 3.

"This is a remarkable fact": Ibid.

96 *"Those ominous, long pine boxes":* Richmond Whig, May 22, 1865.

"The corpse was placed in the casket": "Express Operations During the War," *Express Gazette,* May 15, 1897, 137–38, cited by Jim Schmidt, Dead-Confederates.com, September 24, 2011, https://deadconfederates.com /2011/09/24/can-you-hang-around-a-couple-of-minutes-he-wont-be -long/.

97 *"The instrument was handled"*: Evelyn P. Goodsell, *Some Reasons Why I Am a Spiritualist* (Hartford: Williams, Wiley & Turner, 1861), 35.

"a boy seated, and intently reading": Benjamin Coleman, letter to the *Spiritual Magazine,* February 1863, 86.

98 *"Babbitt's Cytherean Cream of Soap"*: *Louisville Daily Caller,* May 17, 1850.

Boston Chemical Soap Powder: Burlington (Vermont) *Weekly Free Press,* May 11, 1860.

99 *"This is to certify"*: *Banner of Light* 12, no. 12 (December 13, 1862), 4.

10. A CRAVING FOR LIGHT

101 *"There is hardly a block"*: William M. Bobo, *Glimpses of New York City* (New York: J. J. McCarter, 1852), 120.

"the beggars and the takers": "Things in New York," *Brother Jonathan,* March 4, 1843, 250.

102 *"the standing-place for all kinds"*: J. Frank Kernan, *Reminiscences of the Old Fire Laddies and Volunteer Fire Departments of New York and Brooklyn* (New York: M. Crane, 1885), 12.

"ill-looking, ungainly, rambling structure": *New York Times,* July 14, 1865.

"paltry collection of preposterous things": *New York Times,* March 18, 1868.

103 *"As in every art and science"*: Gurney advertisement, quoted in Catherine Hoover Voorsanger and John K. Howat, *Art and the Empire City: New York, 1825–1861* (New Haven: Yale University Press, 2000), 231.

"FIRST PREMIUM NEW YORK": *New York Tribune,* January 8, 1845.

104 *"I felt a craving for light"*: Robert Wilson, *Mathew Brady: Portraits of a Nation* (New York: Bloomsbury, 2014), 8.

105 *"The President and Cabinet," "This collection embraces," "This establish-ment is": United States Commercial Register: containing sketches of the lives of distinguished merchants, manufacturers, and artisans, with an advertising directory at its close* (New York: J. Belcher, 1851), 36.

106 *"composite photography," "I have taken a gentleman's picture":* October 1853 circular, reprinted in *Photographic Times: An Illustrated Monthly Magazine,* January 13, 1888.

107 *"Poetry is in decline": Louisville Daily Courier,* reprinted from the *Albany Evening Journal,* November 27, 1852.

11. THE MESSAGE DEPARTMENT

113 *"battery":* Parker and Day, *Biography of Mrs. J. H. Conant,* 36.

"*Mr. Berry conceived*": Ibid., 98.

"*so thoroughly depleted*": Ibid.

114 *"At first the manifestations":* Ibid., 103.

"*the nicely adjusted magnetic surroundings*": Ibid., 104.

115 *"The great unpopularity of Spiritualism":* Ibid., 108.

"The Spiritualists, or at least some of them": Boston Daily Evening Transcript, April 8, 1862, cited in "Envisioning the Civil War," http://www .iapsop.com/spirithistory/envisioning_the_civil_war.html.

116 *"I've got somebody I want to speak to" and other dialogue purported to be spoken by the spirit of John Dixon: Banner of Light* 12, no. 18 (January 24, 1863).

117 *"Captain?" and other dialogue purported to be spoken by the spirit of Philip Guinon:* Ibid.

118 *"There is much that is genuine": Banner of Light* 12, no. 14 (December 27, 1862).

119 *"On the evening of October 11": Banner of Light* 12, no. 11 (December 6, 1862).

"*The next evening, October 12*": Ibid.

12. A BIG HEAD FULL OF IDEAS

125 *"large," "strong," "mighty"*: Horace Traubel, *With Walt Whitman in Camden*, Vol. 3 (New York: Mitchell Kennerley, 1914), 234.

126 *"I have seen human degradation"*: *Report from the Select Committee on the Health of Towns* (London: House of Lords Seasonal Papers, 1840), xii–xiii.

"In the lower lodging houses": Ibid., 61.

127 *"The employments of these Children"*: *A Supplementary Index to the Life of Robert Owen* (London: Effingham Wilson, 1858), 27.

128 *"by means of the united capital"*: "Documents Related to the Founding of the Clydesdale Company," in James T. Hair, ed., *Iowa State Gazetteer* (Chicago: Bailey & Hair, 1865), 135.

"every stalk of corn": Joseph Hooker, quoted in Edward Porter Alexander, *Military Memoirs of a Confederate: A Critical Narrative* (New York: C. Scribner's Sons, 1907), 252.

129 *"like the war horse"*: *American Journal of Photography*, August 1, 1861, quoted in James Horan, *Mathew Brady: Historian with a Camera* (New York: Crown, 1955), 39.

131 *"a spiritualist's cabinet on wheels"*: E. F. Bleirer, preface to Alexander Gardner, *Gardner's Photographic Sketch Book of the Civil War* (New York: Dover, 1959), vii.

132 *"enlightening the public"*: Alexander Gardner, quoted in Laurel Brake and Marysa Demoor, *Dictionary of Nineteenth-Century Journalism in Great Britain and Ireland* (London: Academia Press, 2009), 251.

133 *"With this exhibition"*: Karl Marx, quoted in George Lichtheim, *Marxism: An Historical and Critical Study* (New York: Routledge, 2015), 136.

"half starved by its own toil": D. Mark Katz, *Witness to an Era: The Life and Photographs of Alexander Gardner* (Nashville: Thomas Nelson, 1999), 5.

"philosophical instruments," "That photography is yet": *Exhibition of the Works of Industry of All Nations, 1851* (London: Royal Commission, 1852), 243.

134 *"*BRADY *(United States, No. 137)"*: Ibid., 277.

"opens a fresh field of philosophical inquiry": Ibid., 245.

13. CHAIR AND ALL

139 *"Ever since I have commenced"*: Mumler, quoted in *Spiritual Magazine*, January 1863.

140 *"Your article of yesterday"*: J. W. Edmonds, letter to the *New York Evening Post*, reprinted in *Photographic News: A Weekly Record of the Progress of Photography*, January 9, 1863, 20.

141 *"They are all Germans"*: "The Confederate Deserters," *New York Times*, June 30, 1861.

142 *"You can rest assured"*: Letter from William Guay, reprinted in *Photographic Journal*, April 15, 1863.

"The result was": Ibid.

143 *"Having since continued"*: Ibid.

"the spirits of those," "These movements became": Isaac Rehn, quoted in Robert Hare, *Experimental Investigation of the Spirit Manifestations* (New York: Partridge and Brittan, 1855), 290. See also "Isaac Rehn and James Cutting Encounter Imponderable Forces," http://www.iapsop.com /spirithistory/isaac_rehn_and_james_cutting_encounter_imponderable _forces.html.

144 *"I have been harassed enough"*: Mumler, quoted in *Spiritual Magazine*, January 1863.

145 *"chair and all"*: Rehn, quoted in Hare, *Experimental Investigation*, 290.

146 *"The noble rock cod"*: Charles Aldrich, *The Life and Times of Azro B. F. Hildreth: Including Personal and Family Letters, Miscellaneous Correspondence, and Selections from His Writings* (Des Moines: Redhead, Norton, Lathrop & Company, 1891), 544.

147 *"the exhibition has already drawn"*: *New York Tribune*, May 24, 1859.

148 *"South African aboriginees"*: Boston Aquarial Gardens advertisement, 1860, quoted in Jerry Ryan, *The Forgotten Aquariums of Boston* (Boston: Finley Aquatic Books, 2002).

"desperation of dullness," "flaming advertisement": *New York Daily Tribune*, November 16, 1860, quoted in Ryan, *The Forgotten Aquariums*.

"We went and found the fish tanks drained": Ibid.

14. DID YOU EVER DREAM OF SOME LOST FRIEND?

153 *"The living that throng Broadway"* and quotes following: "Brady's Photographs: Pictures of the Dead at Antietam," *New York Times,* October 20, 1862.

155 *"From these pictures the historian":* "Photographic Phases," *New York Times,* July 21, 1862.

156 *"Among the many sun-compellers":* Ibid.

159 *"It is not in the Southern character":* "Death in the White House," *Athens* (Tennessee) *Post,* March 14, 1862.

"ever after there was a new quality": Alban Jasper Conant, "A Portrait Painter's Reminiscences of Lincoln," *McClure's Magazine* 32, no. 5 (March 1909).

". . . I have heard you say": William Shakespeare, *The Life and Death of King John,* act 3, scene 4.

"Did you ever dream of some lost friend": Doris Kearns Goodwin, *Team of Rivals: The Political Genius of Abraham Lincoln* (New York: Simon and Schuster, 2005), 423.

160 *"Willie lives":* Jean H. Baker, *Mary Todd Lincoln: A Biography* (New York: Norton, 1989), 220.

"out of regard for President Lincoln": One of Mumler's early images of Mary Lincoln can be seen in Lloyd Ostendorf, "The Photographs of Mary Todd Lincoln," *Journal of the Illinois State Historical Society* 61, no. 3 (Autumn 1968), 269–332.

161 *"Mr. Lincoln was greatly annoyed":* Reverend P. D. Gurley, quoted in Harold K. Bush, *Lincoln in His Own Time: A Biographical Chronicle of His Life, Drawn from Recollections, Interviews, and Memoirs by Family, Friends, and Associates* (Iowa City: University of Iowa Press, 2011), 65.

15. WAR AGAINST WRONG

163 *"Superintending improvements":* Scrap Book and Magazine of American Literature, February 23, 1863.

"Persons residing at any distance": Marc Demarest, "The Actual Likeness of Spirits: The Early Career of William H. Mumler," *Chasing Down*

Emma, March 17, 2015, http://ehbritten.blogspot.com/2015/03/the-actual
-likeness-of-spirits-early.html.

164 *"so much outre":* "Another Spirit-Photograph Recognized," *Herald of Progress,* May 9, 1863.

"Being an investigator": Charles M. Plumb, "'Spirit Photographs.' A Word of Caution." *Herald of Progress,* April 11, 1863.

"Early in the progress": Ibid.

165 *"I propose to go":* Spiritual Magazine, January 1863.

"I wish it distinctly understood": Ibid.

167 *"To think that they should pretend":* Banner of Light 13, no. 2 (April 4, 1863), 5.

"If there were a collection," "I have neither the time nor desire": Ibid.

16. WHOSE BONES LIE BLEACHING

172 *"The whole town, about 3000 inhabitants":* Eliza Farnham, quoted in D. Scott Hartwig, "Eliza W. Farnham—An Unsung Heroine of Gettysburg," March 2, 2002, https://npsgnmp.wordpress.com/2012/03/02/eliza
-w-farnham-an-unsung-heroine-of-gettysburg/.

"Dear friends of the Herald": Eliza Farnham, letter to the *Herald of Progress,* July 18, 1863.

173 *"ghosts and hobgoblins seen there":* Gettysburg Compiler, January 29, 1880.

174 *"Unfit for Service," "The Slaughter Pen," "harvest of death," "thrown behind him":* These and other descriptions of what Alexander Gardner claimed to have found at Gettysburg appear in *Gardner's Photographic Sketch Book of the Civil War* (Washington, DC: Philp & Solomons, 1865–66).

178 *"The musket, rusted by many storms":* Ibid.

179 *A local photographer:* Peter Weaver's images of living soldiers playing dead can be seen at http://civilwartalk.com/threads/the-weaver-photo
graphs-at-gettysburg-nov-1863.83786/.

17. ALL IS GONE AND NOTHING SAVED

183 *"Lincoln was kind":* J. W. Edmonds, *Letters and Tracts on Spiritualism* (London: J. Burns, 1875), 27.

184 *"too torrid for human endurance," "prostrated"*: *New York Herald*, July 1, 1865.

185 *"puffery"*: "Barnum's Museum," *New York Times*, August 13, 1865.

"insatiate want of human nature": Phineas Taylor Barnum, *How I Made Millions: The Life of P. T. Barnum* (New York: Dillingham, 1888), 57.

"The American people . . . like to be fooled": Barnum, quoted in Edward Theodore Page, *Advertising: How to Plan, Prepare, Write and Manage* (Chicago: Publicity Publishing Company, 1903), 111.

187 *"ingenious," "a scientific chemist," "remarkably ghostlike"*: P. T. Barnum, *The Humbugs of the World* (New York: Carleton, 1866), 111.

"Money is in some respect": P. T. Barnum, *The Life of P. T. Barnum Written by Himself* (Buffalo: The Courier Company, 1888), 176.

188 *"best woman in the world"*: Barnum, quoted in his obituary "The Great Showman Dead," *New York Times*, April 8, 1891.

191 *"My 'puffing' was more persistent"*: Barnum, *The Life of P. T. Barnum*, 59.

192 *"hastily put on one of his wife's dresses"*: *New York Times*, May 15, 1865.

"Nobody will attempt": *Green Mountain Freeman* (Montpelier, Vermont), May 23, 1865.

$500 for Davis's dress: *Syracuse Daily Courier and Union*, May 19, 1865.

"Put outside a picture": Telegram from P. T. Barnum received by telegraph operator Ransom Phelps, May 17, 1865, quoted in Clement Augustus Lounsberry, *Early History of North Dakota: Essential Outlines of American History* (Washington, DC: Liberty Press, 1919), 509.

"If Barnum can get possession": *Springfield* (Massachusetts) *Weekly Republican*, May 20, 1865.

"Before a month expires": *Brooklyn Daily Eagle*, May 20, 1865.

"hang Jeff Davis from a sour apple tree": For an example of this lyric's political use from the period, see *Hinds County Gazette* (Raymond, Mississippi), June 12, 1868.

"The Belle of Richmond": Materials related to Jefferson Davis wearing a dress can be viewed on the Library of Congress website: http://www.loc .gov/pictures/item/2008661830/.

193 *"As Jeff made his perilous descent"*: "Disastrous Fire," *New York Times*, July 14, 1865.

"It is suspected": "The Destruction of Barnum's Museum," *Pittsburgh Gazette*, July 17, 1865.

"gave the flames such an impetus": Samuel P. Richards, *Sam Richards's Civil War Diary: A Chronicle of the Atlanta Home Front* (Athens: University of Georgia Press, 2009), 286.

194 *"All is gone and nothing saved"*: "Disastrous Fire."

18. A FAVORITE HAUNT OF APPARITIONS

197 *"We are about making"*: Mumler's Jefferson Davis image and caption can be viewed online at https://www.icp.org/browse/archive/objects /we-are-about-making-a-movement-that-will-astonish-the-world -jd.

198 *"A prophet is not without honor"*: William Mumler, "The Personal Experiences . . . Part 2," 1.

201 *"The great commotion"*: *San Francisco Chronicle*, March 26, 1869.

"Resolved, *That this conference"*: "The Spurious Spirits," *New York Sun*, April 14, 1869.

202 *"Too often in the busy life"*: John William Draper, "President Draper's Address," *Photographic Notes* 5 (June 1, 1860), 151.

"improvements in developing chemicals": Ibid., 152.

203 *"My object of placing this"*: Mumler pamphlet, quoted in Elbridge T. Gerry, *The Mumler "Spirit" Photograph Case. Argument of Elbridge T. Gerry on the Preliminary Examination of W. H. Mumler, Charged with Obtaining Money by Pretended "Spirit" Photographs* (New York: Baker, Vorhis & Co., 1869), 19.

204 *"a brilliant collegiate course"*: "The Laetare Medal," *Donahoe's Magazine*, June 1888.

"immediate and peremptory draft": Samuel Merrill, *Newspaper Libel: A Handbook for the Press* (Boston: Ticknor and Company, 1888), 80.

205 *"What our reporter thinks"*: *New York Sun*, February 26, 1869.

206 *"Many persons would gladly give"*: *New York Times*, April 13, 1869.

"work of the devil": *La Civiltà Cattolica*, 1853, quoted in Christopher M. Moreman, ed., *The Spiritualist Movement: Speaking with the Dead in America and Around the World* (Santa Barbara ABC-CLIO, 2013), 40.

"There is little reason to doubt": "The Second Plenary Council of Baltimore," *New Advent Catholic Encyclopedia*, http://www.newadvent.org/ca then/02235a.htm.

207 *"In the United States"*: *La Civiltà Cattolica*, 1853.

19. THE SPIRITS DO NOT LIKE A THRONG

209 *"sawdust swindle"*: "An Old Complaint Book," *New York Times*, November 28, 1886.

210 *"These books were gathered together"*: *New York Times*, June 27, 1886.

211 *"any violations of the ordinances"*: Jerome Mushkat, *Fernando Wood: A Political Biography* (Kent, OH: Kent State University Press, 1990), 43.

"From 10 to 4 the big space": "An Old Complaint Book."

"a harlot, a gorilla": "Oakey Hall on Horace Greeley," *New York Times*, January 21, 1863.

212 *"Not only is it possible," "The spirits do not like a throng"*: *New York Times*, April 13, 1869.

213 *"produced surprising effects"*: *New York Herald*, April 13, 1869.

"one dozen spirit photographs, ten dollars": Ibid.

20. THE TENDEREST SYMPATHIES OF HUMAN NATURE

215 *"He has a hard class," "penetrating power"*: James D. McCabe, *The Secrets of the Great City* (Philadelphia: National Publishing Company, 1868), 100.

216 *"What is this modern Spiritualism?"*: Gerry, *The Mumler "Spirit" Photograph Case*, 20.

217 *"duty to procure scientific news"*: *New York Times*, April 13, 1869.

218 *"What led you to enter"*: *New York Herald*, April 22, 1869.

219   *"infamously brutal"*: *New York Times*, January 17, 1866.

"The Fighting Lawyer": John Drake Townsend, *New York in Bondage* (New York: by subscription, 1901), xiii.

220   *"marked ability," "recondite themes"*: Adin Ballou, ed., *An Elaborate History and Genealogy of the Ballous in America* (Providence, RI: Press of E. L. Freeman & Son, 1888), 1109.

"Have you, Mr. Tooker, any other name" and quotes following: *New York Herald*, April 22, 1869.

221   *"Bolivar," "Walton," "The Widow Rogers"*: A. E. Costello, *Our Firemen: A History of New York Fire Departments* (New York: A. E. Costello, 1887), 555.

"incisive but never rancorous": *New York Times*, July 8, 1896.

"What promise," "That will do, Mr. Tooker": *New York Herald*, April 22, 1869.

21. WEEP, WEEP, MY EYES

223   *"I have nothing to do with the establishment!"*: *New York Herald*, April 13, 1869.

"Were you present": Accounts of the testimony of William Guay appear in the *New York Herald*, April 22, 1869, and the *Spiritual Magazine*, June 1, 1869, 244.

226   *"I have known Mr. Mumler" and quotes following*: Testimony of Judge Edmonds, quoted in "Spiritual Photographs: Trial of Mr. Mumler in New York," *Spiritual Magazine* 4 (June 1869), 243.

227   *"a man full of sympathy," "warmly attached to her," "Pleurez, pleurez, mes yeux"*: Peyton Farrell Miller, *A Group of Great Lawyers of Columbia County, New York* (privately printed, 1904), 176–77.

228   *"I was at the time withdrawn," "I was invited"*: John Worth Edmonds, *Spiritualism* (New York: Partridge & Brittan, 1858), 71.

229   *"I know a great many persons," "This is the most remarkable"*: Testimony of Judge Edmonds from the *New York Tribune*, quoted in Emma Hardinge Britten, *Nineteenth-Century Miracles* (London: William Britten, 1883), 474.

230   *"Spiritualists reason"*: *Spiritual Magazine*, June 1, 1869, 244.

"I believe that the camera": Ibid., 244–45.

231 *"How do spirits dress?"*: Ibid.

232 *"I was impressed"*: *New York Times*, February 14, 1886.

22. ARE YOU A SPIRITUALIST IN ANY DEGREE?

235 *"Women have long printed"*: *Vassar Miscellany*, November 1872, 116.

236 *"Have you had any experience"* and quotes following: *New York Herald*, April 22, 1869.

23. AN OLD, MOTH-EATEN CLOAK

243 *"Lack of appreciation of art,"*: James Sullivan, *The History of New York State*, Vol. 5 (New York: Lewis Historical Publishing Company, 1927), 2324.

244 *"The miniature in the presence"*: Robin Jaffee Frank, *Love and Loss: American Portrait and Mourning Miniatures* (New Haven: Yale University Press, 2000), 277.

"In his earlier professional life," *"Upon the decline"*: "Samuel Raymond Fanshaw, 1814–1888," National Academy Museum, Index of Artists, http://www.nationalacademy.org/collections/artists/detail/1315/.

245 *"I am a miniature and portrait painter"* and quotes following: *New York Herald*, April 24, 1869.

247 *"In the front rank,"* *"Every one who knew him mourns"*: New York Military Museum and Veterans Research Center, https://dmna.ny.gov/historic/reghist/civil/cavalry/6thCav/6thCavFanshaw.htm.

248 *"If, looking through an old"*: Ibid.

24. BY SUPERNATURAL MEANS

251 Testimonies of David A. Hopkins, Lutheria C. Reeves, and William W. Silver: *New York Herald*, April 24, 1869.

25. FIGURA VAPOROSA

260 *"The Mumler spirit-photography case"*: *Fort Wayne Daily Gazette*, April 27, 1869.

"A very deep interest": *Charleston Daily News,* April 29, 1869.

261 *"It is certainly very strange"*: *Semi-Weekly Wisconsin* (Milwaukee), April 29, 1869.

"I will pay $100": William Slee, letter to the *New York Tribune,* reprinted in Britten, *Nineteenth-Century Miracles,* 479.

"figura vaporosa": *El Criterio Espiritista,* July 1869.

262 *"I have been a photographer"*: Jeremiah Gurney, quoted in Britten, *Nineteenth-Century Miracles,* 474.

264 *"The color is leaden, almost brown"*: *New York Times,* April 25, 1865.

265 "WAR DEPARTMENT, *Washington City"*: Edwin Stanton letter, April 25, 1865, in *Compilation of the Official Records of the Union and Confederate Armies* (Washington, DC: Government Printing Office, 1894), 952.

266 "DICKENS, GURNEY, AND BRADY": *Brooklyn Eagle,* December 27, 1867.

267 *"In justification of our mercantile honor"*: Gurney, quoted in Susan Cook, "Celebrity Circulation I: Dickens in Photographs," *Journal of Victorian Culture Online,* April 16, 2013, http://blogs.tandf.co.uk/jvc/2013/04/16/celebrity-circulation-i-dickens-in-photographs/.

268 *"The effect was produced"*: *New York Herald,* April 27, 1869.

269 *"a veiled figure seated"*: Ibid.

"1. The photographer might take": "Spirit Photographs: How They Can Be Made," *Chicago Tribune,* May 2, 1869.

270 *"The actual developments of the case"*: *New York Tribune,* April 29, 1869.

271 *"Are you a believer"* and quotes following in questioning of Abraham Bogardus: *Oneida* (New York) *Circular,* May 3, 1869.

26. THEY PAID THEIR MONEY, AND THEY HAD THEIR CHOICE

277 *"Do you believe in spooks?"*: The testimony of P. T. Barnum in the Tombs appeared in many newspapers, including the *Philadelphia Evening Telegraph,* April 29, 1869; the *National Republican* (Washington, DC), April 30, 1869; and the *Oneida* (New York) *Circular,* May 3, 1869, from which the account here is drawn.

280 *"If people declare"*: P. T. Barnum, *The Humbugs of the World,* 110.

27. THOSE MORTALS GIFTED WITH THE POWER OF SEEING

283 *"the first time"*: Amelia V. Brooks, letter to the *New York Herald*, April 21, 1869.

284 *"The case under investigation"*: "Argument of Mr. Townsend," *New York Times*, May 4, 1869.

287 *"May it please the court"* and quotes following: Gerry, *The Mumler "Spirit" Photograph Case*, 19.

291 *"After careful attention to the case"*: *Elk County Advocate* (Ridgway, Pennsylvania), May 21, 1869.

28. CALM ASSURANCE OF A HAPPY FUTURE

296 *"Resolved, That the Committee"*: "February 13, 1869," *Journal of the Senate of the United States of America, Being the Third Session of the Fortieth Congress*, 256.

"the pioneer of the photographic art": *New York World*, November 5, 1887.

297 *"the relation of the Bible"*: "Editor's Literary Record," *Harper's New Monthly Magazine* 63, no. 375 (August 1881), 471.

298 *"Here's your flower!"*: Joseph M. Wilson, *A Eulogy on the Life and Character of Alexander Gardner* (Washington, DC: R. Beresford, 1883), 18.

"From all who visited her": *Friend of Progress*, February 1865.

Gurney's final photos of Lincoln: *Life*, September 15, 1952.

299 *"What Barnum was to the circus"*: *New York Times*, December 24, 1882.

"To further mark appreciation": "The Laetare Medal."

300 *"photographic portraits of Abraham"*: *Chicago Tribune*, August 2, 1874.

William Guay in Halifax: *Lawrence* (Kansas) *Daily Journal*, February 3, 1883.

"to aid by all lawful means": "Prevention of Cruelty to Children," *Arthur's Illustrated Home Magazine* 43 (1875), 141.

301 dismemberment, drawing and quartering: See Elbridge Gerry, "Capital Punishment by Electricity," *North American Review* 149, 321–25.

"At the urgent solicitations" *and quotes following:* Parker and Day, *Biography of Mrs. J. H. Conant,* 226–27.

29. THE MUMLER PROCESS

305 *"a clairvoyant remedy":* Port Jervis Evening Gazette, December 29, 1870.

"One of the most powerful imparters": undated *Boston Globe* report, quoted in Mumler advertisement in *Cambridge Chronicle* 49, no. 2 (January 1894), 13.

306 *"Mumler process":* Photographic Times, June 1884, 304.

"'Punch' depends": Boston Post, January 11, 1879.

"Nearly all the pictures": Facts: A Monthly Magazine, June 1886, 158.

307 "MR. WILLIAM H. MUMLER, *a well-known inventor":* Photographic Times, June 1884, 304.

Also by Peter Manseau

Objects of Devotion

Melancholy Accidents

One Nation, Under Gods

Believer, Beware
(COEDITOR)

Rag and Bone

Songs for the Butcher's Daughter

Vows

Killing the Buddha
(WITH JEFF SHARLET)